DALIT WOMEN IN PANCHAYATI RAJ

DALIT WOMEN IN PANCHAYATI RAJ

Dr. Indu Baghel

JNANADA PRAKASHAN (P&D)
NEW DELHI

Published by :
JNANADA PRAKASHAN (P&D)
4837/2, 24, Ansari Road, Daryaganj
New Delhi-110002
Phone : 011-23272047
Mobile : 9212137080

Assisted by :
TEXT BOOK PROMOTION SOCIETY OF INDIA
4837/2, 24, Ansari Road, Daryaganj
New Delhi-110002
Phone : 011-23272047
Mobile : 9212137080

Edition: 2009

Dalit Women in Panchayati Raj

ISBN : 978-81-7139-266-7

Typesetting by :
Vardhman Computers
New Delhi-110017

Published by Mrs. S. Chowdhary for M/s. Jnanada Prakashan (P&D) Daryaganj, Ansari Road, New Delhi-110 002 and printed at Balaji Offset, Navin Shahdara, Delhi-110032.

Preface

The institution of Panchayati Raj has emerged as a powerful tool of emancipation and empowerment of the marginalised and oppressed community of India. More significantly, after the 73rd and 74th constitutional amendments, Dalit Women have been given special protection by way of reserving one-third seats in the institution of local governance.

In the light of the recent changes in the Indian constitution with regard to Panchayati Raj, the author has made a comprehensive and critical study of the role of the women in these institutions. Moreover, it has also been observed that despite these changes in the constitution, the ground situation reflect that there are still violence against Dalit women in different parts of the country.

Empowerment of Dalit women through the institution of Panchayati Raj has made a significant contribution to the very process of democratisation. As a result, it is having enormous influence on the formation and functioning of local government in the whole India.

The author is fully convinced that this book would be an indispensable source for the researchers, academicians as well as policy-makers. Moreover, it would also be a significant contribution to the existing literature on Dalit women in particular and Panchayati Raj in general.

Author

Preface

Author

Contents

1

An Overview of Panchayati Raj in India

As Gandhi often remarked, India lives in villages and unless village life can be revitalised the nation as a whole can hardly come alive. When India became independent in 1947, perhaps one-third of the villages of India had traditional Panchayats and many of them were far from flourishing conditions. The Congress government has made a determined effort to promote the creation of Panchayats and to make them effective units of local self-government. Article 40 of the Constitution clearly declares "The state shall take necessary actions to organize village Panchayats and to endow them with such powers and authority as may be necessary to enable them to function as units of self-government".

The aim was to foster democratic participation, to involve villagers in the development of the community and to reduce the burden of higher level of administration. Though various steps were taken by successive governments to revitalise the system, *Gramswaraj* through village Panchayats remained a distant dream till 1992. Bureaucratic apathy, indifference of the people, lack of political will, lack of uniformity etc were the main factors behind the failure of the system.

Realising the potential of the PR system, Rajiv Gandhi government initiated a process of Constitutional amendment to give sanctity and uniformity to Panchayati Raj system so that it can be immune from political interference and bureaucratic indifference. Rajiv Gandhi introduced 64th Constitutional amendment Bill in 1989. But, the Bill did not materialize. Finally the P.V.Narasimha Rao government introduced Panchayati Raj system in India through the 73rd Constitutional Amendment Act in 1992.

The 73rd Amendment Act has added a new part in the constitution—*Part Nine* - consisting of 16 Articles and the 11th Schedule .The functions of the Panchayati Raj institutions have been clearly spelt out in Article 243G of the Constitution, read with Article 243 ZD and the 1lth Schedule. The PRIs are supposed to be genuine institutions of local self-government, not adjuncts to the implementing agencies of State governments.

The Constitution, which describes them as institutions of local self-government, says that this [status] is [given to them] for two specific purposes: planning for economic development and social justice and implementing these plans. Moreover, it says that this process of empowering them through devolution in order to enable them to plan and implement their own programmes of neighborhood economic development and social justice will be governed by the laws of the legislatures of the States. The Constitution says in the 11th Schedule that this empowerment shall relate or could relate to the 29 subjects listed in the Schedule. Any form of Panchayati Raj that falls short of this cannot be described as genuine Panchayati Raj.

Features of the new Panchayati Raj System

The 73rd Constitutional Amendment Act envisages *Gram Sabha* as the foundation of the PRI system to perform the functions of and powers entrusted to it by the state legislatures. The amendment provides for a three-tier PRI system at the village, intermediate and district levels. Small states with population below 20 lakh have been given the option to not to constitute the intermediate level. The Act provides that the Panchayat bodies will have an assured duration of 5 years with mandatory elections after this period. However it might be noted that under the Act the establishment of Panchayat and the devolution of necessary powers and authority on the PRIs are vested in state governments. In view of this, it may be said that the success of the PRIs as a unit of democracy and thereby ushering an all round development of rural areas will much depend on the intention and support of the state governments. Without sincere intention and political will these institutions would be misused by rural elites and the poor and illiterate masses will remain as mute supporters. The following are the basic elements of the PRI system introduced through 73rd Amendment Act.

Gram Sabha

Article 243A provides that a *Gram Sabha* may exercise such powers and perform such functions at the village level as the Legislature of a State may, by law, provide. *Gram Sabha* means a body consisting of persons registered in the electoral rolls relating to a village comprised within the area of Panchayat at the village level. Thus 73rd Amendment makes *Gram Sabha* as the foundation of PRI system.

Constitution of Panchayats

Article 243B visualises a three-tier PRI system. It provides that in every state there shall be constituted Panchayats at the village, intermediate and district levels. Small states with population below 20 lakh have been given the option to not to constitute the intermediate level. Article 243C further provides that subject to the provisions of these part legislatures of state government may by law make provisions with respect to the composition of the Panchayats. However, the ratio between the population of territorial area of a Panchayat at any level and the number of seats in such Panchayats to be filled by election, shall, so far as practical be same throughout the state.

All the seats in a Panchayat shall be filled by persons chosen by direct election from territorial constituencies in the Panchayat area. For this purpose each Panchayat area shall be divided into territorial constituencies in such manner that the ratio between the population of each constituency and the number of seats allotted to it should be the same throughout the Panchayat area.

The legislatures of the states may by law provide for representation of following persons in Panchayats:

1. The Chairperson of the Panchayat at the village level, in the Panchayats at the intermediate level or I the case of a state not having intermediate Panchayats, in the Panchayats at district level.
2. The Chairpersons of the Panchayat at the intermediate level in the district Panchayat.
3. The members of the Loksabha and the MLAs representing the territorial part of the Panchayat.
4. The members of Rajyasabha and Legislative Council of the state where they are registered as electors.

The Chairperson of a Panchayat and other members of Panchayat whether or not chosen by direct election from territorial constituencies in the Panchayat area shall have the right to vote in the meetings of the Panchayat. The Chairperson of a Panchayat at the village level shall be elected in such a manner as the legislature of a state may by law provide. The Chairperson of a Panchayat at the intermediate level or district level shall be elected by the elected members thereof.

Reservation of Seats

Article 243 D provides that in every Panchayats seats will be reserved for the SCs/STs population in accordance with their population in the village or Panchayat concerned. Moreover 1/3 of the seats in each level shall be reserved for women. The office of the Chairperson in the Panchayats at the three levels shall be reserved for SCs, STs and women in such a manner as the legislatures of each state, may, by law provide. But the number of offices of Chairpersons reserved for the SCs and STs shall be in the same proportion to the total number of such offices in the Panchayats at each level in proportion to the total population of SCs and STs in the state. However not less than 1/3 of the total number of the offices of Chairperson in the Panchayat at each level shall be reserved for women. The number of offices reserved under this clause shall be allotted by rotation to different Panchayats at each level.

Powers and Functions of Panchayats

Subject to the provisions of this Constitution, the Legislature of a State may, endow the Panchayats with such powers and authority as may be necessary to enable them to function as institutions of self-government and such law may contain provisions for the devolution of powers and responsibilities upon Panchayats at the appropriate level, subject to such conditions as may be specified therein, with respect to:

- The preparation of plans for economic development and social justice;
- The implementation of schemes for economic development and social justice as may be entrusted to them including those in relation to the matters listed in the Eleventh Schedule.

The matters listed in 11th Schedule are as follows:

1. Agriculture and extension
2. Land improvement
3. Watershed development
4. Animal husbandry, Poultry and Dairy
5. Fisheries, Social forestry and small scale industries
6. Rural Housing, Khadi, Drinking water and Sanitation
7. Community Health etc.

Powers to Impose Taxes and Funds

Article 243H empowers the legislature of a State to authorize a Panchayat to levy, collect and appropriate such taxes, duties, tolls and fees in accordance with such procedure and subject to such limits and assign to a Panchayat such taxes, duties, tolls and fees levied and collected by the State Government for such purposes and subject to such conditions and limits. Moreover, the article provides for making such grants-in-aid to the Panchayats from the Consolidated Fund of the State. The PRIs are entitled for constitution of such Funds for crediting all moneys received, respectively, by or on behalf of the Panchayats and also for the withdrawal of such money from the funds.

Finance Commission

Article 243 I provides for the establishment of a Finance Commission for reviewing financial position of Panchayats. The Governor of a state shall within one year from the commencement of the Act, constitute a Finance Commission, which should govern—

- The distribution between the State and the Panchayats of the net proceeds of the taxes, duties, tolls and fees leviable by the State, which may be divided between them under this Part and the allocation between the Panchayats at all levels of their respective shares of such proceeds;
- The determination of the taxes, duties, tolls and fees which may be assigned to, or appropriated by, the Panchayat;
- The grants-in-aid to the Panchayats from the Consolidated Fund of the State;
- The measures needed to improve the financial position of the Panchayats;
- Any other matter referred to the Finance Commission by the Governor in the interests of sound finance of the Panchayats.

District Planning Committee

Article 243 ZD provides for District Planning Committees (DPC) comprising representatives elected by the district

Panchayat. It further says that the function of this DPC is to consolidate but not to prepare the district plan. They are to consolidate the plans that have been made by each village Panchayat for the village and, by each intermediary panchayat for the intermediary level, which is described differently in different States, as taluk or block or union. All these different plans are to be brought together in the DPC where they are to be "consolidated" into a draft district.

By way of capacity building, Article 243 ZD provides for a large proportion of the members of the DPC to be nominated by the State government. But, if the State government draws upon local human resources, such as college teachers, ex-servicemen, retired civil servants, retired engineers or even serving ones, doctors, serving or retired, then the community and its best representatives, including businessmen, get involved in the process of developing their own district.

Critical Evaluation

Panchayati Raj was, indeed, one of the most remarkable social and political reforms since independence. However, PRIs today face a number of daunting challenges. Across all states there is a lack of genuine devolution of funds, functions and functionaries in Panchayati Raj. Added to that are social challenges that work against the emergence of leadership from marginalised sections of society, such as women, Dalits and tribals. Further, there is a lack of role clarity among Gram Panchayats, Block Panchayats and District Panchayats.

The socio-political changes expected by the introduction of Panchayati Raj system remained largely unfulfilled for long. Particularly the objectives like social equality, gender equity and the change at grass-root level leadership envisaged as the main were not fulfilled in a meaningful manner. In this regard it was felt that the marginalised groups like the women and other backward castes in the society continue to face many hurdles and found it difficult to participate at the grass-root level developmental process. Some of the shortcomings of the system identified by various studies are as follows:

1. Uniformity of PR system undermines each state's unique history, traditions and consequent structures of local government.
2. Representation of Members of Parliament and state legislatures are often become counter productive. There are clash of interest between the legislatures and PR representatives particularly for getting votes.
3. The Act does not define the role of political parties clearly. It doesn't mention that political parties can enter the election arena in their formal capacity.
4. The Act is silent about the relationship between PRIs and local bureaucracy.
5. The Act doesn't spell out specific grounds for dissolution of PRIs by states. This gives scope for the states to dissolve PRIs on political considerations.

Though the PRI system has so many positive features, yet the elite control over the system, apprehensions of state level leaders of challenge to their power and the lukewarm attitude of the bureaucracy have not yet allowed the PRIs to function as real democratic institutions with people's participation. Studies from different states in India clearly proves that even though some states have shown political activism to implement PRIs, the unequal social structure and rigid caste system prevalent in Indian villages coupled with power-hungry local bureaucracy kill the spirit of the system.

Success of Panchayati Raj: Comparative Study

After the 73rd Constitutional Amendment Act all states in India initiated the process of radical democratic decentralisation. However, the experience of PRIs shows that success of PRIs in India is not uniform throughout the country. In some states the system has played a vital role in changing traditional power structure dominated by local elite-bureaucratic network. In other states the new system has led to empowerment of hitherto marginalised sections of society like women, SC and SC. Unfortunately, in some other states lack of political will and administrative apathy killed the real devolution of power. Using the conventional classification of 'political, administrative and fiscal decentralisation,' the World Bank's three-volume study of Indian decentralisation ranks India *'among the best performers'* internationally in terms of political decentralisation, but 'close to the last' in terms of administrative decentralisation. Most States have held at least one round of elections since 1993. Reservations allowing the participation of women, Scheduled Castes and Scheduled Tribes have been respected.

Finally, voter participation has been high. In its study of 53 villages in Rajasthan and MP, for instance, the World Bank found that voter turnout in *Panchayat* elections was well over 90% for all categories (defined in terms of gender, class and caste). This is significantly higher than the (still high) turnout for the most recent (1998) round of *Lok Sabha* elections, which was 61% for women and 65.9% for men. In its assessment of Indian decentralisation, the Task Force on Devolution of Powers and Functions upon *Panchayati Raj* Institutions (MoRD, 2001) found that 'most of the States' had satisfied only the basic requirements relating to the transfer of functions, functionaries, funds and financial autonomy to the *Panchayats.*

These findings upheld three important limitations, which are commonly associated with Indian decentralisation.

1. The government bodies that operate within their jurisdiction are part of a federal system, in which powers are defined by a written Constitution, and divided among Union, State and sub-State bodies.
2. The institutions empowered by Indian decentralisation are situated in a long standing structure of public administration, whose interests and nature are not necessarily consistent with the provisions outlined in the 73rd Amendment.
3. Finally, this process has happened in a context of political transition, in which customs of discrimination

and inequality in rural areas are thought to have been challenged by forces arising from the green revolution and other forms of guided intervention.

However, some states are ahead of other states in implementing PRIs. For example, Kerala has set a model for decentralised planning with people's participation and an innovative model for allocating fund for PRIs. In Kerala, the local self-governments belonging to higher tiers do not have any control over the lower tiers. The Panchayat presidents are very clear about their role in providing services, and developing panchayat plans and implementing them. The Panchayat presidents take an active interest in the proper running of day care centers, primary schools, and health subcentres. They actively look into the maintenance of buildings housing these institutions, regular attendance of the staff, and other infrastructure needs.

In Kerala, PRIs has initiated the process of participatory natural resource management, water shed management and adult literacy priogrammes. In some districts local Panchayat authorities also introduced training programmes. Participation of women and marginalised community in development process has led to their empowerment to a great extent. However Kerala is also not free from elite capture of political power in grass root level. Over politicisation and interference of local political party leaders often affected the functioning of PRIs making it less objective and more partisan.

Another state, which has shown initial activism in PRI, is Madhya Pradesh. Even before the amendment Madhya Pradesh had a long tradition of local self-governments. So when the Act was implemented, Madhya Pradesh used the district planning committee provision of the 73rd amendment and passed decision-making powers to districts. It has also empowered the Gram Sabha to carry out the functions of Gram Panchayat through numerous committees under the gram swaraj. Madhya Pradesh PRI system is characterised by committee system at the local level managed by members of

Gram Sabha and other higher levels. However, this system is not functioning due to lack of awareness among the members and bureaucratic indifference to provide technical guidance to the representatives on powers assigned to them. Thus, the PRI representatives underutilised the powers and functions delegated to the committees.

In Madhya Pradesh we can see elite capture of the system without giving actual representation to marginalised sections of society even though the Act guarantees it. Yet another problem connected to this is the love-hate relationship between the local level bureaucracy and the elected representative of PRIs. Both use to move in different directions, due to lack of proper coordination and clarity of functions. Moreover, there is also a tendency towards politicisation of local bureaucracy. The *Panchayat* system has been implemented with such pace that the system of governance has not had time to attune itself to these major structural changes.

The elite capture is much stronger in Tami Nadu where Dalit Panchayat members were not even allowed to contest in election. When the hitherto downtrodden people try to establish themselves, assert their opinion and to question the established patrons of authority through constitutional means, traditional caste forces reacted vehemently to revert the natural process of empowerment. This trend was most evident in Tamil Nadu where patriarchal norms and caste equations play vital role in politics. Naturally this has resulted in the creation of several stumbling blocks in Dalit Women's assertion, mobilisation and empowerment. Thus, the chief factor hindering proper functioning of dalit PRIs in Tamil Nadu is strong opposition from upper caste representatives and caste groups. In several panchayats non-cooperation from upper caste members have virtually halted the day-to-day activities of Gram Sabhas and Gram Panchayats. In Pappapatti and Keerippatti panchayats, Dalit Panchayat presidents resigned soon after their election when they failed to challenge the casteist forces.

World Bank studies on PRIs in Andhra Pradesh conclude that decentralisation in AP have emphasised a State that has become decidedly hostile to the interests of *Panchayati Raj*. In contrast to Madhya Pradesh's ambitious 'experiment' in direct democracy the AP government has been associated with a system of governance that has undermined the *Panchayats* in favour of line departments and 'parallel bodies' such as water user groups, joint forest management committees, self-help groups etc.

Conclusion

The experience of different states show that though the PRIs has so many positive features, yet the elite control over the system has not permitted them to work as per the objectives enshrined in Indian Constitution. The need is to evolve a comprehensive concept of PRI system. For this the PRIs has to play three important roles:

1. It should bring about decentralisation of administrative powers in the sense that it has to encourage self-governance and mass participation in its working.
2. The PRIs have to contribute towards strengthening the planning process at the micro level and overall rural development.
3. It has to improve the access of the masses to the highest level of decision-making process.
4. The PRI should ensure the empowerment of the poor and marginalised people and protect them from exploitation of dominant class.
5. PRI members have to be trained for their new role. This is because they have limited knowledge about the Panchayat Act and its provisions, objectives and functions of PR bodies, the dynamics of rural society and the growth potential of their areas. Bureaucracy has to become more committed to PRIs.
6. Since political interference and over politicisation of PRIs lead to dysfunctional, effort should be made to

encourage unanimous election to the PRI bodies without affecting village harmony. In several states PRI election led to violence and local tensions. This kind of disharmony and politicisation affects the legitimacy and spirit of democratic decentralisation. Hence, there is an urgent need to encourage non-partisan elections and procedures of PRIs. Otherwise it will lead to friction and violence. Some states have already initiated this welcoming custom.

Grassroot democracy would seem to have been established in India through 73rd amendment of the constitution. But, even the Act has not resolved the problem of clearly defining the role of local bureaucracy and the elected representatives. Unfortunately the Act has not even defined the role of political parties.

A critical review of the 73rd Amendment and the assessment of the ways in which different States have followed or resisted the stipulations outlined in the 1993 reforms reveals that the grassroot democracy in India still suffers from three limitations- federal constraints, a resistant bureaucracy and local elite capture. Reviewing experiences from different states, studies conducted by Overseas Development Institute [ODI] gives some propositions about the conditions under which decentralisation can lead to improved accountability for poor and marginal groups in society. They are:

- Active participation among broad elements of society, involving activities such as voting, campaigning, attending meetings, running for office, lobbying representatives, etc.
- Fiscal and political support from higher level authorities within government;
- The existence of competitive political parties whose legitimacy depends at least in part on the support of the poor;

- Deeper economic transformations, which embolden traditionally, subordinate groups to challenge local authority structures.

The 11th Finance Commission also came out with similar suggestions. One of the serious concerns the Commission highlighted was that the PRIs have been marginalised by the Central government and state government by sponsoring schemes for rural areas without associating these bodies in their planning and implementation. This is especially true against the context of new central schemes like National Rural Employment Guarantee Act [NREGA] and National Rural Health Mission. Though both these schemes are wide in scope and aim to transform rural India through direct intervention, the process of implementation have marginalised PRIs.

It is imperative to revive PRIs in the era of globalisation and liberalisation. Local initiatives and developmental efforts can indeed enhance competitiveness and income generation among the village community. Thus, rural-urban divide can be minimised using PRIs as an effective catalyst for making villages assertive, self reliant and competitive. Thus revival of PRIs should not undergo another eclipse on the earlier pattern. There has to be genuine commitment to Panchayati Raj as a political value and ideology.

REFERENCES

Bhadouria, B.P.S., *Panchayati Raj and Rural Development*, Commonwealth Publishers, New Delhi, 1981.

Calman, Leslie J., *Toward Empowerment, Women and Movement Politics in India*, Boulder, San Francisco, Oxford West view Press, 1992.

Giri, V. Mohini, *Emancipation and Empowerment of Women*, Gyan Publishing House, New Delhi, 1998.

Kanango, Suhla Deh, "Panchayati Raj and Emerging Women Leadership", *An Overview, Social Action*, Jan.-March, 1996.

Kaushik, Susheela, *Women and Panchayati Raj*, Haranand Publications, New Delhi, 1993.

Maxine Molyneux, *Panchayati Raj from Legislation to Movement,* Concept Publishing Company, New Delhi, 1994.

Mehta, A., "Report on Panchayati Raj Institutions", GOI, Ministry of Rural Development, New Delhi, 1978 .

Santosh, *Cultural Pattern and Economic Participation of Women,* Radha Publications, New Delhi, 1995.

Santosh Nandal, "Equality and Development: Gender Issues in India", *Women's Link,* Vol. 8, No. 1, January-March, 2002.

Jain, Devaki, *The Vocabulary of Women's Politics,* Fredrich Ebert Stiftung, Delhi, 2000.

Moghe, Kiran, "Who Killed the Women's Reservation Bill?" One Indian One People, *Women in Politics,* March, 2004.

Thakur, Rekha "Should It Be Caste or Gender?" *One India One People,* March, 2004.

Thakkar, Usha and Rohini Gawankar "Women in Panchayat: March towards Empowerment", One India, One People-Special Number on *Women in Politics,* March, 2004.

Patel, Vibhuti, *Women's Challenges of the New Millennium,* Gyan Publications, Delhi, 2002.

2

Constitutional Amendment and Panchayati Raj Act

RURAL LOCAL GOVERNMENT IN INDIA

The passage of the 73rd and 74th constitutional amendments in 1994 has been hailed as a landmark in the evolution of local governments in India. The amendments provided rural and urban local governments with a constitutional status that they had previously lacked and reinforced this status by mandating regular elections to locally elected bodies. Further, the amendments mandated reservations of positions in these local bodies for women and for individuals from two traditionally disadvantaged (and constitutionally recognised) groups: Dalits (Scheduled Castes, *i.e.,* castes at the bottom of, or more accurately, excluded from the traditional Hindu caste hierarchy) and Adivasis (Scheduled Tribes, *i.e.,* the indigenous populations of the Indian subcontinent).

Beyond this, the amendments called on—but did not explicitly require—individual states, the highest tier of sub-national government within India's federal setup, to enact legislation to devolve powers and resources to local bodies so as to enable the latter to function as institutions of self-government—to play a central role in the provision of public services, the creation and maintenance of local public goods, and the planning and implementation of developmental activities and programmes to alleviate poverty and promote distributive equity.

At the national level, the ostensible aim of the constitutional amendments was clearly to revitalise local government. This was seen as a means of promoting greater community participation and involvement in developmental efforts, thereby, improving the dismal record of the Indian developmental state in the sphere of human development and public goods provision. In that the impetus for the amendments came from a widespread consensus regarding the failures of the bureaucratic and centralised apparatus of the Indian developmental state, supplemented, in certain circles, with a political agenda of democratic deepening the attempt to revitalize local government in India mirrors attempts in other countries. But, there are several key respects in which the Indian case stands out and these need to be highlighted at the outset.

First, because the Indian Constitution assigns exclusive legislative domain over local governments to the states, unlike in many other countries where the impetus for decentralisation originated at the national level and implementation responsibility also resided at the national level, in India, the final responsibility for the design and implementation of local government reforms lay with the states. Unsurprisingly, given the diversity in their historical trajectories and current sociopolitical and economic situations, across the states there has been tremendous variation in the design, scope and extent of devolution to local governments.

Second, and relatedly, the Indian case also differs from some others in that there have been attempts in the past to empower local governments. Hence, the latest effort to revitalize local government is by no means a "greenfield" initiative. In particular, this means that the novelty of the reforms—the extent to which they represent a significant departure from the pre-1993 scenario—varies across the states. For instance, the provision mandating regular elections to rural local bodies clearly has different implications in the state of Bihar, where elections to rural local bodies were last held in 1978, than it does in the state of West Bengal where elections have been regularly held every five years since 1978.[1]

Lastly, it should also be noted that whereas in some countries the impetus for decentralisation has come from external sources or has been triggered by an economic crisis, in India it was home-grown and there was no single precipitating event that led to the reform. That is not to say, however, that the pressure for reforms came from the grassroots. Instead, the reforms reflected the emergence of a remarkable consensus among India's policy-making and intellectual elites.

The Constitutional Setting and the 73rd and 74th Amendments

That state governments effectively enjoyed in the holding of elections to local bodies, the amendment takes away an option that the state government previously had though it chose not to exercise it. And in politics, as in finance, options have value even if not ultimately exercised.

India is a federal parliamentary democracy made up of 28 states and 7 union territories.[2] At the national level, legislative authority rests with the two houses of the Parliament: the Lok Sabha (House of the People), which consists of 545 members, all but two of whom are directly elected from single-member parliamentary constituencies distributed proportionally on the basis of population among the states and union territories; and to a lesser extent, the Rajya Sabha (Council of States), which has no more than 250 members, most of whom are indirectly elected by the members of the state legislative assemblies of the various states.[3]

The titular head of state is the President. Executive authority, however, resides with the national government—in particular, the Council of Ministers—headed by the Prime

Minister who is the leader of the political party that is able to secure the support of the majority of the members of the Lok Sabha, either directly or through some form of coalitional agreement. Though the government enjoys broad powers and discretion in the design and implementation of programmes and policies, it is ultimately answerable to the Parliament.

The parliamentary structure at the national level is, with some exceptions, replicated at the level of individual states. Each state has a legislative assembly, members of which are directly elected from single-member constituencies organised on the basis of population. The titular head of each state is the Governor, who is appointed by the President. But, as at the national level, executive authority rests effectively with the state government headed by the Chief Minister, the leader of the political party with majority support in the state legislature.

Until the passage of the 73rd and 74th constitutional amendments, the states were the only sub-national units officially recognised by the Indian constitution.[4] And the constitution grants individual states considerable legislative autonomy. Schedule Seven of the constitution explicitly demarcates the respective legislative domains of the state legislatures and the national Parliament. The functional areas over which the national Parliament has exclusive domain are specified in List I, also called the "Union List". Items on this list include among other things, defence, foreign affairs, currency, income taxes, inter-state commerce, and key infrastructure. On the other hand, state legislatures have exclusive authority to enact legislation dealing with the items in List II, known as the "State List". Included in this list are items such as law and order, public health, agriculture, wealth taxes, land tenure and land reforms, and most notably in the current context, functions of local governments. List III, the "Concurrent List" includes items such as electricity, newspapers, education, price controls, etc., over which the national Parliament and the state legislatures share jurisdiction.

As a matter of fact, the Indian constitution recognises and makes special provisions for mandatory political representation—through reservation of seats in the legislative assemblies at both the state and the national levels—of two types of historically disadvantaged groups: Dalits and Adivasis.

The legislative origins of the 73rd and 74th constitutional amendments date back to the the Constitution (64th Amendment) Bill, which was introduced in the Parliament in July 1989 by the government of the then Prime Minister Rajiv Gandhi. The introduction of this Bill represented the first attempt to confer constitutional status on rural local governments. Though the Bill's broader aim of revitalizing rural local government was greeted favourably, some of the details were criticised and the bill was ultimately defeated in the Rajya Sabha. It is worth noting that the main criticism leveled against the Bill was that it offered the states little discretion in the design of local government reforms.

The 73rd and 74th constitutional amendments were introduced in Parliament in September, 1991 by the Government of Prime Minister Narasimha Rao of the Congress(I) Party in the form of two separate bills: the 72nd Amendment Bill for rural local bodies (also known as panchayats) and the 73rd Amendment Bill for municipalities. They were referred to a Joint Select Committee of Parliament and were ultimately passed as the 73rd and 74th Amendment Bills in December, 1992.[5] After the bills were ratified by the state assemblies of more than half the states, the President gave his assent on April 20, 1993. The amendments were then officially enacted through the issuance of government notifications. The Constitution (73rd Amendment) Act, 1992 (commonly referred to as the Panchayati Raj Act) went into effect on April 24, 1993, and the Constitution (74th Amendment) Act, 1992 (the Nagarpalika Act), on June 1, 1993.

With local governments being a state subject in Schedule Seven of the constitution, any legislation reforming the structure of local government has to, ultimately, be enacted at the state level. The first task of the states was therefore to pass conformity acts, which either introduced new legislation or amended existing legislation, to bring the state laws into line with the provisions of the amendment. Under the amendments, states had a year, from the date the amendment went into effect, to do so.

Because the amendments contain both mandatory and discretionary provisions, the degree of flexibility afforded the states in this task varied with the provision in question. The distinction between mandatory and discretionary provisions is embodied in the specific language adopted in the acts and carried over into the newly inserted articles of the constitution. The mandatory provisions were those that contain the word "shall" in referring to the steps that individual states needed to take. In the discretionary provisions, on the other hand, the word "may" figures prominently. And so, while many of the discretionary provisions laid out a vision and created a space for individual states to legislatively innovate in reforming local government, ultimately, the design and scope of particular reforms was left to the discretion of individual state legislatures.

Mandatory Provisions

Of the mandatory provisions of the Panchayati Raj Act, the most critical are those that strengthen the structure of representative democracy and political representation at the local level. The key mandatory provisions are:

- the establishment in every state (except those with populations below 2 million) of rural local bodies (panchayats) at the village, intermediate and district levels (Article 243B).
- direct elections to all seats in the panchayats at all levels (Article 243C).
- compulsory elections to panchayats every five years with the elections being held before the end of the term

of the incumbent panchayat. In the event that a panchayat is dissolved prematurely, elections must be held within six months, with the newly elected members serving out the remainder of the five year term (Article 243E)

- mandatory reservation of seats in all panchayats at all levels for Dalits and Adivasis in proportion to their share of the panchayat population (Article 243D)
- mandatory reservation of one-third of all seats in all panchayats at all levels for women, with the reservation for women applying to the seats reserved for Dalits and Adivasis as well (Article 243D)
- indirect elections to the position of panchayat chairperson at the intermediate and district levels (Article 243C)
- mandatory reservation of the position of panchayat chairperson at all levels for Dalits and Adivasis in proportion to their share in the state population (Article 243D)
- mandatory reservation of one-third of the positions of panchayat chairperson at all three levels for women (Article 243D).

In addition, the Act mandates the constitution of two state-level commissions: an independent election commission to supervise and manage elections to local bodies, much as the Election Commission of India manages state assembly and parliamentary elections (Article 243K); and a state finance commission, established every five years, to review the financial position of local bodies and recommend the principles that should govern the allocation of funds and taxation authority to local bodies (Article 243I).

Discretionary Provisions

Among the discretionary provisions, the two central ones, which in the opinion of many observers are the core of the amendment, call upon the states to:

- endow the Gram Sabha—the electorate of a village panchayat—with powers and functions at the village level (Article 243A)
- devolve powers and authority to panchayats so as to enable them to function as institutions of self-government. In particular, the provision calls for devolution of powers and responsibilities for the preparation of plans and implementation of schemes for development and social justice dealing with an impressively wide range of items, which are listed in a new schedule, Schedule XI, of the constitution (Article 243G).

A further discretionary provision (Article 243H) authorises states to pass legislation aimed at increasing the financial resources available to rural local bodies by increasing the latters' statutory taxation powers and by providing for grants-in-aid from the state government.

The newly introduced Schedule XI of the constitution (shown in Table 1) contains a comprehensive list of functional items, ranging from agricultural extension, implementation of land reforms, poverty alleviation, and promotion of small-scale industries to health, primary and secondary education and family welfare. In fact, there is considerable overlap between Schedule XI and the State List of Schedule VII of the constitution, with one of the notable omissions in Schedule XI being law and order.

Two other points need to be mentioned. The first is that while, for the most part, the 74th amendment act deals with urban local bodies, a key article contained in that amendment applies to rural local bodies as well. The article in question, Article 243ZD, mandates the constitution of District Planning Committees to consolidate the plans prepared by both rural and urban local bodies.

The second point is that the provisions of the 73rd amendment did not apply to what are known as Scheduled

Table 1 : Eleventh Schedule of the Constitution of India

No.	*Description*	*Category*
1.	Agriculture including agricultural extension	Agriculture and allied
2.	Land improvement, land reforms, land consolidation, soil conservation	Agriculture and allied
3.	Minor irrigation, water management, watershed development	Agriculture and allied
4.	Animal husbandry, dairy, poultry	Agriculture and allied
5.	Fisheries	Agriculture and allied
6.	Social forestry, farm foresty	Agriculture and allied
7.	Minor forest produce	Agriculture and allied
8.	Small scale industries	Industries
9.	Khadi, village, cottage industries	Industries
10.	Rural housing	Welfare
11.	Drinking water	Core
12.	Fuel and fodder	Agriculture and allied
13.	Roads, culverts, bridges, ferries, waterways	Core
14.	Rural electrification, electricity distribution	Core
15.	Non-conventional energy sources	Welfare

(Contd. . . . .)

No.	*Description*	*Category*
16.	Poverty alleviation programs	Welfare
17.	Education, including primary and secondary schools	Welfare
18.	Technical training and vocational education	Welfare
19.	Adult and non-formal education	Welfare
20.	Libraries	Welfare
21.	Cultural activities	Welfare
22.	Markets and fairs	Agriculture and allied
23.	Health and sanitation, hospitals, primary health centers, dispensaries	Core
24.	Family welfare	Welfare
25.	Women and child development	Welfare
26.	Social welfare, welfare of handicapped and mentally retarded	Welfare
27.	Welfare of weaker sections, Scheduled Castes and Tribes	Welfare
28.	Public distribution system	Welfare
29.	Maintenance of community assets	Core

Areas, constitutionally recognised areas of the country with large Adivasi populations. The amendment did however contain a provison reserving the right of Parliament to extend the amendments' provisions regarding local bodies to Scheduled Areas at a later date without the need for a further constitutional amendment. Parallel provisions regarding local governments in Scheduled Areas were ultimately enacted through the Provisions of the Panchayats (Extension to the Scheduled Areas) Act of 1996.

Context

The public debate and discussion that preceded the adoption of the 73rd and 74th constitutional amendments revolved almost entirely around the need to correct the multiple failures of the bureaucratic and centralised apparatus of the Indian developmental state—the failure to ensure the efficient and effective delivery of public services, to effectively provide and maintain key infrastructure essential for economic growth, to promote equity, and to eliminate the multiple deprivations associated with poverty.

The basic claim made by proponents of the amendments was that by devolving powers to locally elected bodies the above-mentioned failures would be addressed. The fact that this claim was accepted, at least on the surface, by almost all participants in the public debate—differences of opinion remained on the details—is remarkable given the earlier more contested view of the virtues of localizing government in India's public discourse.

To better understand the roots of this consensus, the scope of the constitutional reforms at the national level, and in particular, the thinking behind the specific provisions of the amendment act, it helps to have a sense of the historical experience with local government, the political constraints imposed by India's federal structure, and the functionings of the Indian developmental state, particularly in rural areas.

- Debates in the Constituent Assembly reflected contrasting positions of Gandhi and Ambedkar on the desirability of decentralised governance structures.
- Phases in the history of panchayati raj in India and the associated committees: Balwantrai Mehta Committee and the phase of ascendancy (1959-64); phase of stagnation (1965-69); phase of decline (1969-77); Asoka Mehta Committee and the revival of panchayats but as political institutions in a few states.
- Elections to local governments frequently postponed at the discretion of the state governments, or in many cases because of writ petitions to the courts.
- Over the years, rural development in the Indian context came to be characterised by a proliferation of government schemes and programmes, staffed by civil servants who, at lower levels, were, at best, accountable only to their superiors in the administrative hierarchy of their respective agencies or line departments, and at upper levels, motivated largely by career concerns in which the responsiveness to state-level elected representatives figured prominently.
- Under the planning approach, preoccupation with narrow sectorally-specific physical targets, little attention to integrated outcomes
- Inefficiencies, leakage, corruption associated with the plethora of government schemes; increasing flow of funds through panchayats in their role as implementing agencies for various schemes led to emergence of collusive networks connecting bureaucrats, local and higher-level elected representatives, and other members of dominant local elites.

  Undermined the legitimacy of the panchayats and wreaked havoc on the the performance of various schemes.
- in 1991, under the pressure of a severe balance of payments crisis, and through a congruence of

favourable political factors, the government then in power initiated a broad package of economic policy reforms, which subsequent governments have, for the most part, maintained and supplemented. Under the new economic policy regime, India's notorious industrial licensing regime has been largely dismantled, domestic industry has been deregulated, trade liberalisation measures have been implemented, and the economy has been opened up to foreign direct investment. Financial sector reforms have also been introduced at a slow but steady pace.

- The timing of 1991 trade and industrial policy reforms happens to roughly coincide with the attempt to revitalize local government, but in terms of the initial impulse as well as the ultimate aim, these reforms are quite distinct. Trade and industrial policy reforms precipitated by balance of payments crisis and the poor performance in terms of economic growth. Aim was to reduce sphere of government influence and control. Consensus behind the need for local government reforms emerged more gradually, and was borne out of the failures of the Indian developmental state in terms of human development and poverty alleviation, particularly in rural areas. The aim was to reconfigure the structure of government.
- The Panchayati Raj amendment has been hailed as a landmark in the evolution of rural local government in India. And they may well turn out to be so in the long run. But, in many ways the provisions of the amendment represent a marginal or incremental reform in that they are specifically tailored to address some of the particular (perceived) problems with previous attempts to empower local government without radically reconstituting the balance of political power at the sub-national level. The clearest indication of this is the seeming gap between the mandatory provisions

requiring regular elections to local bodies and the weaker discretionary nature of the other parts of the amendment.

Assessment of the Design and Scope of Devolution at the State Level

The task of assessing any reform initiative can be subdivided into two stages: a first stage of documenting the extent and scope of the reforms, and a second of evaluating the effects of the reforms. Drawing causal inferences about the impact of particular changes in the policy environment is almost always difficult in the absence of policy experiments. With so-called stroke-of-the-pen reforms that are narrowly focused—for instance, a reduction in tariffs, or the removal of industrial licensing requirements—the first stage is typically relatively straightforward. But, with reforms that are broader in scope, in particular those that aim to bring about fundamental changes in the institutional context and practice of government, even the apparently simple task of documenting the scope and extent of the reforms becomes difficult.

There are two reasons why this is so. The first is the fact that, these reforms are intrinsically multidimensional in nature. An attempt to revitalize local government and institutionalise more decentralised and participatory forms of local governance necessitates reforms along multiple dimensions. The structure and status of institutions of representative democracy need to be altered. Administrative reforms transferring control over civil servants from line departments to local governments have to be initiated. The minutiae of administrative procedures, governing recruitment, promotion, reporting structures, etc. have to be reworked. Functional responsibilities for a wide range of items have to be reassigned. The various aspects of the devolution of financial resources have to be worked out from changes in the assignment of taxes and the adoption of formulae for the transfer of funds to the relative shares of tied vs. untied grants. Keeping track of the changes in all these dimensions is difficult.

A second and more prosaic reason is simply the practical difficulties of empirically distinguishing de jure or nominal reform measures from substantive de facto steps that actually alter day-to-day practices. There is a real danger that too much emphasis is placed on easily recorded indicators of changes in legislative provisions and bureaucratic rules and processes, and insufficient attention paid to whether even clearly mandated changes are effected in practice. This is not to say that changes in the formal legislative and institutional environment are unimportant, only that in contexts where formal structures may be imperfectly applied/enforced, the ground-level reality may differ considerably. Changes in formal structures may well be important as necessary conditions, but are unlikely to prove sufficient.

A further important complication in the Indian context is the fact that though some provisions of the 73rd and 74th amendments were mandatory, the design and degree of implementation of many of the key reforms called for in these amendments were left to the discretion of individual states. Not surprisingly, that has led to considerable variation in the scope and extent of devolution across the Indian states. The assessment is limited to the fourteen major states—states with populations exceeding 15 million that are not special category states. Where relevant (and possible), I also provide some indication of the aggregate India-wide picture as well.

Tables 2(a) and 2(b) provide a basic profile of the fourteen states. The sheer size of many of the states and the tremendous diversity among them, whatever the characteristic one is looking at, is striking. In 1991, the states ranged in population from a low of 16 million in Haryana to 139 million in Uttar Pradesh. West Bengal, with a population density of 767 per square kilometer was nearly six times more densely populated than Rajasthan. Punjab's per-capita state domestic product of Rs. 4336 (at constant 1980-81 prices) was over three times that of Bihar, the poorest state. There was tremendous variation in rural poverty as well, from a low of 6.2% in Punjab to a high of 48.6% in Bihar. In terms of human development, the state of Kerala stood well apart from the other states, a well-known fact that has received much attention in international development circles. The so-called BIMARU states, Bihar, Madhya Pradesh, Rajasthan and Uttar Pradesh lay at the opposite extreme.

These observable differences in key economic, demographic, and human development indicators stem from and are supplemented by less easily quantified differences in the states' colonial histories, political culture, levels of social mobilisation, and internal caste polarisation. To the extent that the prospects for participatory local governance depend in part on a variety of enabling features of the contexts in which it is attempted, as many have argued, this diversity in the initial conditions across the Indian states clearly needs to be borne in mind in considering the design, scope and impact of state-level devolution efforts.

Political Devolution: Voice, Autonomy and Accountability

Of the various institutional reforms, both nominal and substantive, that individual states have initiated since 1993, perhaps the most easily verifiable are the steps taken to meet the mandatory provisions of the constitutional amendment regarding the structure of political representation below the state level. And so I begin by reviewing the progress on this front.

The constitutional amendment mandated the creation of an uniform three-tier structure of local government institutions at the sub-state level.[6] Immediately below the state are the district panchayats, below them, the block panchayats, and at the lowest level, the gram panchayats (village councils). Gram Panchayats have existed in most states since at least the late 1950s (following the recommendations of the Balwantra Mehta Committee). However, in some states, there were no block

Table 2(a)
Basic profile of major Indian states in the early 1990s

State	Total population 1991 (millions)	Area ('000 sq.km.)	Population density 1991 (per sq.km.)	Rural population 1991 (millions)	Fraction of population 1991			Gross state domestic product 1991	
					Rural	Dalit (SC)	Adivasi (ST)	Per-capita	Share from agriculture
Andhra Pradesh	67	275	242	49	73.1	18.0	8.0	2041	48.3
Bihar	86	174	497	75	86.9	15.3	8.2	1308	32.9
Gujarat	41	196	211	27	65.5	7.0	20.9	2823	37.1
Haryana	16	44	372	12	75.4	21.6	0.0	3923	57.5
Karnataka	45	192	235	31	69.1	18.2	5.2	2556	49.9
Kerala	29	39	749	21	73.6	11.0	1.4	2148	41.9
Madhya Pradesh	66	443	149	51	76.8	14.8	29.0	1824	52.5
Maharashtra	79	308	257	48	61.3	11.5	13.2	3799	32.3
Orissa	32	156	203	27	86.6	16.7	24.3	1724	36.5
Punjab	20	50	403	14	70.5	31.9	0.0	4336	68.9
Rajasthan	44	342	129	34	77.1	18.0	15.4	2021	52.6
Tamil Nadu	56	130	429	37	65.8	22.9	1.4	2573	35.6
Uttar Pradesh	139	294	473	112	80.2	23.2	0.2	1849	50.1
West Bengal	68	89	767	49	72.5	27.6	7.3	2505	37.4
India	846	3166	267	629	74.3	.	.	.	.

Table 2(b)
Human development indicators for major Indian states in the early 1990s

State	Rural headcount index 1993	Households with:		Rural female literacy 1992	School attendance rate 1992	Ante-natal care rate 1992	Under five mortality rate 1992	Child vaccin-ation rate 1992
		Electricity 1991	Permanent dwellings 1991					
Andhra Pradesh	29.2	46.3	38.4	23.9	57.8	66	96	44.9
Bihar	48.6	12.6	30.2	17.9	47.3	27	137	10.7
Gujarat	32.5	65.9	56.9	38.6	68.4	50	104	49.8
Haryana	17.0	70.4	50.1	32.5	73.7	67	108	53.5
Karnataka	37.9	52.5	42.5	34.8	64.7	65	102	52.1
Kerala	19.5	48.4	56.0	85.1	85.8	97	41	54.4
Madhya Pradesh	36.6	43.3	30.5	19.7	56.7	36	143	29.2
Maharashtra	42.9	69.4	52.2	41.0	75.1	70	76	64.2
Orissa	43.5	23.5	18.7	30.8	62.9	39	137	36.1
Punjab	6.2	82.3	77.0	43.9	73.3	86	69	61.9
Rajasthan	23.0	35.0	56.1	11.6	52.9	23	108	21.1
Tamil Nadu	38.5	54.7	45.5	41.8	74.1	78	95	64.9
Uttar Pradesh	28.6	21.9	41.0	19.0	56.2	30	162	19.8
West Bengal	25.1	32.9	32.6	38.1	61.6	69	107	34.3
India	33.0	42.4	41.6	30.6	61.6	49	119	35.4

panchayats (or their equivalent) or district panchayats and in these states, these higher tiers of sub-state local governments had to be created. The relevant states all enacted the necessary legislation to meet this requirement. Table 3(a) depicts the structure of representative democracy that resulted. From a single national Parliament and 25 state legislative assemblies, India went to having 238,682 additional constitutionally recognised representative bodies, 499 at the district level, 5905 at the block level, and 232,278 at the village level. And for the first time, there exists an uniform three-tier structure of rural local governments in India. But, as Table 3(a) indicates there remains considerable variation across states in the make-up of the three-tier structure, the details of which were left to the discretion of the states, and were in part determined by varied historical legacies. In particular, village panchayats in Kerala and West Bengal stand out in being considerably larger, in terms of population than village panchayats in other states.

Much of the rhetoric that accompanies initiatives to empower local governments highlights the need to downscale government, to bring "government closer to the people." At least on one dimension, the "closeness" of the electorate to their elected representatives (as measured by the number of individuals represented by each elected representative), that is literally what the mandated creation of these locally elected bodies did. Before 1994, the elected representatives effectively closest to the voters were the state legislative assembly members (MLAs). As Table 3(b) indicates, on an average, this meant a population of nearly 200,000 or more per MLA. After 1994, this number has, in principle, come down to a few hundred in most states with the village panchayat representative being closest to the population . Of course, these numbers overstate the contrast, since village panchayats did exist even prior to the amendment. But, given the irregularity of local body elections in most states, it is not clear that panchayat members could reasonably be considered "elected" representatives. The larger point though is that by increasing the pool of constitutionally protected elected representatives some five hundredfold, the amendment brought about a dramatic broadening of the representative democratic base of India.

Of course, for this new structure to meaningfully increase the closeness of elected representative, elections have to be held regularly. Prior to 1994, with the exception of West Bengal since 1978, local body elections had not been held on a regular schedule in most states. In many cases, elections were delayed as a result of writ petitions submitted to the courts by groups other than the state government. In others, state governments themselves unilaterally postponed elections, putting forward a variety of reasons for the postponement, from natural disasters to civil unrest to school holidays. By mandating regular elections to local government institutions, the constitutional amendment sought to restrict the discretionary authority of the state governments. The amendment even contains a provision (Article 243O) barring interference by the courts in electoral matters.

Have these provisions made a difference? The second column of Table 3(c) provides a partial answer. Shown there are the dates of elections to village panchayats in the last ten years. Since the constitutional amendment calls for an uniform and unalterable term of five years, each state should have had two elections, and the period between elections should not have exceeded five years. Table 3(c) indicates that the first standard has mostly been met. But, less than half the states have met the second, constitutionally mandated standard. And in the case of Orissa and Uttar Pradesh, which did hold elections within five years, elections were held only as a result of court interventions overturning the state governments' decision to postpone elections.

Even when elections have been held, some states have failed to meet the provisions regarding mandatory representation for women, Dalits, and Adivasis. Drawing on the most recent local body elections for which data are available, the second through eighth columns of Table 3(c)

Table 3(a)

State	Number of rural local bodies (RLBs)			Population per elected body (`000s)				Area per village LB	Number of urban local bodies	Population per urban local body (`000s)
				State assembly	Rural local bodies (RLBs)					
	District	Block	Village		District	Block	Village			
Andhra Pradesh	22	1093	21784	66,508	2210.0	44.5	2.2	12	116	154.2
Bihar	55	726	12181	86,374	1364.0	103.3	6.2	14	170	66.8
Gujarat	19	184	13547	41,310	1424.4	147.1	2.0	14	149	95.6
Haryana	16	111	5958	16,464	775.6	111.8	2.1	7	82	49.4
Karnataka	27	175	5673	44,977	1150.7	177.5	5.5	33	215	64.7
Kerala	14	152	990	29,099	1529.9	140.9	21.6	36	58	132.4
Madhya Pradesh	45	459	31126	66,181	1129.8	110.8	1.6	14	404	38.0
Maharashtra	29	319	27611	78,937	1668.8	151.7	1.8	11	244	125.2
Orissa	30	314	5255	31,660	914.2	87.3	5.2	29	102	41.5
Punjab	17	138	11591	20,282	840.5	103.5	1.2	4	137	43.7
Rajasthan	32	237	9184	44,006	1060.6	143.2	3.7	37	183	55.0
Tamil Nadu	28	385	12593	55,859	1313.6	95.5	2.9	10	744	25.6
Uttar Pradesh	83	904	58620	139,112	1343.5	123.3	1.9	5	684	40.4
West Bengal	17	340	3314	68,078	2904.1	145.2	14.9	26	122	153.3
India	499	5905	232278		1259.9	106.5	2.7	13	3682	59.1

Table 3(b)

	Number of elected representatives to:					Population per elected representative to:				
		State	Rural local bodies				State	Rural local bodies		
	Parliament	assembly	District	Block	Village	Parliament	assembly	District	Block	Village
Andhra Pradesh	42	294	1093	14644	230529	1,583,524	226,218	44,484	3,320	211
Bihar	54	324	1585	15344	165452	1,599,527	266,588	47,332	4,889	453
Gujarat	26	182	761	3814	123470	1,588,830	226,976	35,563	7,096	219
Haryana	10	90	303	2418	54159	1,646,365	182,929	40,953	5,132	229
Karnataka	28	224	919	3340	80627	1,606,329	200,791	33,808	9,302	385
Kerala	20	140	300	1547	10270	1,454,926	207,847	71,394	13,845	2,086
Madhya Pradesh	40	320	946	9097	474351	1,654,529	206,816	53,745	5,589	107
Maharashtra	48	288	1762	3524	303545	1,644,525	274,087	27,466	13,733	159
Orissa	21	147	854	5260	81077	1,507,606	215,372	32,113	5,214	338
Punjab	13	117	274	2441	87842	1,560,151	173,350	52,149	5,854	163
Rajasthan	25	200	997	5257	119419	1,760,240	220,030	34,041	6,456	284
Tamil Nadu	39	234	648	6499	97398	1,432,281	238,713	56,761	5,660	378
Uttar Pradesh	85	473	2551	58165	682670	1,636,615	294,106	43,711	1,917	163
West Bengal	42	294	723	8579	50345	1,620,904	231,558	68,285	5,755	981
India	543	4120	13484	128581	2580261	1,558,568				

provide an indication of the extent to which this particular mandate was met. The constitutional provision mandated that a third of all seats at all levels be reserved for women. In most states this mandate was met, and some such as Karnataka, Tamil Nadu, and West Bengal, even exceeded it. However, in Punjab and Uttar Pradesh the mandate was not met. The fifth through eighth columns display the relative representation ratios of Dalits and Adivasis at the lowest and highest tiers of local government. The relative representation ratio of a group is defined as the ratio of the fraction of elected representatives from that group to that group's share in the state's population. By consitutional mandate, this ratio ought to be one. That clearly is not the case in a number of states. The fact that the problem appears to be worse at the level of village panchayats is suggestive of the social and exclusionary dynamics operating in the villages of the states in question. At the district level, with fewer seats to fill in absolute terms, this appears to have been less of an issue, presumably because almost all the major political parties, for purely instrumental electoral reasons, have recruited some members from traditionally disadvantaged groups into their ranks.

Regular elections may ensure, albeit crudely, some degree of accountability and provide some legitimacy to locally elected representatives, but they represent only one step in the process of political devolution. Equally important is the degree of political autonomy afforded locally elected bodies. On this front, there's little variation across the states. Reviews of the various state conformity acts indicate that even at the statutory level—let alone in terms of actual practice—state governments have, against the spirit of the amendment, retained considerable powers over the rural local bodies. As Table 3(d) indicates, in all states, the state-level legislation vests various functionaries of the state government—for instance, the district collector (the chief civil servant at the district level)—with the authority to intervene in the functioning of rural local bodies. These provisions have been criticised by many proponents of local government, not because they do not recognize the need to have some accountability and oversight mechanisms in place, but because the provisions violate the separation of powers and such authority is better retained by the courts.

As indicated in the second column of Table 3(d), all the states also acknowledge a role for elected representatives to higher levels of government, namely Members of Parliament and Members of Legislative Assembly in the two higher tiers of rural local government. Again, this has been criticised because of concerns about the disproportionate influence that MPs and MLAs are likely to enjoy.

The first column of Table 3(d) reveals the state-level variation in one aspect of the design of political devolution that is of particular concern in the Indian context. And that has to do with whether the village panchayat chairperson is selected through direct elections. Apart from Karnataka, Kerala, Maharashtra and West Bengal, all the states require direct elections. The inclusion of this feature of a presidential system of government has been decried by many who see in it the potential for perpetuating the status of panchayat chairperson as a "first among equals." The concern regarding this provision stems from the experience of the last five decades.

Lastly, by explicitly recognizing the Gram Sabha—the electorate of a village panchayat—the constitutional amendment envisioned a more direct channel through which citizens could exercise "voice" and participate in local governance. The hope was that the Gram Sabha, through regular meetings over the course of the year, could become the fulcrum of the community development process, playing a key role in both the planning and subsequent monitoring of development activities. The particular roles and functions entrusted to the Gram Sabha were however left to the discretion of state legislatures. The state-level legislation, in most states, does little more than mechanically list a variety of nominal functions and duties to be performed by Gram

Table 3(c)

State	Elections to village local bodies: 1993-2002		Percentage of elected representatives women			Relative representation ratio				Reservations for backward castes
						Dalits (SCs)		Adivasis (STs)		
			District	Block	Village	District	Village	District	Village	
Andhra Pradesh	1995	2001	33.2	37.0	33.8	0.7	0.9	0.8	0.8	Fixed share
Bihar	-	2001	.	.	.	.	.	.	.	Proportional
Gujarat	1995	2002	33.4	33.4	33.4	1.1	0.5	0.7	0.4	Fixed share
Haryana	1994	2000	33.3	33.4	33.1	1.0	0.2	N.A.	N.A.	Conditional
Karnataka	1993	2000	36.5	40.2	43.8	1.0	1.2	1.0	1.8	Fixed share
Kerala	1995	2000	34.7	36.4	32.9	0.9	1.1	1.0	0.9	None
Madhya Pradesh	1994	2000	33.7	34.2	32.9	1.0	0.9	1.0	1.0	Conditional
Maharashtra	1997	2002	33.3	33.3	33.0	1.0	1.2	1.0	0.9	Fixed share
Orissa	1997	2002	34.4	35.6	35.3	0.6	0.5	0.6	0.6	None
Punjab	1998	-	32.5	13.4	35.4	1.0	1.0	N.A.	N.A.	Conditional
Rajasthan	1995	2000	33.2	33.1	32.5	1.0	0.8	1.0	0.8	Proportional
Tamil Nadu	1996	2001	34.7	35.3	33.7	0.9	0.9	0.3	0.5	None
Uttar Pradesh	1995	2000	25.4	24.1	25.5	0.7	0.6	1.4	0.6	Proportional
West Bengal	1993	1998	34.0	35.1	35.6	1.4	1.0	1.3	1.0	None

sabhas. Only in Kerala, has there been an effort to seriously engage the Gram Sabha.

Functional and Financial Devolution

Article 243G of the constitutional amendment, which calls upon state governments to devolve power, authority and responsibilities to rural local bodies so as to enable them to "function as institutions of self-government," captures the core ostensible aim of the constitutional reform. And that was to empower and enable rural local bodies to play the central role in the provision of public services, the creation and maintenance of local public goods, and the planning and implementation of developmental activities and programmes to alleviate poverty and promote distributive equity.

At the time the constitutional amendments were introduced, the situation in most states was almost farcically far from this ideal. The functional domain of rural local bodies was largely limited to the provision of some core services such as street lighting, water supply, sanitation, and local roads. To the extent that panchayats were involved in developmental activities, they played the role of implementing agencies at the local level for various schemes sponsored by either Central government or state government departments. In this capacity, panchayats helped identify beneficiaries for a number of transfer schemes, and oversaw the management and implementation of various local infrastructure schemes funded through various state government departments.

The picture presented above is an aggregated one. There have been attempts at various points in time and in various states to enhance the role of local governments. At the national level, the initiative for community development following the Balwantrai Mehta Committee has already been mentioned. The experience of a few selected states also bears mentioning. The states of Gujarat and Maharashtra were early reformers, passing legislation in the 1960s transferring many activities, including primary health care and education to district

Table 3(d)

State	Head of VP directly elected?	MPs/ MLAs members of local bodies?	State government has power to…					
			… suspend/remove head of local body		… suspend/dissolve local body		…countermand orders of local body	
			Village	District	Village	District	Village	District
Andhra Pradesh	Yes	Both	Yes	Yes	Yes	Yes	Yes	Yes
Bihar	Yes	Both	Yes	Yes	Yes	Yes	Yes	Yes
Gujarat	Yes	MLAs	Yes	Yes	Yes	Yes	Yes	Yes
Haryana	Yes	Both	Yes	Yes	Yes	Yes	Yes	Yes
Karnataka	No	Both	Yes	Yes	Yes	Yes	Yes	Yes
Kerala	No	Both	Yes	Yes	Yes	Yes	Yes	Yes
Madhya Pradesh	Yes	MLAs	Yes	Yes	Yes	Yes	Yes	Yes
Maharashtra	No	Both	Yes	Yes	Yes	Yes	Yes	Yes
Orissa	Yes	MLAs	Yes	Yes	Yes	Yes	Yes	Yes
Punjab	Yes	MLAs	Yes	Yes	Yes	Yes	Yes	Yes
Rajasthan	Yes	MLAs	Yes	Yes	Yes	Yes	Yes	Yes
Tamil Nadu	Yes	Both	Yes	Yes	Yes	Yes	Yes	Yes
Uttar Pradesh	Yes	Both	Yes	Yes	Yes	Yes	Yes	Yes
West Bengal	No	Both	Yes	Yes	Yes	Yes	Yes	Yes

panchayats. In both states, funds were devolved as well and a separate administrative service—the Panchayat Service in Gujarat and the Maharashtra Development Service in Maharashtra—was set up to facilitate the transfer (or deputation) of state-level civil servants to work with the district panchayats.

More recently, in the mid-1980s, the southern state of Karnataka undertook a significant and in many respects, far-reaching devolution of functional responsibilities to the district panchayats. But, as in the cases of Gujarat and Maharashtra, the original vision behind the decentralisation effort has not been sustained. Significant attempts to broaden the functional domain of village panchayats have been rarer. West Bengal, since 1978, has made a concerted attempt to more directly involve village panchayats in the implementation of various programmes.

To what extent has the passage of the constitutional amendments changed the situation? While a definitive response to this question is not possible without a detailed empirical study, which has yet to be done, of the institutional arrangements under which local governments operate on a day-to-day basis, anecdotal reports, media accounts and a myriad of case-studies suggest that, with perhaps a couple of exceptions, the progress by the states in genuine functional and financial devolution has been extremely limited.

At the statutory level, almost all the states have enacted new or amended previous legislation to broaden the functional domain of panchayats. But, as Vijayanand points out, statutory provisions, unless they are extremely detailed, provide "only the skeletal framework and form" for the day-to-day workings of government and for the design and implementation of public programmes. The "flesh and blood of administration," in practice, comes from the myriad of administrative rules and procedures—procurement rules, reporting structures, compensation schemes, accounting systems, etc.—that are put in place by the executive branch of government.

Table 4(a)

State	No. of Schedule Eleven items for which legislation enacted and/or government orders issued transferring:			Status (as of 2001) of District Planning Committee	
	Functions	Functionaries	Funds	Constituted?	Chairperson
Andhra Pradesh	13	2	5	No	-
Bihar	-	-	-	No	-
Gujarat	-	-	-	No	-
Haryana	16	-	-	Partially	-
Karnataka	29	29	29	Partially	-
Kerala	29	15	15	Yes	District panchayat head
Madhya Pradesh	23	9	10	Yes	State minister
Maharashtra	18	18	18	No	-
Orissa	25	3	5	Yes	District panchayat head
Punjab	7	-	-	No	-
Rajasthan	29	-	-	Yes	District panchayat head
Tamil Nadu	29	-	-	Yes	District panchayat head
Uttar Pradesh	13	9	12	Yes	State minister
West Bengal	29	12	12	Yes	District panchayat head

Table 4(b)

State	Restrictions on powers of village panchayats to sanction expenditures (as of 1999)
Andhra Pradesh	Capped at Rs.10,000
Bihar	
Gujarat	Uncapped for own resources
Haryana	Capped at Rs.25,000
Karnataka	Capped at Rs.10,000
Kerala	Uncapped regardless of source
Madhya Pradesh	Rs.300,000 for own resources
Maharashtra	Uncapped for own resources
Orissa	Capped at Rs.1,000
Punjab	Capped at Rs.10,000
Rajasthan	Capped at Rs.100,000
Tamil Nadu	Uncapped for own resources
Uttar Pradesh	Capped at Rs.20,000
West Bengal	Uncapped regardless of source

A number of reports that review the state-level legislation indicate that, in most instances, the statutes merely provide a "shopping list" of various activities and sectors for which panchayats would be newly responsible (Government of India (2001), World Bank (2000)). Little detail is provided in the legislation in terms of the specific roles and responsibilities of the different tiers of panchayats relative to the other tiers and to the existing line departments of the state governments.

Whether the lack of specificity and clarity in the state conformity legislation was strategic, as some have argued, can be debated. State legislatures were under some pressure to enact the conformity legislation within a prescribed time frame. Articulating a detailed road map for administrative devolution may not have been feasible within this time frame. However, if that were the sole reason for the omission of details regarding the framework for functional devolution, one would expect to see, subsequent to the initial legislation, significant administrative steps being taken.

In ascertaining the extent of administrative devolution, it is, therefore, necessary to go beyond the legislative statutes and review whether the administrative steps—issuance of government orders and circulars, notification of changes in administrative rules and procedures—needed to fully operationalize the intent of any new legislation have in fact been taken.

One such study is the Report of the Working Group on Decentralised Planning and Panchayati Raj Institutions (Government of India (2001)), a high-level task force of the Central government. Table 4(a) displays the report's findings, based upon information compiled by the Ministry of Rural Development, on the extent to which functions, funds, and functionaries have been transferred to rural local bodies. The second column displays the count of activities—of the 29 listed in Schedule XI of the constitution—that individual states have transferred to local governments. In several states, all the functions appear to have been transferred though what exactly this means is unclear. But from the third and fourth columns it is clear that even when functions have been statutorily or even administratively transferred to panchayats, in most states, the funds and personnel necessary for meaningfully carrying out these functions remain under the administrative control of the state-level bureaucracy (departments of the state governments). Karnataka, Kerala, Maharashtra and West Bengal are the exceptions to this norm.

Yet another indicator of the failure of the states to make any serious efforts to implement the spirit of the amendment comes from looking at the status of the District Planning Committees, the constitution of which was mandated by Article 243ZD. As can be seen from the last two columns of Table 4(a), many states have yet to establish the District Planning Committee. The significance of this is that it indicates that funds for a variety of central and state-sponsored schemes are still being routed through the District Rural Development Agencies and line departments. It is also an indication that the rural local bodies are yet to be genuinely involved in the planning process. Even when the District Planning Committee has been constituted, in some states, contrary to the spirit of the amendment, it is headed by a state minister rather than the chairperson of the district panchayat.

A central theme in the economic literature on decentralisation is that the functional and fiscal domain—taxation and spending authority—of local governments should, to the extent possible, overlap. In a perverse sense the pre-amendment situation in most Indian states satisfied this basic tenet in that the severely circumscribed functional domain of panchayats described above was mirrored by an equally limited fiscal domain. In principle, panchayats, and in particular, village panchayats, did have powers to impose local taxes and assess a variety of fees. In practice, given the limited capacity and effective authority of village panchayats to enforce tax collection, and the even more limited incentives they had to do so under the prevailing system of transfers

Table 5(a)

State	Annual per-capita own revenues (Rs.)						Ratio of own revenue to total revenue: all RLBs		
	Village local bodies			All RLBs					
	90-95	95-98	% chg.	90-95	95-98	% chg.	90-95	95-98	Diff.
Andhra Pradesh	13.5	20.2	49.7	16.2	23.9	48.2	6.1	6.1	0.0
Bihar	0.0	0.0	.	0.0	0.0	.	0.0	0.0	0.0
Gujarat	8.4	10.1	21.0	11.2	13.1	17.3	2.6	1.9	-0.7
Haryana	28.5	32.2	12.9	28.5	32.3	13.2	68.4	61.8	-6.7
Karnataka	6.3	8.6	37.5	6.3	8.6	37.5	1.1	0.9	-0.2
Kerala	19.3	39.5	104.1	19.3	39.5	104.1	31.3	17.7	-13.6
Madhya Pradesh	3.1	4.7	53.8	3.3	5.6	69.9	6.0	4.1	-1.9
Maharashtra	8.8	16.8	90.6	9.7	18.2	88.2	3.1	3.3	0.1
Orissa	2.6	2.4	-6.2	2.6	2.4	-6.2	3.0	1.2	-1.8
Punjab	18.7	28.5	52.0	22.1	33.2	50.6	24.3	34.0	9.7
Rajasthan	4.0	3.4	-13.6	6.7	7.7	14.1	3.0	2.1	-0.9
Tamil Nadu	3.9	6.8	72.2	5.4	8.9	62.8	5.7	8.2	2.4
Uttar Pradesh	0.4	0.3	-24.6	2.7	3.3	23.2	6.3	5.9	-0.4
West Bengal	1.7	1.9	13.5	2.9	3.1	7.8	7.6	3.2	-4.4
India	5.1	7.4	44.4	6.2	8.9	42.5	4.5	3.7	-0.7

Source: own calculations from Annexure VIII of Government of India (2000), Report of the Eleventh Finance Commission.

from the state and central governments, local revenue collection was negligible and revenue dependency—the share of panchayat total income that came from external sources—was in most states very high.

Sources of Revenue of the Panchayats

Panchayat revenues fall into two main categories: own revenues and transfers from higher levels of government. Own revenues, *i.e.*, revenues that are collected locally, come from two sources: non-tax sources such as user fees for local public goods and commons, income from panchayat-owned properties, etc., and own tax revenues. Own taxes are those that are statutorily assigned to local bodies and collected by the local bodies. Typically own taxes have included items such as entertainment taxes, dwelling taxes, taxes on professions, levies on pumps, tractors, etc.

The other main category of revenues, intergovernmental transfers, can be sub-divided into tax and non-tax components as well. The tax component consists of revenues from both assigned taxes—taxes statutorily assigned to local bodies but collected by the state government and transferred to the local body—and shared taxes—taxes assigned to the state and entirely collected by the state government but subsequently shared with local bodies. The non-tax component of intergovernmental transfers takes the form of grants from the central and state governments, tied in most cases to a variety of state-sponsored and centrally-sponsored development schemes.

On the expenditure side, because their effective functional domain was so limited, panchayats had few areas over which they have enjoyed discretionary decision-making authority and budgeting autonomy. The bulk of the expenditures that were incurred by—*i.e.*, nominally routed through—the panchayats were financed by the tied grants linked to specific state and centrally-sponsored schemes. That panchayats lacked genuine spending authority for much of their expenditures is indicated

Table 5(b)

State	Annual per-capita total revenues (Rs.)						Ratio of RLB revenues to state revenues: all RLBs		
	Village local bodies			All RLBs					
	90-95	95-98	% chg.	90-95	95-98	% chg.	90-95	95-98	Diff.
Andhra Pradesh	55	58	5.5	268	397	48.2	25.0	24.2	-0.8
Bihar	31	38	22.8	39	47	21.5	3.7	5.8	2.0
Gujarat	27	35	31.3	439	709	61.5	36.5	33.3	-3.2
Haryana	38	47	24.6	42	52	25.8	2.7	1.7	-0.9
Karnataka	46	69	52.0	592	992	67.4	49.3	50.4	1.1
Kerala	63	199	217.0	63	274	335.5	5.3	12.9	7.7
Madhya Pradesh	51	91	77.9	54	176	223.0	6.1	12.5	6.4
Maharashtra	38	81	114.7	310	555	78.9	20.4	26.0	5.7
Orissa	38	47	26.1	94	202	114.1	10.2	16.2	5.9
Punjab	76	78	1.8	89	100	11.3	5.9	3.9	-2.0
Rajasthan	93	192	105.7	231	367	58.7	22.5	23.5	1.0
Tamil Nadu	40	72	80.5	97	110	13.6	.	5.5	.
Uttar Pradesh	41	51	24.7	42	56	33.0	5.9	5.4	-0.5
West Bengal	41	54	34.0	58	97	66.4	6.1	8.8	2.7
India	43	69	59.3	142	239	68.0	13.2	14.5	1.4

Source: own calculations from Annexure VIII of Government of India (2000), Report of the Eleventh Finance Commission.

Table 5(c)

	Annual per-capita expenditures on core services (Rs.)						Ratio of core services to total expenditures: all RLBs		
	Village local bodies			All RLBs					
	90-95	95-98	% chg.	90-95	95-98	% chg.	90-95	95-98	Diff.
Andhra Pradesh	9.0	16.3	81.4	26.4	55.9	111.5	9.8	13.8	4.0
Bihar	.	.	.	0.0	0.0	.	.	.	.
Gujarat	4.0	5.0	25.2	4.0	5.0	25.2	0.8	0.7	-0.1
Haryana	.	.	.	0.0	0.0	.	.	.	.
Karnataka	8.4	15.9	89.1	53.8	96.2	78.9	9.9	10.0	0.1
Kerala	18.0	24.2	34.5	18.0	27.8	54.6	28.4	12.0	-16.5
Madhya Pradesh	1.9	4.1	115.5	2.4	8.7	261.5	4.4	6.1	1.7
Maharashtra	8.1	14.2	76.6	30.6	59.9	95.9	6.9	8.1	1.2
Orissa	1.6	1.5	-1.3	4.8	2.9	-39.6	5.8	1.5	-4.3
Punjab	37.9	38.0	0.2	37.9	38.0	0.2	41.6	33.5	-8.1
Rajasthan	0.0	0.0	.	0.9	2.8	218.7	0.4	0.8	0.4
Tamil Nadu	16.3	26.4	61.8	19.4	33.4	72.0	30.5	30.7	0.1
Uttar Pradesh	0.4	1.7	296.6	45.0	59.6	32.4	0.9	2.6	1.6
West Bengal	0.1	0.1	-3.6	0.4	0.4	-4.9	0.7	0.4	-0.4
India	4.6	7.2	57.4	10.3	18.7	80.8	6.6	7.3	0.6

Table 5(d)

State	Annual per-capita total expenditures (Rs.)						Ratio of RLB expenditures to state development expenditures: all RLBs		
	Village local bodies			All RLBs					
	90-95	95-98	% chg.	90-95	95-98	% chg.	90-95	95-98	Diff.
Andhra Pradesh	50	55	9.8	268	398	48.3	30.5	27.8	-2.7
Bihar	35	43	23.6	65	74	13.7	12.4	13.6	1.2
Gujarat	13	17	33.2	477	687	44.1	39.5	36.7	2.8
Haryana	61	82	34.5	66	89	35.4	5.5	4.8	-0.7
Karnataka	43	68	60.3	538	968	79.7	54.4	61.1	6.7
Kerala	64	156	143.6	64	235	268.0	6.9	14.6	7.7
Madhya Pradesh	52	94	83.2	54	178	227.1	6.9	15.3	8.4
Maharashtra	51	77	49.2	449	749	67.0	39.0	40.1	1.1
Orissa	38	47	26.1	94	202	114.1	11.5	17.8	4.3
Punjab	75	90	19.8	90	111	23.6	6.6	6.5	-0.1
Rajasthan	94	196	109.5	230	369	60.2	22.8	26.0	3.2
Tamil Nadu	34	57	67.0	63	109	71.2	.	6.3	.
Uttar Pradesh	41	52	25.1	45	60	33.1	8.7	8.0	-0.7
West Bengal	51	62	20.9	69	103	49.9	12.1	11.0	-1.1
India	45	69	52.5	154	256	66.2	17.7	19.6	1.9

by the restrictions that most states placed on the power of village panchayats to sanction expenditures above a pre-specified cap.

The second, fifth, and eighth columns of Tables 5(a) to 5(d) give some sense of the state of panchayat finances in the years, from 1990 to 1995, immediately preceding and subsequent to the passage of the constitutional amendments, and before, presumably, any reforms had taken[7] effect. A couple of disclaimers need to be made about the information presented in these tables. First, data on local government finances in India (and it must be said, in most poor developing economies) are extremely hard to come by and can be quite unreliable when they are available, which in itself is an indication of the status of local governments. The scale of the problem is reflected in the fact that the Eleventh Finance Commission, a statutory body at the national level that prescribes the rules for transfers between the national government and the state governments, specifically set aside funds to assist panchayats in the maintenance of accounts and to set up a database on local government finances (Government of India (2000)). The second caveat is simply that data on the flow of funds through panchayats, no matter how accurate, do not indicate which tier of government has ultimate decision-making authortity.

Table 5(a) clearly indicates the dismal record of rural local bodies in collecting revenues locally. On a per-capita basis, own revenues were laughably low. What revenues were derived locally were generally collected by the village panchayats with whom the statutory powers of taxation resided in most states. Village panchayats in ten of the fourteen states reported own revenues of less than Rs. 10 per year on a per-capita basis. Given the relatively small populations of most village panchayats, these figures translate into aggregate own revenues—for instance, Rs. 760 for Uttar Pradesh, or Rs. 11,310 for Tamil Nadu—that are insufficient to cover even minimal establishment costs. The only exceptions to this generally bleak picture were Haryana, Punjab and Kerala.

Not surprisingly, given the low absolute levels of own revenues, revenue dependency levels were high in most states, with Haryana, Kerala and Punjab again being the exceptions. The level of revenue dependency is a normalised measure that obscures differences in scale. From Table 5(b) it is clear that there were significant differences in the volume of revenues flowing through local governments in different states. Per-capita total revenues of all rural local bodies combined were highest—an order of magnitude higher than in some of the other states—in the states of Gujarat, Karnataka and Maharastra, reflecting their respective legacies of devolution to the district level.

Since own revenues were likely to be the sole source of funding for the discretionary expenditures by village panchayats, the low levels of own revenues are mirrored, as one would expect, by low levels of expenditures on core services by village panchayats. This is apparent from Table 5(c). Somewhat surprising in light of the fact that the core services in question are truly local in nature is the fact that in a few states—Andhra Pradesh, Karnataka, Maharashtra, and Uttar Pradesh—there is a jump in reported expenditures on core services in going from the village panchayat to the higher tiers of local government.

To address the weak financial position of panchayats, in Article 243H, the constitutional amendment authorises states to pass legislation aimed at increasing the financial resources available to rural local bodies by increasing the latters' statutory taxation powers and by providing for grants-in-aid from the state government. To assist the state governments in this process, the amendment mandates the constitution of a State Finance Commission every five years. Under this provision, the State Finance Commissions are charged with advising the state governments on the principles to be adopted in determining the allocation of funds to local bodies and the range of taxes to be devolved to local bodies.

The fourteen major states all constituted State Finance Commissions by the prescribed deadline, *i.e.*, within a year of the amendment coming into effect. Thereafter, however, the record of individual states has varied significantly. It is worth spelling out the sources of this variation, not so much because the work of the State Finance Commissions represents a key element of the constitutional reforms, but rather because it provides yet another example of how, within India's federal structure, even a mandatory constitutional provision can be ignored or deliberately misimplemented. In four of the states, Bihar, Gujarat, Madhya Pradesh, and Orissa, the commission had to be reconstituted because the original commission was not, for a variety of reasons, able to submit its report. In most states, there were delays of two to three years before the commission was able to submit its report, often because the information on local government finances and needs was not readily available. There were further delays still, often over a year after the submission of the commission's report, before the state government submitted an Action Taken Report to the state legislative assembly. And even then, only in some states, for instance Kerala, did the government accept and pledge to implement all of the recommendations made by the finance commission.

A number of studies have examined the reports of the State Finance Commissions in some detail. These suggest that for the most part the finance commissions have attempted to balance the natural limits, both economic and political, to the tax base of local governments, the need for interjurisdictional equity given the heterogeneity in local economies and the need to preserve the incentives of local governments to raise revenue locally.

From an economic perspective, the natural tax base of local governments consists of taxes on immovable property and user fees for local public goods and commons. In rural India the predominant form of property is agricultural land. There is a levy on agricultural land in most states—based not on the value of the land but on the potential income from it as determined by its productivity— but it is not seriously enforced.[8] The "settlement rates", *i.e.*, the assessed productivity of the land used to calculate the levy, have been so rarely revised and updated that revenues from this particular source have become insignificant (Rajaraman, 2000). Perhaps anticipating the political constraints on doing so, none of the State Finance Commissions appear to have seriously considered proposals, such as that put forward by Rajaraman and Bhende (1998), to revive the land levy as a source of income for rural local bodies. Instead, the recommendations have largely been limited to reassignment of some minor taxes, *e.g.*, imposition of surcharges and the like.

If, indeed, as many claim, there are few elastic sources of local revenue for rural local bodies, the only real avenues that remain for enhancing the financial resources of rural local bodies, while ensuring some degree of budgeting autonomy, are on the one hand, to identify mechanisms for improving the tax effort—*i.e.*, better collection and enforcement of existing taxes and fees—of local bodies, and on the other, to increase the transfer of untied block grants from the state governments. Concerns have been expressed about the incentive effects of a move towards untied block grants on the tax effort or more broadly, own resource mobilisation efforts, of rural local bodies. These concerns are, in principle, legitimate but given the empirical evidence on the limited tax effort of rural local bodies even in the absence of untied grants, they seem misplaced. It is hard to see how tax effort could get any worse.

The way forward would therefore appear to be to consider increasing the use of untied block grants while exploring ways of improving the tax effort of local bodies. The use of matching grants as incentive devices risks worsening cross-jurisdictional inequality. Matching grants, though ideally based on tax effort relative to the tax base, in practice, tend to be based on observed tax revenues because tax effort is difficult to directly ascertain. In settings where the tax bases of local bodies vary greatly because of inherited disparities in infrastructure and levels of economic activity, the use of these matching grants is clearly likely to exacerbate, rather than mitigate these existing disparities. The alternate route considered by some of the State Finance Commissions was therefore to make "obligatory" the collection of certain taxes and fees and moreover to specify a floor on the minimum tax rates that local bodies could impose.

The State Finance Commission reports, even when they have been accepted in principle, do not of course, reveal the extent to which financial devolution has actually taken place. Again, without further detailed empirical research, it is impossible to say definitively what the situation is in individual states. But a sense of the overall trend can be obtained by returning to the data on panchayat finances presented in Tables 4(a) to 4(d).

The third, sixth and ninth columns of these Tables present the summary statistics on local government finances at the state level for the most recent three years, 1995 to 1998, for which they are available. Table 4(b) indicates that in a few states, whether or not there was genuine financial devolution, there was at least a dramatic rise in the flow of funds to rural local bodies. Nationwide, per-capita total revenues of village panchayats rose by nearly 60% in the relatively short span of 5 years or so. In Kerala, Madhya Pradesh, Maharashtra, Rajasthan and Tamil Nadu the growth in village panchayat revenues exceeded the national rate, in the case of Kerala (217%), Maharashtra (114%) and Rajasthan (106%), by a considerable margin. In Kerala and Madhya Pradesh the total revenues of all rural local bodies combined also grew at a rate far exceeding the national average. The numbers for Madhya Pradesh suggest a bias in favour of district panchayats relative to village panchayats. In contrast, in the case of Maharashtra there appears to have been some movement towards redressing the previous focus on district panchayats. Rajasthan and Tamil Nadu are the only two other states where the recorded per-capita revenues of village panchayats grew at a faster rate than did the revenues of block and district panchayats.

In terms of the impact of increased grants-in-aid to local bodies on the own revenues of local bodies, some of the worst fears seem to have been unfounded. Though measured levels of revenue dependency did increase in some of the states (*e.g.*, Kerala and Madhya Pradesh) that had the highest rates of overall revenue growth, in absolute terms own revenues increased appreciably in the same states.

Overall, the available information suggests that in most states there has been very limited progress in terms of administrative and financial devolution. What is one to make of this? Certainly it suggests a lack of political will and significant bureaucratic resistance. But, to attribute it entirely to efforts to preserve "rents" would be to risk oversimplifying the nature of the problem.

A more nuanced perspective would also recognize that the process of transferring funds and functionaries can be quite complicated. In terms of transferring personnel, two sets of issues arise. The first is a practical one—the need to adequately address bureaucratic career concerns in order to retain and attract suitably qualified individuals to these positions. The smaller scale of the bureaucracies supporting local governments potentially limits the upward promotion possibilities for civil servants and practical ways have to be devised to get around these limits.

A second issue that arises is the tension between the need to, on the one hand, make bureaucrats accountable to elected representatives, and on the other, ensure some degree of insulation for the bureaucracy from political pressures. The basic tension between bureaucratic accountability and autonomy does not of course exist only at the local level—see Krishnan and Somanathan (2001) for a lucid discussion of this point in the context of the Indian Administrative Service—but it does complicate the process of reconfiguring bureaucratic structures.

An Aggregate Index of Devolution

Having provided a more disaggregated account of the scope and extent of devolution attempted (or not) by individual states along the various relevant dimensions of devolution, and at the risk of considerable oversimplification, in this section has been made an admittedly crude and speculative attempt to partition the fourteen major states into categories based on the overall extent of devolution. I do this for two reasons. First, such a categorisation provides an initial reference point, a sort of benchmark, through which the more detailed case-study investigations of the specifics of each state can be filtered in a way that facilitates cross-state comparisons. Second, without some degree of aggregation, the task of empirically assessing the impacts of devolution, even in a very exploratory fashion, becomes unmanageable.

Needless to say the entire exercise is quite ad-hoc and others reviewing the same information may have arrived at a different way of organizing and categorizing it. The first is a study by the Eleventh Finance Commission, which put together a state-level index of decentralisation.[9] This index was used by the Eleventh Finance Commission in its formula for allocating funds to the states. The second is a study sponsored by the World Bank looking intensively at the experiences in seven major states.

The outcome of this crude exercise yields the following categorisation of states. Kerala and West Bengal emerge as the only two states to have undertaken significant devolution. Maharashtra, Madhya Pradesh, Karnataka and Rajasthan come next as states with modest records of devolution.

Kerala—People's Campaign for Decentralised Planning

In 1996, the Left Democratic Front (LDF) coalition returned to power in Kerala and the Communist Party of India-Marxist (CPM)—led government immediately fulfilled one of its most important campaign pledges by launching the "People's Campaign for Decentralised Planning". All 1,214 local governments in Kerala—municipalities and the three rural tiers of district, block and village panchayats—were given new functions and powers of decision-making, and were granted discretionary budgeting authority over 40% of the state's developmental expenditures. The Campaign however went well beyond the devolution of governance functions. As structured by the implementing agency—the Kerala State Planning Board—the campaign was designed to create an active role for local citizens in shaping local development policy-making and budgeting. Thus, not only were local governments charged with designing and implementing their own development plans (which included designing and financing projects across the full range of development sectors), but were mandated to do so through an elaborate series of participatory exercises. The building block of this process was the holding of 2 annual Gram Sabhas (ward-level assemblies), one at the beginning of the planning cycle and one at the end of the budgeting process.

The first Grama Sabha serves as an open forum in which residents identify local development problems, generate priorities and form sub-sector development seminars in which specific proposals first take shape. The Gram Sabhas are open meetings, presided by local elected officials, and facilitated by "key resource persons" trained by the State Planning Board. They are always held on weekdays, and in public buildings (usually schools). Preparations for the assemblies include extensive publicity, and the distribution of various planning documents. Minutes are kept, and each sub-sector group presents a report of its deliberations and produces a list of "felt needs". These are in turn translated into specific projects by Task Forces and submitted to the elected Panchayat council for final budgetary approval.[10]

Beyond its institutional design, there are two critical features of the campaign that need to be highlighted. The first is that in addition to providing the fiscal resources, the procedural templates, the enabling regulations and laws, key oversight functions and administrative capacity, the Kerala state government—and specifically the SPB—also orchestrated a massive training exercise, described by one observer as "the largest non-formal education programme ever undertaken in India." In the first year, in seven rounds of training at state, district and local level, some 15,000 elected representatives, 25,000 officials and 75,000 volunteers were given training. About 600 state level trainees—called Key Resource Persons (KRP)—received nearly 20 days of training. Some 12,000 district level trainees—District Resource Persons (DRP)—received 10 days of training and at the local level more than a 100,000 persons received at least five days of training. In subsequent years these training programmes were extended, and were more specifically targeted at women and Dalits and Adivasis.[11] The second point is that at every stage of this process, a range of civil society organisations have played an active role. Most notable has been the role of the Kerala Sastra Sahitya Parishad (KSSP)—the Kerala People's Science Movement. With its 50,000 strong membership recruited predominantly from the white-collar professions of civil servants and school teachers, the KSSP has an organised presence in almost every village in Kerala, and is by far the most active and influential non-party affiliated, secular organisation in the state. In addition to playing an active role in the campaign itself (supplying for example many of the local Key Resource Persons) it is important to emphasize that in designing the campaign the SPB relied heavily on a stock of practical knowledge, ideas and experiences drawn from twenty-five years of local-level experiments in sustainable development conducted by the KSSP.

Inter-state patterns in the scale and scope of devolution

Combining the picture of the inter-state variation with the various case studies that have been done looking at individual states, some preliminary observations may be made:

- Economic prosperity, far from being a facilitating contextual factor, may actually provide a disincentive for devolution. Of the high and middle income states, only Maharashtra, West Bengal, Kerala and to a lesser extent, Karnataka appear to have attempted any meaningful measure of devolution. On the other hand, Madhya Pradesh and Rajasthan, usually lumped together with Bihar and Uttar Pradesh in the BIMARU group of underperforming states, have taken measureable steps towards devolution.

- Imperatives of electoral politics appear to figure prominently; in particular the combination of a change of government within a bi-polar party system is a common feature of all instances but Maharashtra: CPIM in West Bengal in 1978 with Congress in opposition, Janata Party in Karnataka in 1983 with Congress in opposition, CPM in Kerala in 1995 with Congress in opposition, Congress in Madhya Pradesh in 1994 with BJP in opposition, BJP in Rajasthan in 1994 with Congress in opposition. Important to note however that this particular combination is at most a facilitating factor. Andhra Pradesh, Tamil Nadu and Gujarat are all exceptions.
- If we limit our focus to the states where there have been meaningful (if not entirely successful) attempts at devolution, three separate approaches to devolution are evident:
- Phased or stepping-stone approach in West Bengal
- Big bang approach in Kerala
- Thematically-oriented demand-driven approach in Madhya Pradesh
- Increasing emphasis on participatory approaches often in the context of increasing involvement of non-governmental actors

Impact of the Reforms

A growing literature in economics has used policy variation across political jurisdictions to econometrically estimate the effects of key policy innovations on various outcomes of interest.[12] The typical approach involves the use of longitudinal data on outcomes for a panel of jurisdictions (*e.g.*, states in India) coupled with data (often categorical) capturing the timing and magnitude of reforms. The basic intuition behind this approach—often labeled "difference-in-differences"—is that the difference between the changes (*i.e.*, difference) over time in the outcome of interest in a jurisdiction that experienced a policy change and the changes in outcomes in a jurisdiction that did not, ought to, subject to some caveats and complications, provide a rough estimate of the impact of the policy change. In the Indian context, a number of papers have adopted this approach. These include, among others, Banerjee, Gertler and Ghatak (2002), who look at the efficiency effects of tenancy reform in the state of West Bengal, Besley and Burgess (2000), who consider the poverty-reducing and growth impacts of land reform legislation more broadly, and Pande (2002), who examines the effects of mandated political representation in state legislative assemblies for traditionally disadvantaged groups, on patterns of public expenditure.

For a number of reasons, all of which have been previously mentioned in other contexts, a formal implementation of this approach is not feasible in tracing the impact of the constitutional amendments at the state-level. To begin with, given the paucity of information regarding the substantive reform measures adopted by individual states, even a crude assessment of the true extent of the devolution in individual states is difficult. In principle this problem can be gotten around by reframing the problem as one of estimating the reduced form effect of what is acknowledged to possibly be only a nominal reform effort, i.e., an estimate of the impact of the promulgation of a new policy that incorporates and reflects the possibility that the policy may have been imperfectly implemented.[13] And in fact, a case can be made that this reduced form effect should be the object of inference since the impact of institutional reforms is inevitably mediated through the political and societal context within which they are attempted.

However, even if a reduced form approach is adopted, other hurdles remain. One is the multidimensional nature of the reforms; in particular, given the heterogeneity across the states in the scope of devolution along different dimensions, a complete overall ordering is simply not possible. Another is the relatively short time since the introduction of the reforms.

The task is complicated further by the fact that the panchayati raj initiative roughly coincided with a major programme of economic liberalisation at the national level. The liberalisation programme initiated in 1991, by reducing the span of central government control, opened up the space for a variety of state-level initiatives to promote industrial development and economic growth, for instance, by offering tax incentives to attract private investment. This makes it yet more difficult to disentangle the impact of local government reforms from that of these other initiatives.

In the light of these difficulties, what appears below can only be described as a highly exploratory analysis, loosely motivated by the differences-in-differences intuition underlying more formal investigations. The state-level outcomes I consider, along with the relevant dates at which they are observed, are:

- per-capita state domestic product from agriculture (1991-93 average, 1995-97 average).
- mean rural per-capita expenditure (1993, 1999).
- the rural headcount index of poverty (1993, 1999).
- the fraction of households with electricity connections (1991, 2001).
- the fraction of households living in permanent structures (1991, 2001)
- the rural female literacy rate (1991, 2001).
- the school attendance rate of school-age children (1992-93, 1998-99).
- the fraction of pregnant women who receive ante-natal care (1992-93, 1998-99).

- the under-five mortality rate (1992-93, 1998-99).
- the percentage of children between 1 and 2-years old who are fully vaccinated ((*i.e.*, who have received vaccines for BCG, measles, and three doses of DPT and polio) (1992-93,1998-99).

The first three measures, and in particular, the rural poverty rate, though certainly affected by the quality of governance in rural areas, are also obviously influenced by the overall economic conditions in the state and in the country. The remaining indicators, on the other hand, are likely to more directly reflect the quality of public service delivery.

For each of the variables, the first column displays the level of the variable in the early 1990s, prior to the passage of the constitutional amendment. This column basically reproduces the information from Table 2(b), which documented the diversity in the state of human development across India's major states. The second column displays the level in the late 1990s (or in some cases, 2001), five years or more after the state conformity acts were enacted. The third column displays an index of the progress made by each state between the two dates.

For the two straight economic variables, per-capita state domestic product from agriculture and rural per-capita expenditures, the index of progress is simply the percentage change between the two dates.

All the remaining variables admit of a natural target level, *i.e.*, a maximum or minimum attainable level, and for these variables the index of progress (between two dates) is defined as the proportionate reduction in the distance to the target. So, for instance, a reduction in the headcount index of poverty (for which the natural target level is 0) of five percentage points from 25% to 15% would translate into an index of progress of 40% (=100 × (10/25)). Similarly, an increase in the school attendance rate from 50% to 60% translates into an index of progress of 20%. For aggregate welfare indicators that have a natural upper bound (or lower bound), defining the index of progress in this way avoids some of the conceptual difficulties that arise in simply measuring progress in terms of changes. For instance, in assessing progress in poverty reduction, if we adopt as our index, the percentage point difference in poverty rates at two dates, we would end up attributing greater progress in poverty reduction to a state where the poverty rate decreased by 10% points from 30% to 20% than we would a state where poverty was eradicated starting from an initial rate of 5%, and further reductions were simply not possible.

The question then is can some of the variation across states be traced back to differences in the scope and extent of devolution? A very crude way of getting at this question is to overlay the pattern of deviations at the state level from the mean index of progress across the fourteen states with the crude categorisation of states in terms of devolution. The mean across the fourteen states controls for any common factors, *e.g.*, increases or decreases in allocations for centrally sponsored schemes, that might influence the index of progress for a particular indicator. The deviation from this mean then captures the influence of any factors specific to the state, among them, the degree of devolution. Of course this is a very crude proxy for the actual extent of devolution. In particular, it is likely to be confounded by other state specific factors that are unrelated to the process of devolution, for instance, a variety of economic shocks, and so I also construct a set of adjusted deviations that account for growth in *per-capita* expenditures in the state. It should be noted that by examining deviations in the index of progress for an indicator, which is constructed from changes in the indicator across two points in time, I am implicitly controlling for any time-invariant state specific effects.

Figure 1 provides a sense of how the deviations are constructed. The indicator shown is the school attendance rate, and the index of progress is calculated between the years 1992

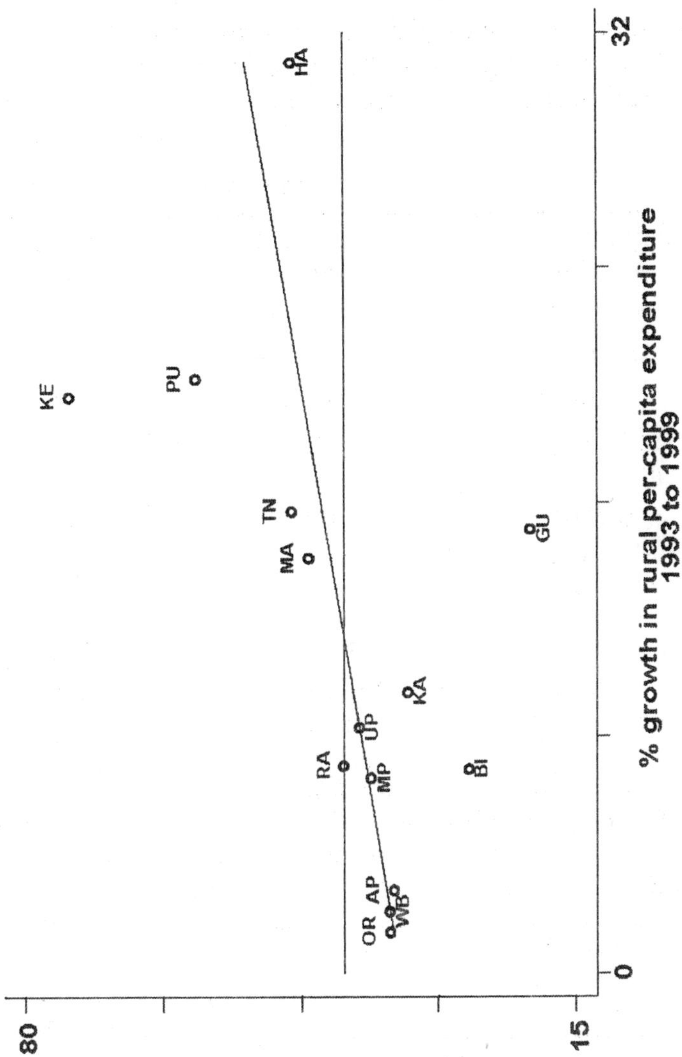

Figure 1

School attendance rate:
% index of progress 1992 to 1998

and 1998. The unadjusted deviations are simply the vertical distances from each individual data point (representing a state) to the horizontal line set at the mean index of progress across the states. The adjusted deviations are the vertical distances between the data points and the regression line predicting progress on school attendance rates in terms of *per-capita* expenditure growth. So, for instance, in the case of Haryana (HA), the unadjusted deviation is positive, but once we take account of the high rate of per-capita expenditure growth, the adjusted deviation turns out to be negative.

Observations

The relative merits of the two approaches to reform—"big bang" vs. "stepping-stone", "shock therapy" vs. "gradualism"—can and have been debated, if not in the Indian context, certainly in the case of the reform programmes in Eastern Europe and the former Soviet Union. The usual line is that, whatever the domain of the reforms, the choice between the two depends on the institutional and political context in which the reforms are being contemplated. At some level this claim obviously is right. But the Kerala approach suggests the intriguing possibility that what may be a more critical element in the long-term success of a reform process than the choice that is made at the outset, is the conscious recognition of the power of agency and the adoption of a learning-by-doing mentality. As Thomas Isaac, the principal architect of the Peoples' Campaign describes it: "...in short, the pre-conditions for successful decentralisation are to be created in the very process of decentralisation."(Isaac (2000)). Essentially this approach treats as central, the dynamic and contingent nature of directed institutional change. Similar themes are stressed in the literature on participatory democracy—participation inculcates the capacity for participation—and in a more recent literature on the constructability of collective capacities for change:

- This point about the need to incorporate or at least recognize the dynamic and contingent elements of the processes of institutional change carries over to the economic literature on decentralisation. There are three separate strands of the literature, distinguished by the implicit or explicit view that is taken of the nature of state-society interactions. The literature on fiscal federalism, dating back to Tiebout and Oates, implicitly views government (and governmental actors, whether bureaucrats or politicians) as benevolent, if not omniscient, decision-makers, motivated only by the disinterested pursuit of economic efficiency, and limited only by informational constraints *vis-à-vis* the population at large. As Bardhan (2002) points out the realities of governance in most developing economies make this framework largely irrelevant in that context. A subsequent literature, Seabright recognises potential agency problems between the electorate and bureaucrats/politicians, for instance by viewing government as a set of elected representatives motivated by electoral imperatives. But this literature too is of limited relevance in the Indian context because it implicitly assumes reasonably well-functioning representative democracies in that the channels of political influence are limited to the act of voting and hence influence is equitably distributed. A third strand, Bardhan and Mookherjee explicitly incorporates the possibility of uneven influence and capture by elites at both the local and higher level, and hence provides a much more useful framework for thinking about decentralisation in developing countries. But even this strand of the literature ignores the possibility of dynamic agency.

- However, even if, as I suggest above, pre-existing conditions at the local level are less immutable than much of the current thinking presumes—which is to say that the possibility of local capture may itself be diminished and the prospects for participation enhanced through the process of decentralisation—there are clearly contextual prerequisites at higher levels, of which the most important is the political will and capacity at the level of government contemplating decentralisation. Put another way, while local context may be less important to the "normative" questions of how and whether to decentralize, the primacy of politics and the broader context manifests itself in the "positive" questions of "where" and "when" and "if meaningful decentralisation is attempted in the first place.

Prospects

With the slow progress that is evident in most Indian states on genuine functional devolution, and the many instances where pre-existing inequities and patterns of social exclusion and domination have thwarted even genuine attempts at devolution, some observers are worried that this latest initiative to revitalise local government will also fail. Clearly institutional reforms initiated through state-level legislation are not irreversible. The decline of panchayats in the 1970s and 1980s in most states, or the failure to sustain the Karnataka reforms, all attest to that.

The question then is whether the one element that thus far has distinguished this latest attempt to foster panchayati raj, the fact that it has constitutional backing, will make a difference in the long run. There is undoubtedly considerable uncertainty about how exactly events will unfold this time around. But constitutional reforms lie at the top of the reform hierarchy in terms of their purported impact and degree of irreversibility. And while it is true that, in practice, the Indian experience has revealed that the implementation of constitutional mandates remains vulnerable to various forms of "filibustering" because constitutional contracts are inevitably "incomplete," it is also the case that they can be made more "complete" by more clearly outlining the consequences of non-compliance. And that increasingly is happening in the Indian context.

The courts have begun to play a more assertive role as witnessed by the intervention of the Supreme Court and the Andhra Pradesh High Court, respectively, in ensuring that panchayat elections went ahead as scheduled in Orissa and Andhra Pradesh. The Indian government too has begun considering introducing progress in devolution as a key element in the forumulae determining intergovernmental transfers.

Ultimately though, the main reasons for optimism are scattered but numerous accounts of developments at the community level, where the space created for participation is being occupied and contested by those previously excluded. If participatory democratisation involves learning-by-doing, there is increasing evidence that the learning is taking place in disparate communities all over India. The learning may be slow and sporadic and much of rural India is still on the flat portion of the learning curve, but it does appear to be taking place. And just as the extension of the franchise and mandatory representation manifested itself, albeit with considerable lags, in the growing political participation of subordinate groups (other backward classes), there is the distinct possibility that just the sheer numbers of individuals, the 2 million plus locally elected representatives who now have a stake in the system will make a difference. In effect a new interest group has been created that potentially cuts across preexisting lines of division providing a new axis along which interests may align.

NOTES

1. It is important to recognize that this does not mean that this particular provision has no implications in the case of West Bengal because it does by reducing the discretionary powers.
2. The number of states has increased over time, with various state re-organization initiatives. The latest occurred in 2000, when three new states were created: Chhattisgarh, by partitioning the state of Madhya Pradesh, Jharkand, from the state of Bihar, and Uttaranchal, from the state of Uttar Pradesh.
3. Two members of the Lok Sabha and 12 members of the Rajya Sabha are directly appointed by the President to represent,

respectively, the small Anglo-Indian community and various fields of human endeavor such as literature, sciences, the arts and social service.

4. The constitution of India came into effect on January 26, 1950, just over two years after India attained its independence on August 15, 1947.
5. In the fifteen months between the time the Bills were introduced and the time they were finally passed, the numbering changed.
6. Smaller states with populations below two million are exempt from this requirement.
7. Other potential sources of funds are loans from financial institutions, public and private, and voluntary contributions from panchayat residents. Historically, these have been uniformly negligible though this may change with proposals to set up a Panchayat Finance Institution.
8. The distinction between a tax on the value of land and a tax on the potential income from the land would be irrelevant with well-functioning land markets since the potential income stream from the land would be capitalized into the value of the land. In rural India, as in many poor agrarian economies,
9. The index aggregates ten different design elements and implementation steps that states incorporated or undertook: enactment/amendment of state panchayat and municipal legislation; intervention/restriction in the functioning of the local bodies; assignment of functions to the local bodies by state legislation; actual transfer of functions to these bodies by way of rules, notifications and orders; assignment of powers of taxation to the local bodies and the extent of exercise of such powers; constitution of the SFCs and the extent of action taken on their reports; elections to the local bodies; and constitution of District Planning Committees as per the letter and spirit of article 243ZD.
10. The design and politics of the campaign created a wide range of mechanisms that make elected panchayat councilors de facto—if not de jure—accountable to the Gram Sabha mandates. Needless to say, the degree of accountability varied widely, and calls for further research. However, previous field work, other research and some simple but significant aggregate shifts in expenditure leave little doubt that popular mandates significantly impacted budgetary outcomes.

11. As of the 1991 Census, Dalits and Adivasis represented 11.9% of Kerala's rural population.
12. A parallel and much more established (though still very active) literature uses microeconometric techniques to evaluate the effects of particular programs on a range of outcomes at the individual and household level. The literature on policy impacts at the aggregate level, using aggregate jurisdiction-level data, has increasingly drawn upon this literature in framing the analysis in terms of estimating "treatment" effects, and in taking the seriously the possibility that "treatments" may be endogenous.
13. The analog in the programme evaluation literature is the distinction between the "intention-to-treat" effect and the effect of "treatment-on-the-treated". The former incorporates the possibility of selective compliance with the treatment and therefore provides, in some senses, a more robust estimate.

REFERENCES

Ahluwalia, M., "Economic performance of the states in post-reforms period," *Economic and Political Weekly*, May 6, 2000.

Banerjee, A., P. Gertler, and M.Ghatak, "Empowerment and Efficiency: Tenancy Reform in West Bengal", *Journal of Political Economy*, 110(2), April 2002, pp. 239-80.

Bardhan, P., "Decentralisation of governance and development," *Journal of Economic Perspectives*, Fall, 2002.

Besley, T. and R. Burgess, "Land reform, poverty reduction and growth: evidence from India," *Quarterly Journal of Economics*, 105 (2), May, 2000, 389-430.

Crook, R. and J. Manor Deaton, A. and J. Dreze, "Poverty and inequality in India: a re-examination," *Economic and Political Weekly*, September 7, 2002, 3729–3748.

Ghatak, M. and M. Ghatak, "Recent reforms in the panchayat system in West Bengal: toward greater participatory governance?," *Economic and Political Weekly*, January 5, 2002.

Government of India, *Administrative arrangements for rural development—a perspective: proceedings of the national workshop held at NIRD*, Hyderabad: National Institute for Rural Development, 1985.

Government of India, *Report of the Eleventh Finance Commission,* New Delhi: Ministry of Finance, 2000.

Government of India, *Report of the working group on decentralized planning and Panchayati Raj institutions,* New Delhi: Ministry of Rural Development, November, 2001.

Government of India, *Report of the task force on Panchayati Raj institutions,* New Delhi: Planning Commission, December, 2001.

Government of India, *National Human Development Report,* New Delhi: Planning Commission, March, 2002.

Kohli, A. Kohli, *The state and poverty in India,* Cambridge: Cambridge University Press, 1987.

Manor, J., *The political economy of democratic decentralisation,* Washington, D.C.: World Bank, 1999.

Mathew, G., "Panchayat elections: dismal record," *Economic and Political Weekly,* January 20, 2001.

Mookherjee, D., "Combating the crisis in government accountability: a review of recent international experience," *Boston University Institute for Economic Development Discussion Paper* No. 117, December, 2001.

PRIA, *The State of Panchayats: A Participatory Perspective,* New Delhi: Samskriti, 2001.

Rajaraman, I., "Fiscal features of local government in India," in *Governance, decentralisation and reform in China, India and Russia,* ed. Jean-Jacques Dethier, Boston: Kluwer Academic Publishers, 2000.

Rajaraman, I. and M.J. Bhende, "A land-based agricultural presumptive tax designed for levy by panchayats," *Economic and Political Weekly,* April 4, 1998.

Seabright, P., "Accountability and decentralisation in government: an incomplete contracts model," *European Economic Review,* 40, 1996, 61-89.

Tiebout, C., "A pure theory of local expenditures," *Journal of Political Economy,* 64, 1956, 416-424.

Vijayanand, S.M., "Issues related to administrative decentralisation and administering decentralisation: lessons from the Kerala experience," Workshop on Decentralisation, Institute for Social and Economic Change, Bangalore, May 31-June 1, 2001.

3

Political Empowerment of Women through Panchayati Raj Institutions

Introduction

The purpose of this chapter is to explore whether a 'quantitative' rise in the representation of women in political decision-making would translate into 'qualitative' changes in the status of women thus paving the path for real political empowerment of women. The paper does so by examining political institutions at the sub-national level or rather the sub-provincial level. Understanding the impact of the 73rd Amendment Act, which reserved 33% of all seats for women in the Panchayati Raj Institutions (PRIs) (village self-governing institutions), is of great scholarly interest, as there is a high degree of variation in the results of the implementation of this Act.

However, studies of the transformative role of PRIs have generally been the concern of policy-making institutions (both governmental and non-governmental) and there are actually very few academic works that specifically study the theoretical impact of this type of representation, which goes well beyond the federal and provincial level. At the same time, both governmental and non-governmental studies fail to move beyond their view of women as a single unitary "category" and do not inform us of the manner in which the processes of reservations at the village level are impacting the marginalised within the marginalised (*i.e.* women belong to the Scheduled Castes, Schedule Tribes and religious minorities).[1]

To a large extent the paucity of theoretical work on this phenomenon is a function of the methodological choices. As Stephen Castles says, "Top-down approaches to understanding social transformations tend to focus on the realities of powerful institutions and privilege groups at both the global and local levels, and may be blind to the differing realities of disempowered groups" (1999, 26). In order to bridge the theoretical challenge posed by the representation of women in PRIs, the paper will examine the case of political empowerment of minority women through affirmative action in India's PRIs. Studies of the reservation of seats in legislatures for women (Dahlerup 2002; Malami & Kenworthy 1999) tend to limit their view of affirmative action, to the formal institutional reservation of seats in national-level legislative bodies.[2] While we view their contribution as extremely critical for the study of gender politics, it is our aim to draw attention to the fact that the processes by which representation at the sub-national or sub-provincial evolve is very different. In fact we have to also take into cognisance, informal institutional[3] and cultural practices, that have an impact during the implementation stage. We take issue with works that believe that, "As we enter the twenty-first century, the extent to which socialised norms and traditional family structures impede women's entrance into politics is diminishing".

The case of affirmative action in India is crucial, as the identity of a woman is layered in the various intersecting forces of caste, class, religion and ethnicity and is not manifested only in terms of 'gender.' This social reality gets reflected in political institutions like PRIs (Vyasulu & Vyasulu 1999). Hence although women as a group itself can be viewed as a minority, the special conditions surrounding the plight of marginalised women within the larger group makes it imperative to study minority groups within this minority, i.e. women belonging to Scheduled Castes (SC), Scheduled Tribes (ST) and religious minorities.

Historical Background

The term 'Panchayat' traditionally implies a body of five elders in a village set-up who were responsible for resolving conflict and meting out punishment to the offenders, and the entire village held them in reverence. In this traditional conception of a 'Panchayat', women and lowers castes were not allowed membership. During the Indian National Movement, Mahatma Gandhi came to champion the cause of local self-government at the village level as he considered village as the true center of knowledge. In the post-independence (1947) era, the idea of village self-administration found place in Part IV of the Constitution that is known as the Directive Principles of State Policy.[4] However, Part IV of the Constitution is only in the nature of directives to the government and not enforceable in a court of law. Hence it was not mandatory for the state governments to implement its provision and set up Panchayati Raj Institutions.

The Panchayati Raj as a system of self-governance was introduced for the first time in 1959 following the Balwant Rai Mehta Committee report (1958) that recommended a three-tier structure of local self-government consisting of Gram Panchayats at the village level, Taluka Panchayat Samitis at the sub-district level, and Zilla Parishads at the district level. The Balwant Rai Committee had further recommended that at the Panchayat Samiti level there should be two women as co-opted members besides the official 20 members. However, this system of Panchayati Raj gradually lost momentum under conditions of one-party rule. The Asok Mehta (1978) Committee was set up for further investigation in local self-government. The Committee in fact recommended greater decision-making power to the local councils.

During this phase, few states such as Maharashtra and Karnataka even went to the extent of reserving 25 to 30 per cent council seats for women on their own initiative. Demands for the reform of local self-government were also accompanied by active civil society movements that agitated for greater participation with the representation of women being an important platform. The National Perspective Plan for Women (1988-2000) recommended the reservation of at least 30 per cent of the total seats for women in local government institutions. The 64th Constitutional amendment Bill was introduced in the Parliament in 1989, which provided for 30 per cent reservation for women. However, the Bill could not passed as it was defeated by a narrow margin in the Upper House. The Bill was reintroduced in September 1991 as the 73rd and 74th Constitutional Amendment Bills and they were finally passed by the Parliament on 22 December 1992. The 73rd Amendment deals with rural local self-government (Panchayati Raj[5]), while the 74th Amendment concerns urban local-self administration (municipalities).

The Acts constitutionally reserved 33% of all seats in Panchayats and Municipalities for women.[6] The scope of the present paper, however, only covers the 73rd Amendment Act (Part IX of the Constitution). As per the 73rd Amendment Act, the Panchayati Raj Institutions (PRIs) are divided into three tiers. At the base of this structure is the Gram Sabha that comprises of the entire body of the citizens in a village. It constitutes all the eligible voters within a Gram Panchayat area and serves as a principal mechanism for transparency and accountability. Above the Gram Sabha is the first level elected body - the Gram Panchayat (GP). It covers a population of around five thousand people and may include more than one village. At the district level is the Zilla Panchayat (ZP) that is the link with the state government.

The most crucial aspect of the 73rd Amendment Act, that the present paper aims to study, is the provision whereby one-third of all seats in the PRIs are reserved for women (including women belonging to SC and ST).[7] Seats for Scheduled Castes (SC) and Scheduled Tribes (ST) are in proportion to their number in the population of each region. In the country as a whole, SCs constitute 16% per cent and STs 6% of the population and about 22.5 per cent of the total seats reserved for women are to be allotted to women belonging to these categories.

Theoretical Background

The idea of democracy in its purest form, as J.S. Mill argues, is to ensure "a government of the whole body by the whole people, equally represented" (1962, 256-57). A legislature "should be an exact portrait, in miniature, of the people at large, as it should feel, reason and act like them" (Adams 1951, 205). A focal point of the current discourse on democracy is the concept of political representation. The "politics of ideas" have come to be "challenged by the alternative politics of presence" (Philip 1995, 5). Political presence or 'empowerment through representation' is crucial since in a liberal democratic set up the actions and deliberations of some people or some institutions at one place affect the lives of many at various other places. As Iris Marion Young states "Representation is a cycle of anticipation and recollection between constituents and representative, in which discourse and action at each moment ought to bear *traces* of the others."

Jane Mansbridge highlights three most vital functions of a representative because of which, the disadvantaged groups may want to be represented by individuals who in their own backgrounds 'mirror' the typical experiences and outward manifestations of belonging to the disadvantaged group (2000, 99-100). Firstly, the representative is an instrument of ongoing communication and consultation. The members of the dominant groups have failed to listen to the grievances of the subordinate groups and the subordinate groups, in their turn, have developed a keen sense of distrust and hence they want to be represented by members who belong to their own group in the belief that such representatives would be able to understand their grievances better and hence would be able to communicate it in a much better manner.

Secondly, at the legislative level the representatives engage in an "organised deliberative process"; and they need to communicate with each other in an effective manner. In this process of deliberations, the issues that are taken up are largely "uncrystallised" and the representative who does not personally share the experiences of the disadvantaged groups would not be able to spontaneously contribute to such deliberations. Only those representatives who belong to these disadvantaged groups would be able to convince the advantaged groups as regards to the problems faced by the people they represent by drawing instances from their personal experiences.

Finally, in the case of a polity, which has a history of legally excluding the members of a particular group from voting and other political rights, there are traces of the feeling that the dominant cultures did not consider the specific group to be fit to rule. Under such historical conditions, it is important that their own people, who would instil the feeling that they are capable of functioning successfully and competently as lawmakers, are representing such groups.

With the feminist cry 'political is personal', there is a growing demand for increasing presence of women in political decision-making. It is argued that women need to be 'empowered' in the realm of political decision making so as to facilitate their 'real' empowerment. Anne Philip divides the arguments favouring increased political presence of women into four broad categories: one, successful women politicians act as kind of role models for the others; secondly, increasing the proportion of the women elected would ensure the principles of justice between the sexes; thirdly, this would ensure the fulfilling of certain interests of women, which may otherwise be neglected; and finally, it is argued that women's presence would enhance the quality of political life. It is claimed that an enhancement in the inclusion and influence of the social groups that are unrepresentative or underrepresented would help the society in confronting the problem of structural social inequality and to find remedies for it. For instance, a study conducted on the women in Norwegian politics concluded that with a relative increase in the number of women in public office has enabled a greater amount of gender equality in the country's governance and has also contributed towards a change in the national political agenda and legislation. Drude Dahlerup argues that in South Africa women networking across party lines have been responsible for coming up with very clear agendas dealing with a host of issues, for instance, clean drinking water, better HIV-AIDS programme for women, and tough rape laws.

Within the broad contours of the ongoing theoretical debate on representation, the line of argument that favours a numerical rise in the political representation of disadvantaged groups fall within the ambit of 'descriptive' or 'mirror' representation. It is argued that the democratic political institutions that are committed to political equality need to resort to specific measures to ensure the representation of those socially deprived groups which would fail to voice its interests and concerns without such measures. Most of the democratic countries in the world, including, for instance, Germany, Sweden, Australia and New Zealand use a form of proportional representation, which is thought to be more favourable to disadvantaged groups like women because parties have the chance to compete for and win several seats, allowing them to go further down the party list where women are usually listed. In certain democracies, political parties tend to balance their ticket by including women in order to attract a diverse electorate. In some countries political parties receive financial benefits for nominating women candidates. In various countries such as in Russia and Iceland, there have even been attempts at founding all-women political parties.

Of all the varied ways of addressing the issue of women's political representation, the one that generates maximum debate and counter-debate is the system of quotas. Electoral quotas for women—itself worked out in various ways—may be constitutional, legislative or take the form of voluntary political party quota. The Scandinavian countries have had a great deal of success in changing the gender balance by using quotas. A number of democracies in the developing world, such as Costa Rica, and South Africa, are adopting quotas of various types and at different levels. Somewhat older democracies, have introduced quotas recently. Even in an authoritarian communist polity like China has recently declared its decision to reserve 22% seats in the Parliament for women.

However, as opposed to the 'descriptive' argument that favours affirmative action for increasing the political representation of disadvantaged groups, we have the 'substantive' representation argument that claims that with an emphasis on numerical increase in representation in the institutions of political decision-making, the focus is on "being something rather than doing something". If one looks at the legislature as a "pictorial representation or representative sample of the nation" then the emphasis would automatically lie on the composition of the legislature (who they are) rather than on the activities of the legislature . The task of the representatives is to act in the "interests of the represented in a manner responsive to them".

Melissa Williams argues that the mere presence of marginalised groups in the decision making process does not guarantee positive outcomes and in order to ensure positive policy outcomes decisions should be based "not only on the counting of votes but also on the sharing of reasons". Pennock rather cynically comments, "no one would argue that morons should be represented by morons." It is true that the responsibility of being a politician cannot be relegated as "just another kind of job" and hence "while men have no 'right' to monopolize political office, there is something rather unsatisfying in basing women's claim to political equality on an equal right to an interesting job."

Thus, on the issue of political empowerment through representation, we have one set of arguments that favour a "top-down" approach whereby advocating a "symbolic recognition" of the disadvantaged groups, while another set of arguments favour a "bottom-up" approach that argue that disempowered groups need to be first made aware of their "disempowered status" and then measures should be taken to facilitate their empowerment in various fields. Summing up, we find it useful to conclude this with Dahlerup's analysis of the quota debate.[8] According to her there are eight major arguments that are for the system of quotas and five against:

Arguments for Quotas

- Quotas for women do not discriminate, but compensate for actual barriers that prevent women from their fair share of political seats.
- Quotas imply that there are several women together in a committee or assembly, thus minimizing the stress often experienced by the token women.
- Women have the right as citizens to equal representation.
- Women's experiences are needed in political life.
- Election is about representation, not qualifications.
- Women are just as qualified as men, but women's qualifications are downgraded and minimised in a male dominated system.
- It is in fact the political parties that control the nominations, not primarily the voters who decide who gets elected.
- Introducing quotas may cause conflicts, but only temporarily.

Arguments Against Quotas

- Quotas are against the principle of equal opportunity for all, since women are given preference.

- Quotas are undemocratic, because voters should be able to decide who is elected.
- Quotas imply that politicians get elected because of their gender, not because of their qualifications and that more qualified candidates are pushed aside.
- Many women, who do not want to get elected, get elected just because they are women.
- Introducing quotas creates significant conflicts within the party system.

It is within this theoretical backdrop that the political empowerment of minority women in India through affirmative action at the subnational level (village local self-governing institutions or PRIs) becomes a crucial case study. Following the 73rd Amendment Act, the first two rounds of elections that were held in 1993 and 1995 saw one million women becoming elected members of the PRIs. However, it needs to be examined whether this massive rise in the numerical strength of women has brought about substantive changes in the status of women, especially in the status of traditionally deprived SCs and STs women.

A Critical Assessment of the Position of Marginalised Women in PRIs

A critical overview of the existing literature (mostly empirical) on the working of the Panchayati Raj Institutions over the past one-decade and role played by women therein reveal two contrasting trends. One trend shows that women in the PRIs are mere proxies who act at the instance of their husbands or other male members of the family. In case of SCs and STs women societal restrictions, due to the prevalence of the 'purity-pollution' concept, act as a further deterrence to political representation. However, the second trend indicates that these women are 'first generation learners' who have been gradually becoming more and more aware of their political rights and many have slowly started to make a difference in grassroots politics. It is our view that more exploratory studies are required to determine the underlying conditions that result in such contrasting outcomes. We thus undertake a preliminary attempt at outlining the nature of these contradictory processes.

Women as 'Rubber Stamps'/'Proxies'.

One of the most striking aspects of Panchayat elections is that there is qualitative difference in the meaning of the vote when it comes to federal and state elections, versus voting for Panchayats. While, federal/state elections are extremely well organised, village level politics are inherently problematic. In fact, some of the historical electoral malpractices especially the use of violence and the stuffing of ballot boxes, which are said to be diminishing, are making their presence felt in village level elections. It is at this level that we see informal institutional practices reinforcing the structural biases against women candidates.

The most crucial obstacle in the way of real political empowerment of women through Panchayati Raj occurs at the stage of the filing of the nomination for candidature itself. Most women file their candidature for elections to PRIs not out of their own will, but due to the pressure of husbands, sons or other male member of the family or the village or due to the pressure of some political party. This phenomenon is even more apparent in case of women belonging to SC or ST. In order to fulfill the reserved quota, the political workers have to deploy various strategies to convince the women and one of the most adopted strategies is to influence the women through the family members. Zenab Banu argues that it is extremely difficult to make tribal women stand for Panchayat elections as they consider Panchayats as bad and full of quarrels. The following table based on her study of tribal women representatives in PRIs clearly illustrates this point.

Corruption in panchayat elections (Chauhan 2003) is also responsible making the participation of women in the process a mere tokenism since due to the constraints of village societal norms, indulgence in such practices fall strictly within the male domain. Bribes in the form a liquor or cash are offered. Muscle power and money power are used extensively. Women would not stand a chance in the elections if they do not have the support of the male members of the family. For instance, in one election, in Salumber Panchayat Samiti of Udaipur district, wives of the three PRI members—Sarpanch (President), Upa-sarpanch (Deputy President), and ward Panch got elected. Even in the case of election expenditure, the management of it is left in the hands of the husband or other male members of the family, thus leaving no power in the hands of the woman (Banu 2001, 123). Corruption[9] is also rampant in the allocation of resources and contracts at the Gram Panchayat level.

Table 1: Factors of Motivation and Incentives for Tribal Women in Filling up Nominations

	Influencing Agency	*Frequency*	*Percentage*
1.	Family Members	18	18%
2.	Kinsmen	19	19%
3.	Tribal Community	17	17%
4.	Panchayat Officials such as Panch, Sarpanches, Pradhan and MLAs	08	08%
5.	Party Workers	24	24%
6.	NGOs	10	10%
7.	Candidates own desire	4	4%
	TOTAL	**100**	**100%**

Violence has also come to dominate the PRI elections in many states thus making participation of women more difficult.[10] Most such violence seems to have been resulting from the existence of 'caste war'[11] (Panchayati Raj Update 2001) where people belonging to lower castes are tortured and murdered for daring to stand against upper caste candidates.[12] In such a situation, participation and performance of women belonging to SCs or STs become absolutely impossible.[13] Moreover, in places that suffer from armed conflicts, booth capturing and bloodshed is common in panchayat elections thus marring the participation of women.

Table 2 : States that have gone beyond the 33% Reservation Quota

State	*Percentage (%)*
Andhra Pradesh	33.04
Assam	50.38
Chhattisgarh	33.75
Gujarat	49.30
Kerala	57.24
Karnataka	43.6
Tamil Nadu	36.73
Uttar Pradesh	37.85
West Bengal	35.15

Further, societal restrictions require that women do not venture into public spaces alone. The traditional concept of women's real place being within the four walls of the house is strongly prevalent in rural India. PRIs are mainly regarded as political entities that are associated with power; and power is traditionally a masculine concept, women are not associated with it.[14] Women who mix around openly with their male counterparts in political meetings are looked down upon as women of dubious character.[15] Therefore, although women can freely attend meetings that are held inside the Panchayat office, the presence of women in Gram Sabha meetings is meager as such meetings are mostly held in open spaces and are mainly attended by males. It is also the case in many villages that the daughter-in-laws (bahu) of the house who generally belong to a different village are hardly allowed to have social intercourse with men of her husbands village.[16] Hence participating in PR activities in public space is totally out of question (Hust 2002).

Sometimes it also so happens that a number of villages come under one GP, in such cases representation and participation of women become difficult as women have much less mobility than men (Vyasulu & Vyasulu 1999, 12). Household responsibilities also restrict the mobility of women. Another major impediment is the 'two-child norm' that has been made a criterion for contesting elections in many a state like Haryana, Madhya Pradesh, Rajasthan and Himachal Pradesh. Rural India has a high fertility rate and children are borne early. Hence due to such norm it becomes extremely difficult for women to enter the PRIs and even when they enter they are mostly confined to household responsibilities letting the male members of her family run the office for her. As a result, a new class of *sarpanch patis* has emerged who manage the affairs of the Panchayat on behalf of their wives (Mathew 2002; Hust 2002, Palanithurai 2001; Vyasulu & Vyasulu 1999; and Leiten 1996).[17]

In case of a woman belonging to Scheduled Caste, such restrictions become further binding since both upper caste female and male members refuse to intermingle with them[18] in Panchayat meetings due to the 'purity-pollution' practices. Lower caste representatives do not get much cooperation from the higher castes and women members would not dare speak in front of the high caste representatives. While in case of ascribed status, the lower caste women get discriminated against, in case of social groups; it is the scheduled tribes who become mere 'rubber stamps' in the decision making process of the panchayat.[19] If not the husbands, they are dependent on the other male members of the family, villagers, *sarpanch,* political parties or government officials. Despite reservation, there is little change in the customary patterns of exclusion (see World Bank 2001).[20]

Moreover, due to the dominant male discourse, women in Panchayats find it difficult to raise issues that would run contrary to that discourse.[21] Such handicaps are more blatant in case of women belonging to SCs or STs category, as they cannot dare to take up issues that would provoke the ire of the upper caste male. There have been number of instances when tribal women members in the Panchayat faced violence and rape when they dared to challenge the authority.[22] Moreover, political parties also play a crucially significant role in directing the affairs of the panchayat. Winning an election requires political party backing. Due to this the elected candidates (men/women) remain loyal to the party line.

Since political parties are most controlled by the non-tribal lobby, tribal women find it extremely difficult to make their voices heard or had to become mere 'rubber stamps' to the dictates of the party.[23] The ability to take up issue pertaining to gender sensitive discourse is also limited due to the resource restrictions, as money has to be spent as per the dictates of the government schemes and there is very little flexibility. Issues such as violence against women, female foeticide and infanticide, women health, livelihoods etc are rarely taken up (Institute of Social Studies Trust 2005).

Further, if one looks at how the benefits coming out of PRIs are being shared, it is observed that female-headed households are mostly excluded from these benefits (see World Bank 2001, 19). Such discrimination turns out to be even more blatant towards women headed households of the lowers castes. In an interview, a widow from a SC household in Ajmer district, Rajasthan revealed, "My husband died about 15 years ago. I have two young sons and a daughter. I and my son go out for labour work early every morning and return late in the evening. I have no idea of what happens in the panchayat and how they take decisions. I have approached the ward panch several times for a loan, but nothing has happened. We have nobody to tell is the right way. Had my husband been alive he would have mixed with the other men and found out". Therefore, in such a situation, the argument that having more women in political decision-making would bring about gender-related equality and justice is seriously questioned.

Women as 'First Generation Learners'

The paper had so far explored how the prevalence of corrupt practices, violence, societal cleavages based on caste/class/religion clubbed with the dominant male discourse in rural Indian society have created a situation where women in political decision making have been reduced to mere 'proxies' thereby impeding the mission of empowering women politically through affirmative action. On the other hand, however, there are several cases of positive changes brought about by the implementation of the quota system where SC/ST women have been observed to bring about socio-economic and political changes.

It may be argued that the women members in the PRIs today are 'first generation learners' who are gradually learning to adjust to the new political conditions. The political knowledge of women is increasing and gradually a sense of confidence is getting instilled in them, as they are now aware of the problems being faced by their locality. However, one has to keep it mind that without the system of reservation women would have had no role to play in grassroots politics in India. As statistics show, 95% of women claimed they would never come to acquire positions in Panchayats, if there were no provision of reserving seats for them (Centre for Women's Development Studies 1999).[24] Talking about the non-election of women to PRIs in the general seats in the state of Orissa, Hust suggest that there could be two explanation for this phenomenon: one, women failed to successfully compete with men in the non-reserved constituencies; or two, women did not compete at all from general non-reserves seats. Men are not willing to let women contest from a general seat and lose their own chance of being in the decision making position. Hence, reservation has at least succeeded in bringing the womenfolk in rural India into the political forum. Hust's study shows that at least 25% of the elected women could now imagine standing against a man in future.

There are many instances of women members of the Panchayat taking a keen interest and playing a significant role in the workings of grassroots politics. For instance, Jesumary, the President of the Michalepattinam Gram Panchayat in Mudukulanthoor Block of the Ramnathapuram district in Tamil Nadu, was conferred with the Seva Ratna as the best performing Panchayat president by the Tamil Nadu Gram Panchayat Leaders Association. Fatima Bi of Kalve village in Kurnool district in Andhra Pradesh received the UNDP award for the Asia Pacific region for her work in the area of poverty alleviation. In Madhya Pradesh, there is the case of a proactive woman sarpanch who had done remarkable work in the area of maternity and infant care; another woman sarpanch was responsible for checking the high rate of school drop outs in her village and also worked for constructing more class room for girl students. Women Panchayat members in Himachal have been successful in getting all marriages and births registered (Institute of Social Studies Trust.

A number of studies conducted in Madhya Pradesh, Karnataka and Andhra Pradesh list the cases of various women who used their position in the PRIs to engage in developmental work in their respective localities and bring in positive changes. Even tribal women are gradually getting integrated into the village organisations. In fact, it is revealed that as against the prevalent notions, the PRIs in the tribal Madhya Pradesh comprised of young and educated women.[25]

No doubt, women are constantly under pressure from their family especially the dominant male members), 'village community' or are facing societal restrictions and cleavages in performing their role as Panchayat members. However, in some cases women are gradually learning to hold their own. For instance, in the recent PR elections held in Almora, Uttaranchal, Durga Devi, the president of the women's group of Chaura village, was approached by a political party to contest elections under the party banner. The party offered her monetary and logistical support. However, when she realised that she would not be able to take up programmes for women's development on her own will and would have to follow the party agenda, she refused the party backing and contested the elections with the support of the women's group.

All Women Panchayats have also come up in number of states. In Madhya Pradesh there are nine such villages that have all women Panchayats. There are few villages in West Bengal, Karnataka, Maharashtra, Haryana and others, which have all women Panchayats. Moreover, dismantling the argument that claimed majority of the women representatives in the PRIs to be drawn from the rural elite (barring the seats that are reserved for SCs/STs), Hust in her study brings out that since families belonging to the higher strata in the villages are not yet ready to introduce their womenfolk to the public space, it is women belonging to the lower castes or lower class who get entry to the PRIs. In Kotgal Gram Panchayat of Gadchiroli district in Maharashtra, for the first time 11 candidates from the lower castes won the elections in 2002. A study conducted by Centre for Women's Development Studies also revealed that a large number of women from the poor families and women having no political connections have found their way to PRIs through reservation.

In fact, in 2004, there were at least nine states where going beyond their reserved quota women acquired more than 33 per cent seats taking a revolutionary step, the Bihar government went on to reserve 50 per cent seats for women in all the three tiers of the PRIs in all categories of seats as against the constitutional requirement of reserving one-third seats.

Normative Implications

In a country like India, where society is "highly gender-segregated", quotas for women have "an additional relevance". It is possible for womenfolk in a village to approach the female members of the PRIs with their grievances. Women members of the Panchayats very often receive petitions from other village women on issues such as family disputes, disputes over land, employment and housing. They may not be able to find solution all such problems, but they are now "exposed to a whole new world of public service". Moreover, women have come to value their newfound freedom to move out of the four walls of the house and are finding a space for themselves in the public realm. There is a higher visibility of women and they are increasingly recognizing their self-worth and gaining respect for their work.[26]

However, it needs to be emphasised that although changes are happening, they are occurring gradually. It may also be observed that villages that are socio-economically more advanced are ones where women have more exposure to information and education.[27] There is, therefore, the need to take various proactive measures if political empowerment is to be translated into real empowerment and not mere lip service. As Hust argues "reservation for women in political bodies can only be an enabling condition for the larger project of women's empowerment." For actualizing real political empowerment of women, quotas cannot be disassociated from the larger structural elements of social relations. Moreover, the lack of education is a serious obstacle[28] that has marred the real empowerment of women despite their numerical strength in the Panchayats.

Women who are educated and have access to information have often been more successful in bridging "social differences associated with gender."[29] There is also a need to impart political training to the women panchayat members so that they are able to understand the workings of the system. Provisions need to be made to offer financial assistance to the female candidates so that their dependence on the male members of the family for election expenditure is considerably reduced. A monitoring mechanism needs to be set up whereby the workings of the PRIs could be evaluated and necessary changes initiated.

Again, compared to the upper caste and non-tribal women, the lower caste and tribal women require more encouragement in terms of education and training due to the history of discrimination meted out to them. Reservation of seats has either willingly or unwillingly made the SC and ST women enter the political forum at the grassroots. Proper measures need to be taken so that this phenomenon could be molded to the advantage of the cause of women's political empowerment.

CONCLUSIONS

In a fractured democracy like India, where the identity of a woman is not manifested only in terms of gender, it would be an error to expect that women would work as a single group towards their empowerment. Rather, studies should take into account the differential impact of PRI quotas and the role of class, caste, ethnicity and religion. Affirmative action through the 73rd Amendment Act had created a massive rise in the numerical strength of women in PRIs. However, the elected women members continue to suffer under the "dichotomy" of their roles: "their ostensible power in the panchayat and their relative powerlessness within the home". In addition, SC/ST women face structural inequalities that cannot be captured through conventional social scientific methods. Rather, explanations must also look at culture and the mechanisms of social stratification to account for outcomes.

Democratisation occurs at many different levels, with substantial differences between each level. In other words, as a process, democratisation at the federal level is different from the processes occurring at the level of the states and at the village level. Similarly, within this larger process, the debate over the reservation for women in PRIs, is extremely critical, as in most cases we see women bearing the brunt of unprogressive social practices. Thus, a change in political status may bring about a larger transformation in socio-economic processes. It is our contention that social scientists who are studying the impact of quotas for women in political systems must go well beyond the federal and state legislatures, and take into account the extremely important processes of change occurring at the village level.

NOTES

1. The terms Scheduled Castes and Schedule Tribes are essentially legalistic categories, which are a sub-part of a larger term "backward classes." Under the Government of India Act of 1935 a separate schedule was created to govern relations between the state and the classes/castes/tribes under the category of backward classes. Scheduled Castes include all those castes that were originally considered "untouchables" while scheduled tribes referred to all aboriginal and hill tribes (See Mathew Zachariah. 1972. "Positive Discrimination in Education for India's Scheduled Castes: A Review of Problems." *Comparative Education Review* 16(1): 16-29). Schedule Castes make up about 16% of the total population while Scheduled Tribes make up about 6% (See Rohini Pande. 2003. "Can Mandated Political Representation Increase Policy Influence for Disadvantaged Minorities." *The American Economic Review* 93(4): 1132-1151.
2. It is important to indicate that dominant paradigm of the electoral systems literature finds its way into the study of quotas, and does not tell us about why or how informal institutional practices impinge upon representation through quotas. For example Malami and Kenworthy's (1999) concern with the variation in the share of parliamentary seats occupied by women led them to identify certain factors that have significant impact. They find that electoral system structure, the presence of a left party government, the timing of women's suffrage, and the share of women in professional occupations, and cultural attitudes towards the role of women each play a significant role. However, what we do not know is how exactly these factors determine reservations (an answer which can only be provided through historical case study methods). Similarly Pande's (2003) methodological choices in the study of reservation of SC/STs in general, in the states, led her to examine the provincial legislatures, which are based in the cities.
3. Informal institutions have been defined as "socially shared rules, usually unwritten, that are created, communicated, and enforced

outside of officially sanctioned channels" (Helmke & Levitsky 2004, 727). would be on SC and ST women as there is a complete paucity of empirical observations of the representation of religious minorities within these institutions.

4. Article 40, Part IV, of the Constitution says, "The State should take steps to organize village panchayats and endow them with such power and authority as may be necessary to enable them to function as units of self-government".
5. Article 243 of the Indian Constitution says 'Panchayat' means an institution of self-government. Article 243G entrusts the State legislatures to "endow the panchayats with such powers and authority as may be necessary to enable them to function as institutions of self-government".
6. It ought to be noted that at the federal level a Bill known as the Women's Reservation Bill (WRB) to reserve 33 per cent seats for women at the national and state legislatures was introduced in the Lower House of the Indian Parliament on 12 September 1996. The Bill was kept in the "storage" in order to achieve consensus by the members of the Parliament, but is yet to get codified into law.
7. Article 243D of Part IX of the Constitutions states, "(1) Seats shall be reserved for—(a) Scheduled Castes; and (b) Scheduled Tribes... (2) Not less than one-third of the total number of seats reserved under clause (1) shall be reserved for women belonging to the Scheduled Castes or, as the case may be, the Scheduled Tribes. (3) Not less-than one-third (including the number of seats reserved for women belonging to the Scheduled Castes and the Scheduled Tribes) of the total number of seats to be filled by direct election in every Panchayat shall be reserved for women.... "(4) The offices of the Chairpersons in the Panchayats at the village or any other level shall be reserved for the Scheduled Castes, the Scheduled Tribes or women in such manner as the Legislature of a State may, by law, provide...."
8. It is extremely crucial for us to point out that neither the definitions of the term "reservations" or "quotas" fully capture the type of affirmative action being carried out in the PRIs. For example Mala Htun tries to distinguish between the two terms in the following manner. Quotas are understood to function "by taking a category of people who belong to, but suffer from discrimination in mainstream political parties and propel them

to positions wherein they stand a chance of popular elections." Further, "Reservations take a different approach. They introduce group-specific avenues of representation that circumvent the party system and create new electoral incentives. These include the creation of: separate electoral rules, special electoral districts that limit competition to group members, exceptions to counting rules, and provisions for direct elections to legislatures (*Ibid*).

9. One of the major causes of corruption is that the salaries paid to PRI-members are extremely low. The remuneration varies from 10 rupees (INR) per sitting to 50INR. The *sarpanch* can get upto 100INR. Hence in case of a SC or a ST woman who works outside their house as wage laborers in order to contribute to the household income, if the choice is between attending a Panchayat meeting and earning their daily wage, they most certainly would opt for the latter. A World Bank study on exclusion and inclusion within PRIs in Rajasthan and Madhya Pradesh reveal that 42% of men are highly active as compared to only 11% of women. 52% of women fell within the least active political category as compared to 30% of men.
10. Ms Leelavathy from Villapuram, Tamil Nadu, was murdered in broad daylight by armed men since she was working towards getting permanent water supply to Villapuram as part of her election campaign and it ran contrary to the interests of the mafia henchmen who sold drinking water to the people (see Mythily Sivaraman, 'Blow to Goodness', *The Hindu,* May 18, 1997).
11. It must be pointed out that the problem of violence towards SC/ ST women is very extensive. A measure of the degree of violence can be seen in the following statement of the All India Dalit Adhikar Manch (All India Dalit Women's Rights Forum): "On an average 27,000 incidents of serious atrocities and human rights violations are registered under the SC/ST (Prevention of Atrocities Act), annually. Despite the lack of disaggregated data on the extent of violence on Dalit women, there is no doubt that women are affected disproportionately in these incidents. A micro study of 124 cases by the Centre for Dalit Rights of atrocities in 5 districts of Rajasthan between October 2004 and January 2006 showed that 55 of these cases were directly inflicted on Dalit women and girl children. They ranged from rape, gang rape, rape of minor girls, murder and attempt to murder, physical assault, battering and acid attacks. Another 28 women were affected along with their

families through land related violence, social boycott, murder of husbands and sons. It is clear that Dalit women are the prime victims in violence against Dalit communities" (2007,2).

12. "The classic case is that of a village in Madurai district of Tamil Nadu, a southern state in India. In Melavalavu, the dominant castes of the area murdered the panchayat president and the vice-president who both belonged to a lower caste, merely because they dared to fight the panchayat elections."
13. There have been reports from four districts of Madhya Pradesh —Raigarh, Chattarpur, Raisen and East Nimar of a lady Sarpanch being stripped naked, another lady sarpanch being gang raped, an *upasarpanch* (deputy president) being tortured and a dalit panchayat member being beaten up.
14. In an interview, a prominent young politician in Bhilwara, Rajasthan, said (Aug 1999), "Development has been in a setback by at least a decade in villages where a female has been *sarpanch* for the last five years" (World Bank 2001, 28).
15. Maya (a member of Vadal Gram Panchayat, Maharashtra) along with her colleague from another village had gone to attend a women's organization program that was held in the hall of a hotel. On being spotted there, a vulgar rumor was spread in her village that these two women went to hotel rooms and hence were of stained character. There were accused of misconduct and were treated as outcastes in their village and even the other women in the village stopped talking to them (Women's Environment and Development Organisation 2007).
16. To quote a young ward member from Gania block, Orissa, "I have no problem to speak with men in the [Panchayat] meetings. They do not belong to my village. I do speak to them like I do speak to the women. Outside the panchayat office I do not speak to the men. After the meeting I go home immediately and stay in the house.... I do not go the *gram sabha.* My husband attends the *gram sabha.* I am a *bahu* (daughter-in-law) of the village" (Hust 2002,11). A very important factor for the election of women is also age. The elder women have a more liberated position in the village and can therefore freely intermingle socially with men. Hence they are the preferred candidates to enter PRIs. However, the younger females (most particularly daughter-in-laws) fail to get elected because of the strict social norms. However, it is the young women who are educated and

hence could fare better if given a chance to enter the PRIs (World Bank, 2001,17).

17. A crucial study (2001) carried out with 60 gram Panchayat members who had undergone a free phased training in Tumkar district, Karnataka, revealed that one-third of the members were still functioning as proxy candidates while the actual control remained with either their husbands or sons. Another one-third, who did not face such constraints at home, was faced with gender subordinations within the Gram Panchayats. Only the remaining one-third was found to be effectively functioning as members and they have also gained some amount of power and respect in the family (Murthy 2001:134).
18. In a case from Uttar Pradesh, it has been reported that the an elected woman member of the PRI belonging to the lower caste was not allowed to sit inside the panchayat office along with the upper caste members and she had no freedom of expression. In Panchayat meetings in Rajasthan, lower caste women members sit veiled and in a corner without contributing to the proceedings (World Bank 2001, 18).
19. In her study of tribal women in PR in MP, Abha Chuahan revealed that nearly 63 per cent did not raise any issue in the panchayat of their own accord and the few who did mainly confined their concerns to health, women, child welfare, and drinking water. While 62 per cent attended the meetings, 48 per cent did not attend the meetings at all or did attend at times. Those who did not attend the meetings, 50 per cent of them said that their husbands were managing their affairs for them (2003, 22). Tribal women in Dungarpur district in Rajasthan revealed that they were satisfied working in a women's savings group, as there were many benefits from it. They claimed, "...There is no work for the individual in the panchayat, and especially women. What will we gain from participating there? Whether we go or not does not make a difference" (World Bank study 2001, 26).
20. Gangamma Jayakar, a ST candidate (studied up to Class IV), was made the GP President following the elections in 1993 in Haleuru Gram Panchayat, Malgudi, Karnataka as the seat was reserved for a ST woman candidate. While the other members of the GP had no qualms in a ST woman becoming an "ordinary" member of the GP, they refused to serve under a ST

woman President and demanded her resignation. When she refused to comply with their requests, the others stopped cooperating with her. She later had to approach the High Court who ruled in her favour. However, the others still did not cooperate and since the quorum for holding a meeting is the presence of 3 members, she held meeting with the help of two other SC members and had to continue like that throughout her tenure. Jayakar feels that she could have initiated a lot of developmental work if she got the cooperation of the others (Vyasulu & Vyasulu, 1999).

21. In Gania block in Orissa, although a young and energetic female *sarpanch* wanted to tackle the issue of alcoholism in the area she could do nothing about it as the elite class male of the village who would be instrumental in deciding her re-election were the liquor consumers. Antagonizing them would make her lose her political support (Hust, 2002, 16).

21. In Gania block in Orissa, although a young and energetic female *sarpanch* wanted to tackle the issue of alcoholism in the area she could do nothing about it as the elite class male of the village who would be instrumental in deciding her re-election were the liquor consumers. Antagonizing them would make her lose her political support (Hust, 2002, 16).

22. A tribal woman *sarpanch* was stripped naked while unfurling the national flag on 15th August 1998 (Independence day) in a district in Rajasthan. In another case a tribal women *sarpanch* in Madhya Pradesh was stripped naked in a Gram Sabha meeting because she was not consulting the leader of the dominant caste.

23. George and Krishnan give the instance that the first ever tribal woman Block Panchayat President in Attappady block in Palakkad district of Kerala could hardly do any work due to the boundaries laid by the political party, which she represented (2006, 213).

24. George and Krishnan, 2006. They argue that only because of the presence of the policy on reservation a tribal woman was elected as the president of the Attappady Block Panchayat, Palakkad district, Kerala.

25. The study reveals that 70 per cent of women in PRIs in tribal MP are below 49 years of age and 30 per cent are educated. Moreover there are nearly another 30 per cent who call themselves 'literates' i.e., they can sign their names.

26 In case of Orissa, 40% of female incumbents perceived that their status has been elevated in the family as well as in the village community with their election into the PRIs (Hust, 2002,16). One OBC ward member in Balipatna (Orissa) said: "Before my election I [....] never went out or mixed with people. But now I am more confident and mix with others. When I met our *sarpanch* the first time [a very respected senior *Brahmin]* I was very nervous, but after the meeting I was very happy. Also the other ward members helped me to overcome my nervousness and it helped that there were also other women, not just me. I also adjusted slowly to sit together with men, and now I can also speak to men in the village. Before I could not talk to them, but now I think that they do respect me" (*Ibid*).

Shubhatai of Vitner village, Maharashtra, is much more confident following her election to the Panchayat as her husband had stopped battering her and her status in the family and the village had also improved (Baviskar 2005, 340). A positive change can be observed in the image and status of the tribal women through participation in PRI activities. They feel that their status has been elevated and they are now treated with respect (see Chauhan 2003).

27. Hust found that in case of Orissa, women belonging to more forward blocks like Baltipana gained more than their colleagues in Gania (2002,17).

28. Hira Devi, a SC candidate and Panchayat Pradhan of Soloi Gram Panchayat, Gongri village, Himachal Pradesh, was very confident of her abilities and was involved in initiating a number of village development projects. However, being educated only till class five, she claimed that education was the main obstacle that came her way as she failed to understand clearly various schemes and policies of the government (Institute of Social Studies Trust 2005).

29. We have the case of a well-educated female *sarpanch* in Ujjain district in Madhya Pradesh who exercised total control over the activities of her Panchayat (World Bank 2001, 18). Savita Rathi, *sarpanch*, Gopalpura gram panchayat, Jaipur, Rajasthan, has an LLB. Education which has helped her to get an intricate understanding of the working of the system. She has been able to handle the administrative officers, the local press and the MLAs. She has been successful in renovating the infrastructure

of the panchayat in the area. A woman with a vision she has drafted and computerized a 2005-25 master plan for the development of her area that includes phased proposals, census figures, maps and such considerations as the ideal populations density for the village centre (Karnard 2007).

REFERENCES

Adams, John, "Letter to John Penn, 1776", in *Works of John Adams,* Boston: Little, Brown, 1951, Vol.4.

Alsop, Ruth, et al, "Inclusion and Local Elected Governments: The Panchayati Raj System in India" Social Development Paper 37, *World Bank, South Asia Region, Social Development Unit,* Washington D.C., 2001.

Banu, Zenab, *Tribal Women Empowerment and Gender Issues,* New Delhi: Kanishka Publishers, 2001.

—, *Disempowerment of Tribal Women: Perspectives on 73rd Constitutional Amendment,* New Delhi: Kanishka Publishers, 2004.

Baviskar, B.S., "Impact of Women's Participation in Local Governance in Rural India" in L.C. Jain (ed.), *Decentralisation and Local Governance,* New Delhi: Orient Longman, 2005.

Buch, Nirmala, "Women and Panchayats: Opportunities, Challenges and Support" in L.C. Jain (ed.), *Decentralisation and Local Governance,* New Delhi: Orient Longman, 2005.

—, "Women's Experiences in New Panchayats: The Emerging Leadership of Rural Women" Occasional Paper 35, *Centre for Women's Development Studies* (CWDS), Delhi, 2000.

Bystydzienski, Jill M., (ed), *Women Transforming Politics: Worldwide Strategies for Empowerment,* Bloomington: Indiana University Press, 1992.

Castles, Stephen, "Studying Social Transformation," *International Political Science Review* Vol. 22, No.1, 2001, pp. 13-32.

Centre for Women's Development Studies, "From Oppression to Assertion: A Study of Panchayats and Women in M.P., Rajasthan, and U.P.", *CWDS,* New Delhi, 1999.

Chauhan, Abha, "Women's Participation in Panchayats in Scheduled Areas With Special Reference to Madhya Pradesh",

A Decade of Women's Empowerment Through Local Government in India, Institute of Social Sciences/South Asia Partnership Canada/International Development Research Centre, October 20-21, 2003.

Dahlerup, Drude, "Using Quotas to Increase Women's Political Representation" *Women in Parliament,* International IDEA, 2002.

Fox, Richard and Jennifer Lawless, J., "Entering the Arena? Gender and the Decision to Run for Office," *American Journal of Political Science,* Vol. 48, No.2, 2004, pp. 264-280.

George, Alexander and Andrew Bennett, *Case Studies and Theory Development in Social Sciences,* Boston: MIT Press, 2005.

George, Abey and Jyothi Krishnan, "From the Other End: Tribals and Democratic Decentralisation in Kerala", *IDPAD,* 2006.

Helmke, Gretchen and Steven Levitsky, "Informal Institutions and Comparative Politics: A Research Agenda," *Perspectives on Politics,* Vol. 2, No. 4, 2004, pp. 725-740.

Hust Evelin, "Political Representation and Empowerment: Women in the Institutions of Local Government in Orissa after the 73rd Amendment to the Indian Constitution", *Heidelberg Papers in South Asian and Comparative Politics,* Working Paper No.6, August 2002.

Institute of Social Studies Trust, "Beyond Practical Gender Needs —Women in North-Eastern and Hill States", *Study for the UNDP-Panning Commission National Research Programme on Growth and Human Development,* ISST, New Delhi, July 2005.

Institute of Social Studies Trust, "Women in Leadership Positions: A Scoping Paper", ISST, New Delhi, July 2005.

International Fund for Agricultural Development, "India - Participation of Tribal Women in Village Organisations", *IF AD,* 19 January, 2007.

Kenworthy, Lane and Melissa Malami, "Gender Inequality in Political Representation: A Worldwide Comparative Analysis", *Social Forces,* Vol. 78, No.1, September 1999, pp.235-268.

Leiten, G.K., "Panchayats in Western Uttar Pradesh: 'Nameless Member", *Economic and Political Weekly,* XXXI, No. 39, 1996, pp. 2700-2705.

Mansbridge, Jane, "Should Blacks Represent Blacks and Women Represent Women? A Contingent "Yes"," *The Journal of Politics*, Vol. 61, No.3, 1999, pp.628-657.

Mathew, George, "Panchayati Raj Institutions and Human Rights in India", *International Council in Human Rights Policy*, 2002.

Oppressed?", *Economic and Political Weekly*, Vol. XXXI, No. 27, 6th July 1996, pp. and Ramesh Nayak, "Panchayats at Work: What it Means for the *E* 1765-1771.

Mill, J.S., *Considerations on Representative Government*, Chicago: Reguers, 1962.

Moser, Caroline, O.N., "Practical and Strategic Gender Needs and the Role of the State" in Caroline Moser (ed.), *Gender, Planning and Development: Theory, Practice and Training*. London: Routledge, 1993.

Murthy, Ranjani (ed.), *Building Women's Capacities: Interventions in Gender Transformations*, New Delhi: Sage, 2001.

Karnard, Raghu, "A Thar Spring: A Women Sarpanch Rewrites the Script of an 'Injured' Rajasthan Village", *Outlook*, October 15, 2007.

Palanithurai, G., "New Panchayati Raj System in Tamil Nadu", *South Asian Journal of Socio-Political Studies*, January-June 2001.

Panchayati Raj Update, Institute of Social Sciences, Vol. VIII, April 2001.

Pande, Rohini, "Can Mandated Political Representation Increase Policy Influence for Disadvantaged Minorities." *The American Economic Review* 93(4), 2003, pp. 1132-1151.

Phillip, Anne, *The Politics of Presence*, Oxford: Clarendon Press, 1995, Reprinted 2003.

—, "Democracy and Representation: Or, Why should it Matter Who Our Representatives Are?" in Anne Phillips (ed.), *Feminism and Politics*, New York: Oxford University Press, 1998.

Pitkin, Hanna F., *The Concept of Representation*, Berkley: University of California Press, 1967.

—, "Rethinking Representation", *American Political Science Review*, Vol.97, No.4, 2003.

Rai, Manoj, et al, (eds.), *The State of Panchayats: A Participatory Perspective,* New Delhi: Sanskriti, 2001.

Rai, Shirin M., "Reserved Seats in South Asia: A Regional Perspective", *Women in Parliaments Beyond Numbers* 2005.

Ravi, Venkata *et al,* "Women participation in Decentralised Local Self Governance" *South Asia Politics,* Vol. 3, Issue 4, August 2004, pp. 26-30.

Sivaraman, Mythily, 'Blow to Goodness', *The Hindu,* May 18, 1997.

Uma Prachar (A Resource Letter on Panchayati Raj), Vol. 13, No. 1, 2006.

Vyasulu, Poornima and Vinod Vyasulu, "Women in Panchayati Raj: Grassroots Democracy in India, Experience From Malgudi" Background Paper No.4, UNDP, 24-26 March 1999.

Williams, Melissa, "The Uneasy Alliance of Group Representation and Deliberative Democracy" in Will Kymlicka and Wayne Norman, eds., *Citizenship in Diverse Societies,* New York: Oxford University Press, 2000.

Women's Environment and Development Organisation, "Women in Local Self Governance.... In an Indian Context", *WEDO* 2007.

—, *Voice, Trust and Memory: The Failings of Liberal Representation,* Princeton: Princeton University Press, 1998.

Young, Iris Marion, *Inclusion and Democracy,* Oxford: Oxford University Press, 2000.

Zachariah, Mathew, "Positive Discrimination in Education for India's Scheduled Castes: A Review of Problems." *Comparative Education Review* 16(1), 1972, pp. 16-29.

4

Reservation for Women in Local Panchayats

Since independence, both governmental and non-governmental organisations have initiated a number of projects and programmes in India with the intention of empowering and advancing women in society. While there have been attempts to empower women in all areas of society, including the social, economic and religious sectors, some of the most visible attempts have occurred in the political realm. The most recent policy change in government occurred in 1992, when Parliament passed the seventy third amendment of the Constitution, reserving 33% of the seats for women in the panchayats, the local governing system.

While this constitutes a positive step for women, it is necessary to assess the extent to which this legislative action has affected women's position in Indian society. In order to do this one must first consider carefully the nature of women's power in society, and then determine to what extent women's power in government influences the other spheres of women's lives. Are there other modes of exercising power within society that are not affected by this so-called progressive action for women? Some questions that must be addressed are: What were the motivations behind implementing this seat reservation? Who supported the amendment? What types of programmes actually assist women assimilate into this structural system? What aspects of the political structure limit women's power in politics? And finally, what factors outside of the political sphere affect women's position of power within politics?

While advancements in the political sphere are essential for the overall "empowerment" of women, the implementation of seat reservations with the intention of empowering women carries a number of assumptions concerning power. One of these assumptions is based on the overall importance of political power in comparison with power exercised in the social or economic spheres. Increasing the number of women in governmental positions does open doors for women in terms of presence and visibility. Moreover, the critical mass of women in political life itself increases the potential for the transformation of gender consciousness. However, it does not guarantee it. Numbers alone do not indicate that the situation for women has improved. This is the case for a few reasons, the most important being that there are certain norms, values and everyday practices that legislation simply cannot change or even affect. It is very important that those who fill the seats are aware of the problems that women face and are interested in creating change within the community. Often, it is argued that changes in legislation will be ineffective without the support of educational or training programmes that promote gender consciousness. The presence of women in politics alone has very little effect on the status of women in society. Therefore, if the actions taken by women in positions of political power do not benefit women outside of politics, then this legislative change provides a limited form of agency for women.

This study was conducted in a Hindu community and all the women interviewed were Hindu women. Although women are subjected to many similar forms of oppression across religious boundaries in India, the situation for Hindu women does differ from that of Muslim and Christian women. For example, there are fundamental practices within the religion that serve as barriers to women in both the public and private realms. And with the recent rise of Hindu fundamentalism in government, Muslims and Christians have increasingly faced religious prosecution and oppression. Since Hindus are the majority in India, it makes sense that Hindu women are more prevalent in politics and generally hold more political power than Muslim and Christian women. However, under the Hindu fundamentalist government, Muslims and Christians face more than just oppression from numbers.

Deconstructing Power

The concept of power itself must be deconstructed, along with its relationship to gender and repression, in order to understand why quotas in the legislature may not lead to women's agency in the long run. In his evaluation of the history of sexuality, Michel Foucault refutes the typical Victorian view of sexual repression. He explains,

> We are informed that if repression has indeed been the fundamental link between power, knowledge, and sexuality since the classical age, it stands to reason that we will not be able to free ourselves from it except at a considerable cost: nothing less than a transgression of laws, a lifting of prohibitions, an irruption of speech, a reinstating of pleasure within reality, and a whole new economy in the mechanisms of power will be required. For the least glimmer of truth is conditioned in politics.

However, Foucault believes we have been misinformed. Foucault attacks the views projected by previous Victorian thinkers by questioning the source of repression and society's ability to reverse it. While Foucault's argument dealt more with the issue of sexuality and the repression of sex itself in society, his argument carries over into the discussion of the repression of women. At some point women were imbedded into their roles in society, and Foucault acknowledges an interesting connection between power, knowledge, and sexuality. However, he goes on to ask if sex is so repressed, why then was it so widely discussed in Victorian times. Foucault examines the widely discussed "repression hypothesis" put forth by Freud, and others similar thinkers and comes up with his own new set of questions and in fact refutes this hypothesis. He does not believe that women are confined to these positions in society as the "repression hypothesis" suggests. Foucault chooses not to focus on the outward limitations and the reasons the situation has evolved in this manner, but rather he focuses on the values in each person that support these repressions, thus arguing counter to the Freudian analysis of Victorian values. The Victorian values assume that if women simply became oppressed by the laws of society, a removal of these laws will remove the oppression. Foucault chooses to "to locate the forms of power, the channels it takes, and the discourses it permeates in order to reach the most tenuous and individual modes of behaviour, the paths that give it access to the rare or scarcely perceivable forms of desire, how it penetrates and controls everyday pleasure..." Following Foucault, it is important to further analyze the extent to which the patriarchy, defined as male structural dominance, is rooted in society in order to evaluate the type of power women embody in different realms of life. If the governmental system is based on a patriarchal structure, then admittance into and acceptance by that structure will only be effective in advancing women in that structure but will fail to bring women to an equal status in society.

Power, Patriarchy and the Problem of Gender

As Foucault suggests above, there are many forms of power that dictate behaviour and patterns within every culture. Before further evaluating the role of power in society, there must first be an understanding of what power actually is and what type of power the governmental structure provides. V. Spike Peterson and Anne Sisson Runyan argue that there are a variety of ways of looking at power. Political power offers what they refer to as "power-over," which is basically the ability of one person to make someone do something they previously had no intention of doing. They argue that the conceptual notions of power themselves are based on masculine qualities and ideals. "This definition of power is masculinist to the extent that it presupposes androcentric notions of strength, competition, aggression, and coercion, and because it focuses on power understood only in terms of public-sphere activities that are dominated by men." Historically, women have been able to effectively assert this type of power on an individual level, but it can be argued that they are merely becoming part of a patriarchal power structure that omits other important forms of power. This is the reason definitions of power exercised by women that pertain to the private-sphere and the public sphere outside the realm of politics are often overlooked. Peterson and Runyan go on to argue that the more "power-over" power that women receive; the more their gender becomes invisible, simply because they are taking on a male-dominated definition of power.

They state: "....not only are very few women 'at the top,' but even those who succeed in achieving positions of power remain largely gender-invisible in conventional accounts of how power works in the world." To follow this point, traditionally feminine qualities are not recognised as powerful qualities, which could explain why women often are seen as abandoning the women's image to become more 'powerful' in the political structure. Women's gender often becomes invisible because "....feminine women (passive, dependent, domestic; engaged in meeting private, familial needs) are by definition inappropriate political agents (active, autonomous, public oriented; engaged in meeting collective, not personal needs)." They further their argument by asserting the importance of this dichotomy between the public and the private sphere. Because many of the qualities valued in the public sphere are labeled as unfeminine, women's ability to break out of the private sphere is thwarted.

Patriarchy by definition is a social system in which the father is the head of the family and men have authority over women and children. The structure of the governmental system, which exists in India and throughout much of the world, is based on a patriarchal system. However, it is important to acknowledge that the forms patriarchies take depend on cultural and historical factors. "Patriarchy" does not look the same in every society. Relating to politics in India, even if there are members of government and policies within the government that support women or give particular powers to women, the basic system still benefits men over women. But the goal of many feminists is not to establish a matriarchal governmental structure in its place, but rather to find a way to remove the engendered structure that causes the oppression of one gender over another. Peterson and Runyan address this issue in discussing gender ideologies. They emphasize that, "although not all whites endorse racism, all men masculinism, or all heterosexuals homophobia, *all* whites, men and heterosexuals *benefit* from their positions of relative privilege within the structures of racism, sexism and heterosexism. It is in this sense that the hierarchies are *structural* and not simply individual or idiosyncratic." Therefore, in order to create long-term change for women's involvement in politics, there must be structural changes. Individual advancement does not promote the progression of all women in society. Peterson and Runyan also point out that those who hold positions of power within these structurally biased systems are typically the people responsible for adjustments and changes within these structures. Government legislation and quota systems are an excellent example of this type of situation.

When making this policy change in a patriarchal system, it is often the case that those creating the change do not fully understand the complexity of the position of women in society and especially how women came to take on the roles that they did. Before an effective method of eliminating these barriers can be found, the key issues that women face must first be evaluated. The patriarchal ideology that stems from this type of structure can be found in other realms of life besides the public political sphere. However, the origin and the role of the ideology within the structure are essential, given that it dictates the policies and actions visible in government today.

Robert Connell has done extensive research on the role of gender in politics. He argues, "If the modern state is itself 'the general patriarch,'...then demanding that the state redress injustices worked by the 'individual patriarch' in the family (or any other setting) is merely appealing from Caesar unto Caesar. Seeking reform through the state is an exercise in futility, perhaps even in deception." He creates a convincing argument that the state cannot assume control of removing 'power-over' type relationships since the state itself is responsible for this type of relationship that is found within the public and private spheres. They are in many ways strengthening this relationship rather than breaking it down since the same type of relationship is being translated from the private sphere to the public sphere and vice versa. However his argument goes much further than this point. At the forefront of his argument, there is an understanding that "the state as an institution is part of a wider social structure of gender relations." The "power over" relationship that Peterson and Runyan refer to is widely found in gender relations. Connell's argument emphasises the importance of legislative change by showing that the gender relations found in government or state institutions extends to the gender relations in the social and economic sphere. Both the private and public spheres do have an affect on each other.

Quotas for women's representation in governing institutions are largely a response to liberal feminist demands for equality. Liberal feminists believe that the answer to women's subordination is the acquisition of individual and equal rights. Since individual rights and the state are interconnected, Connell maintains, the liberal feminist argument is based on the assumption that the state can reverse this subordination and lesser status of women. Furthermore, he asserts that liberal feminism lacks a solid understanding of the actual structure of government and the extent to which gender is institutionalised. Connell suggests that,

> Liberal feminism has brought to the surface the suppressed truth that the state is gendered, and has used this truth to inspire a formidable and sustained politics of access. But it has not been able to grasp the character of gender as an institutional and motivational system, nor to develop a coherent analysis of the state apparatus or its links to a social context.

While the efforts of liberal feminists have been influential to a degree, their theory's effectiveness is limited by its failure to comprehend the nature of gender relations within the public and private sphere. Connell explains that liberal feminism assumes patriarchy is a surface problem that can be really removed with laws. He asserts that liberal feminism "understands men as a category overrepresented in the state structure." Under this assumption, it seems logical that a seat reservation quota would be implemented as an effort to reverse men's "overrepresentation." But the patriarchal structure of the state goes much deeper than the overrepresentation of men. The state's role in women's oppression is often difficult to identify because it is not always direct and is often combined with other oppressive cultural factors. According to Connell, perhaps one of the most influential factors of oppression in the state's structure is the state's ability to appear neutral on issues, specifically those affecting women, while operating under gender biased procedures and systems. Connell contends that the state "plays a part in establishing or regulating 'systems' (the family, wage labour) in which women are oppressed. But the state can appear in itself to be gender-neutral; and this is a vital aid to legitimacy." The state's neutral stance comes from the fight for equality and sameness between the sexes. This creates an excuse for the state to ignore problems related to women by ignoring their differences and thus operating under a neutral system.

Simplistic notions of patriarchy and male domination suggest falsely men intentionally oppress women and consciously attempt to hold power over them. However, often it is more the support of a system that is built on patriarchal ideals that endorses the further oppression of women, rather than individual viewpoints and individual actions. Women's entrance in politics may simply further support this patriarchal structure than reverse women's position in society. Connell insists that generally there "is a broad *similarity* between women's and men's political attitudes, interests, and partisanship. This contradicts the theoretical idea that men's domination of the political apparatus arises from natural differences in motivation or outlook between the sexes."Assumptions of Male Dominance and Cultural Differences

In theory the state is the central location of power. Connell makes the argument that the family, while an important source of power, is peripheral and isolated into individual situations, or "cells." Connell is referring to the state of power relations in the modern era. Foucault would agree with Connell's assessment of the present day allocation of power and its implications in relation to the private sphere. Connell believes that the state is the central location of all power relations. Through laws, programmes and policy, according to Connell, the state is able to assert this power in an administrative and far more central way than the family structure ever could. However, Connell fails to account for the inability of the state to implement these state laws and policies which they create. While potentially the state could hold power over violence, property, sexual violence and other male-dominated practices, it is often unable to influence these actions as much as it claims it will. He overestimates the effectiveness of the state to have total control over the everyday life of people. Therefore, it may not be the state's power that dominates the private sphere but rather a different type of power relationship that does not necessarily result from the state's laws, programmes or policies. In India, seat reservations for women are based upon a similar assumption about state power. The implementation of the reservations differs greatly from its conception in theory.

However, Connell does argue that women's economic and religious involvement in society has placed gender at the base of the state structure. This, he argues, proves that the political structure of government is much more complex than a simple "male state."

Seat reservation for women in government at the local level is advancement towards empowerment in the political realm and a step forward in the dismantling of the repression of women in this sphere since this is a visible change for women. However, questions that follow this statement must be: To what extend does the seat reservation translate into changes in the rest of society? Is this policy change as monumental for women's advancement as it appears from an outside perspective? If it does not translate into other realms of society then other questions need to be addressed. What are the factors that cause this method of change to be a limited form of empowerment for women? And, What are the reasons behind this limitation? These factors include social values, patterns of governance, limitations in or gains from political parties, basic modes of establishing political power and the lack of a gender-conscious education.

Some of the greatest obstacles in cross-cultural research are the assumptions embedded in the differing perspectives. The Western perspective especially creates barriers for researchers and impinges our ability to make accurate assessments of women's roles in developing societies. In her article "Under Western Eyes: Feminist Scholarship and Colonial Discourses," Chandra Talpade Mohanty criticised earlier work by Western feminists who failed to acknowledge their own assumptions about non-Western women. Liberal feminists, specifically during the 1970s, typically characterised "third world women" as one large homogeneous group under the heading of the "Other." Certain Western feminists gave the impression that women in India, Africa, and the Arab world are all culturally bound by something that men of the same culture are not also bound by. Their assumptions removed women from their culture and lives by alienating them to this position of an "oppressed individual" in society. However, women cannot be looked at apart from their culture. By doing this, women's roles in society are largely discredited. Women's roles are necessary and often recognised within their cultures as being important. While women may experience oppression in both the public and private spheres, they are certainly still members of their culture and not an entirely separate entity simply bound by shared oppression. Women still have agency even in the context of being oppressed. Western feminists often overlook this fact. Mohanty reasserts that "this is what the 'colonizing' gaze of Western feminism does not acknowledge."

This notion of the "other" that Mohanty found in modern Western feminist writings has been very influential in anthropological research as well. Kamala Visweswaran finds this notion of the "other" extremely prevalent in most cross-cultural anthropological research. She emphasises that the elimination of ethnic studies from ethnographic and anthropological research, as well as the elimination of gender studies, makes it impossible to ever remove this concept of the "other." Without the understanding of the use of this concept of the "other," the researcher will not be able to adequately represent the situation as it actually is.

Mohanty goes on to address the issue of "male dominance." She believes that the misinterpretation of the concept of male dominance is one of the greatest barriers when performing anthropological research in third world countries. She argues, "An analysis of 'sexual difference' in the form of a cross-culturally singular, monolithic notion of patriarchy or male dominance leads to the construction of a similarly reductive and homogeneous notion of what I call the 'third world difference' that stable, ahistorical something that apparently oppresses most if not all the women in these countries." This implies that women in third world nations are held down by a singular force in a way that women in the

Western world are not. By making that sort of statement, feminists discount the importance of the cultural, political and social history of the country in which these women live. They are almost implying that women have not been affected by the changes in culture, let alone played a role in forming the culture, based on the fact that they have been oppressed by this "monolithic notion of patriarchy." If the researcher enters the field with this assumption, it becomes difficult to evaluate what the actual situation for the female interview subjects is since they have already placed a barrier between themselves and those they plan to interview. A solid knowledge of the history behind the Indian women's movements as well as a clear understanding of present-day efforts by Indian women themselves, are two important forms of understanding that would be helpful to acquire before beginning the research. Similarly, this should also be the case when implementing legislation such as the seat reservation. The implications of the women's movement in India and other factors that affect the seat reservation will be discussed below.

Mohanty also highlights the tendency among feminists to omit an analysis of the cultural basis of particular societies and attempt to create what she calls a "basis of secondary sociological and anthropological universals." The first example of generalisation is the homogenisation of all women under the assumption of "shared oppression." She emphasises that by eliminating the biological make up of women as the common factor among women and replacing it with "oppression," women have thus been labeled as powerless and in a lower position in all realms of life throughout history. "This results," Mohanty explains, "in an assumption of women as an always already constituted group, one which has been labeled 'powerless,' 'exploited,' 'sexually harassed,' etc., by feminist scientific, economic, legal, and sociological discourses." This eliminates the drastic cultural and religious portions of women's lives that define their power and position in society differently from each other. Finally, Mohanty argues that there is no such thing as universal male dominance or patriarchy. Rather she says: "There is, however, a particular world balance of power within which any analysis of culture, ideology, and socioeconomic conditions necessary has to be situated." This is relevant to this particular study because the governmental structure, cultural practices and religious ideology in India differ significantly from other nations and therefore cause a very different effect on the women who are subject to them. Studies such as this one must be very culturally specific. Generalisations, whether it is through assumptions of male dominance or of shared oppression, can hinder the evaluation of legislation and creation of other strategies to clarify women's status in the society.

Research Methodology and Setting

My research was conducted in Amreli District, Gujarat in May, 2003. Gujarat is located in central India, and Amreli District is situated in the southeastern section of the state. The district has a total population of 1,393,295, with the male population of 701,384 and a female population of 691,911 making the sex ratio 986 females to every 1,000 males. The data was collected through a series of twelve interviews with women in nearby villages and towns, who are presently, or who have in the past, held positions on the panchayats at the district, taluka or village level. Gujarat was chosen for a number of reasons. It is presently a very politically active state under the domination of the Bharatiya Janata Party (BJP). The BJP plays a large role in politics in the state of Gujarat and will be addressed later in this paper. As a result, in recent years there has been a great deal of tension over religious issues and violent outbreaks directed at Muslims and more specifically at Muslim women. Gujarat is also the birthplace of Mahatma Gandhi. As a result, there are numerous individuals and programmes in existence today dedicated to the Gandhian values aimed at bettering society in general and the status of women specifically.

The panchayat raj itself was a body instituted in 1957 as a method of decentralizing the government and allotting power to the village for the purpose of local developmental needs. It is composed of three levels: the gram panchayat at the village level, the panchayat samiti at the middle level and the zilla parishad, at the district level. While the panchayats lost much of their power throughout the 1960s and early 1970s, by 1977 the Janata Party, a predecessor of the BJP, decided it was necessary to strengthen this unit of government. While the panchayat raj system has attempted to implement economic and rural developmental programmes, especially during the 1980s, a number of factors that prevent the success of these types of programmes still exist. The first limitation in implementing developmental programmes is the structure of the body of the panchayat. Due to the structural set up of the panchayats, the councils have difficulty communicating with the development administrators. Hoshiar Singh pinpoints the major constraint of the panchayat system. He believes that not only is the increase in number of power elites in the panchayat a problem, but also the fact that many of these members are "discarded" state officials who are either highly corrupt officials or unqualified political leaders. Singh insists the panchayat raj,

> ... is working for elite groups or for groups of big farmers and rich businessmen, and the system has thus lost its appeal...[furthermore] State level leaders began to see these local institutions as rivals, and they started withdrawing important functions from them, making them dumping grounds for discarded state cadre administrative officers.

A significant change occurred in the panchayat system when the 73rd amendment was passed in 1993. The amendment was introduced under Rajiv Gandhi in 1989, and faced difficulty getting passed in the Rajya Sabha, or the upper house of the national government. For the next three years there was a struggle as the bill was reintroduced multiple times. Finally, on December 22 of 1992, the bill was passed in Parliament and then ratified by 17 state assemblies, including the state of Gujarat on April 24, 1993. Along with the 33% seat reservation for women the amendment also proposed a variety of changes in other areas. First, it established the three-level provincial government mentioned above. Second, it established direct elections for panchayat members. Third, it established that members would have the right to vote in meetings, but could not vote in elections for other panchayat members at the gram, intermediate, or district levels. Fourth, the amendment established five-year terms with control of the state over the elections.

However, the portion of the amendment that is most relevant to this study is the section that reserved seats for women. Along with the seat reservation for women, it also designated that seats be reserved for members of Scheduled Castes and Scheduled Tribes at all three levels of the panchayats. In the Hindu religious structure there are certain castes that are designated as below all other castes and this amendment provided special provisions to integrate these castes, known as Scheduled Castes, into the political structure of society alongside women. While Hoshiar Singh feels there are many beneficial aspects to this act, he argues that there are some limitations as well. Singh admits that, "it offers little to the *panchayats* by way of functions, powers, and resources to shape them as 'units' of self government."

Since the 73rd amendment was passed in 1993, it is useful to take a comparative look at the statistics for men and women in 1991 and in 2001 to gain a sense of the changes that have occurred statistically over the past ten years. The district of Amreli has a total population of 1,393,295. In 1991, the sex ratio for Amreli district was 985 females for every 1000 males, showing fewer women than men, and in the 0-6 year age group the ratio of girls to boys was even lower at 923 females for every 1000 males. But in 2001, while the overall ratio stayed the same, the 0-6 age group shows a drop in females with a ratio of 894/1000. In 1991 women had a 49.68% literacy rate, compared with a 71.21% male literacy rate. In 2001 both genders showed an increase in literacy rates with women at 57.77% and men at 77.68%. As expected, the statistics differ somewhat in rural and urban areas. In 1991, the rural literacy for women was at 46.22% and at 68.18% for men, compared with urban statistics of 61.16% for women and 80.73% for men. In 2001, the rural literacy rate was 54.51% for women and 75.24% for men and the urban literacy rate was 69.26% for women and 85.72% for men. In both the rural and urban setting, the gap between literacy rates seems to have been closed by 2% or 3%.

Currently in the district of Amreli, the total number of workers is at 43.12%. Of these workers, 55.15% are male workers and 30.93% are female workers. As expected, when looking at non-workers, the percentage of non-working women is greater than that of non-working men, at 69.07% to 44.85% respectively, which is important since non-workers make up 56.88% of the population. Women hold a much higher percentage in the marginal workers section than do the men at 15.94% to 2.8% in a category that makes up 9.33% of the people. The men well outweigh the women as the full time workers, as opposed to marginal workers. 33.79% of the population is fulltime workers outside of the household with 52.35% of them male and only 14.99% female. There are more men in the work force than women. This most likely means that women are taking care of the domestic responsibilities while men are working outside of the home.

Lack of experience working outside of the home is an inhibiting factor for women entering politics. Furthermore, women maintain their domestic responsibilities when they become involved in politics and often find themselves caught between their domestic and political duties. Therefore, family support is a necessity for women who want to become involved in the village panchayats. Generally women do not want special consideration based on the fact that they bear the burden of the domestic responsibilities. In a study done in the state of Kerala, the researcher found that "the familial responsibilities of all respondents seemed to conflict with their public duties, but women generally did not like partisan considerations to enter the field of panchayat work."

The base of my research was in Babapur, a small village just outside the city of Amreli. The population of Babapur itself is 2,838. Babapur is the location of Gunvantrai S. Purohit's ashram and Gandhian school which he and his wife started over forty years ago. This ashram is a community residence in which all the members contribute in some way to the school, whether through teaching, cooking, sewing or other necessary tasks. Although all the members of the ashram are Hindu, they belong to a variety of different castes. The Purohits moved to this area from Mumbai in order to educate the children living in this rural setting. The children in this area had previously not had access to quality education or, in a number of cases, had no access to education at all. When the Purohits first arrived, this was the case for almost all the women and girls in the area. Mrs. Purohit worked for nearly forty years to convince girls and their mothers in the area to leave their houses and begin attending school. She said, "At 10:30 every morning I would go to the village and ring a bell as a way to tell all the girls in the village to complete their household chores and then go for their education." Resistance came from both the fathers and mothers, who failed to see the necessity and benefits of educating their daughters.

According to the parents, education was merely an impingement on the domestic chores and could only have negative results. Girls were not expected to find work outside the home, so there was, in the eyes of the mothers, simply no need. The parents' objective was to have a daughter who would be a desirable candidate for marriage.

One of the greatest changes that has evolved in recent years which contributed to a widespread increase in women's education is that education became a prerequisite for marriage. According to many of the women I interviewed, men started to demand that their prospective wives receive an education. Following this turn, mothers and fathers encouraged their daughters to attend school. Mothers and fathers were supportive of this because "an investment in education is seen to benefit their conjugal families and, once again, is known to be tied to notions about paraya dhan (someone else's wealth). These refer to practices of dowry-giving and the giving away of daughters, thus defining the outflow and inflow of property, consumer goods, money, and even sills derived through education."

Today the Purohit's school has expanded to include a teachers training school. Nearly twenty years ago Mrs. Purohit served on the village panchayat. At this time, when the seat reservation had not yet been implemented, there were three women panchayat members. Mrs. Purohit was a member of the district panchayat for ten years. Over the years she was a member of the Taluka and Gram panchayats as well. Their daughter, Mendalieni Purohit, known as Miniben by her family and friends, has worked at the school since she graduated from college. She has also since started an orphanage for underprivileged children. Recently Mini was elected as the head of the village panchayat of Babapur. She was a guiding source in my research not only as a useful source of knowledge, but also as a translator for all the interviews.

Background of Setting

The conflict between Hindus and Muslims in India plays an important role in the region's dynamics. Gujarat has severely suffered from communalism since India gained independence from Britain in 1947. There has been an upsurge in communal violence in Gujarat in recent years. The most recent instances of violence occurred in February, 2002 when a train full of Hindus, returning from a pilgrimage to a temple in Ayodhya, was burned. Following this incident was an extreme backlash against the Muslim community. The violence that followed extended from the burning of houses, to the rape of women to the looting of stores and homes. Many scholars attribute the continued violence and heightened tensions to the Hindu fundamentalist political regime presently in power in the state of Gujarat. Cynthia Keppley Mahmood argues that "the changes underway in India today clearly reach far deeper than electoral politics, many commentators continue to look to campaigning, voting and the competition for political office as keys to understanding the obviously increasing communalism."

The attacks have appeared to be planned and supported by members of government. There have been reports that the police force, backed by governmental support, not only ignored the attacks, but actually encouraged them. Apparently, during attacks on the Muslims in Gujarat, "not only did the police remain inert, when the army arrived on the scene, [the army] was not deployed." While modern politics did not form these distances between the two communities, the BJP's policies and actions certainly promote the divide between the two religious groups. The Muslim community has therefore been extremely alienated from politics in the state of Gujarat. Muslims remain peripheral to the political structure. Arundhati Roy believes that the violence will drive the Muslims to "learn to keep quiet, to accept their lot, to creep around the edges of society in which they live." The serious violence that occurs in Gujarat does not take place in any other state.

The tension between the Hindus and the Muslims has an effect on the status of women in political positions. While Chandra Talpade Mohanty acknowledges that Indian women are often subjected to this concept of "other" by Westerners, Roy believes that Muslim women are seen as subjected to a similar alienation within their own country. She insists that "increasingly, Indian Nationalism has come to mean Hindu Nationalism, which defines itself not through a respect or disregard for itself, but through a hatred of the Other. And the Other, for the moment, is not just Pakistan, it's Muslim." Since Muslim women face both gender and religious oppression in Gujarat, they are at a much lower status than Hindu women socially, politically and economically. Since the Purohit family is Hindu, all the subjects interviewed consequently were also Hindu since all the contacts for the research were made through this family. Had some of the interviewees been Muslim, the findings would have been different.

However, I was able to interview women from a range of different castes within the Hindu religion since the Purohit family is of the Brahmin caste, and thus was accepted by the most elite of caste members. The Brahmin caste is extremely important in Hindu tradition and this carries over into other realms of life. Mahmood claims that "the Brahmins... [are] the key definers of group identity." The caste system has been the basis of the social structure in Hindu society since it emerged between the years 300 and 500 AD. The caste system has thus had a huge impact on women's lives. However each caste and sub caste follows its own specific practices. In this case, women are subjected to different limitations depending on which caste they belong to. Customs relating to marriage are also interrelated with the caste hierarchy. Carol Anne Douglas believes that "the custom of marrying girls before they reached puberty was developed to ensure that girls were unavailable to men of lower castes than their families." Castes are extremely divided through a hierarchical stratification and tend to remain socially within their castes. Marrying outside of one's caste, especially marrying someone of a lower caste is considered taboo in Hindu society. However, the Purohit family was extremely dedicated to what Miniben referred to as socialist values.

The "socialist values" that she refers to are mainly Gandhian values based on dedicating one's life to helping those in need and providing education and welfare for people in the rural areas of India. Since the Purohit family was very supportive of these ideas, as a result they strongly supported the increased representation of lower caste women, especially in local political institutions. Dalits, who are outside the traditional caste structure, are excluded from the public realm of politics. Even with their efforts, caste remains one of the greatest barriers for 'universal' women's advancement both in and outside of politics. However the Purohits have been very influential in their community through their support of dalits.

Research Methods and Limitations

The language barrier was a limiting factor in the research. While it was extremely helpful to have a translator who understood the nature of the research being conducted, which in itself lowered the chance of a misunderstanding, the possibility of mistranslation still exists. Moreover, there is also the possibility that the translator, in this case Mini Purohit, could unknowingly insert her point of view into the translation. However, her viewpoint was extremely valuable to the research, given her understanding of the situation, but it is worth noting that the interviews are heavily influenced by her assessment of the situation.

The final aspect of the interview crucial to my analysis is body language. When men were present, women often felt held back and as a result did not seem to share as much as they might have in the interviews. It is important for the researcher to be able to read a woman's silences. When attempting to assess the amount of control the husband has over his wife's political position, or how held back a woman is by her colleagues and the government corruption. Kamala Visweswaran has done extensive work on anthropological research of women by looking past the outside image of a woman's position within society to find out what the actual situation for women is. She argues that both male and female anthropologists have struggled with this for years because they simply cannot break down barriers with the women subjects. In her essay "Defining Feminist Ethnography," Visweswaran argues that feminist anthropologists stand to learn not only from women's speech, but women's silences as well." Most silences occurred when the husband was present. One of the most telling actions is when women immediately glance at their husbands, following each question, almost looking for approval or assurance, before either answering the question hesitantly or having the husband take over the answer. This could mean that she was either unsure of the policies due to her own lack of involvement in the position's work, or she was worried about her husband's reaction to the answer she wanted to provide. This was a common feature of interviews with women carried out in front of male family members.

WOMEN'S POSITION IN POLITICAL STRUCTURE

Women's decision making power in the panchayats is limited by male dominance in the domestic sphere, political party dominance in the region, corruption and state control, and religious and caste limitations. While the acquisition of power in politics itself does not necessarily affect the cultural morals and values that contribute to the male dominated atmosphere that exists in the areas that lie outside the political sphere, women also have not attained full decision-making power within the political realm itself, even at the local level. After evaluating the factors above that serve to limit this power, it becomes obvious that a change in legislation requires the support of programmes and time to establish a significant form of change. Women's ability to attain and exercise power, as well as create programmes, are essential. As explained above, the governmental structure contains gendered power relations that have been present since the creation of the system. This makes it difficult to create a reversal of these power relations through policy changes within the same system. This simply means that if women attain positions in the government, they should attain the type of position that gives them the power to institute the programmes that deal with issues they feel are the most important in society and they should be able to institute them by using their own methods. Otherwise, women's presence in government is simply reinforcing a male dominant structure. Women's fortification of the patriarchal system does, in fact, happen quite frequently. Often, when women individually achieve positions of authority in government, instead of creating change for women, they support a gender biased structured system. Indira Gandhi, for example, was a very powerful prime minister and exercised strong authority during her term, but it is questionable whether she changed the system simply by being a woman in a high ranking position. On an individual level, the sex of a person holding the position may not be as important as restructuring the actual system because the presence of women in political office holds no guarantee of commitment to the betterment of women's position in society.

Not only do women and men differ in their responsibilities within society, they can differ in their modes of affecting change on their communities. Joanna Liddle and Rama Joshi claim that "the contradiction between women's experience and male constructions of that experience, [create] an instability in individual consciousness upon which external factors can act to affect a change." Women are given much more freedom outside of politics to effect change in their communities and often find themselves to be much more successful. This makes politics less enticing to women. Two of the women interviewed said that they would be much more influential in their community outside of politics, where they could effectively take part in and initiate constructive and socially beneficial programmes without all the limitations that politics presents. This often discourages women from even attempting to run for reelection or continuing a career in politics. This is a typical problem that arises from top-down approaches to empowerment of women. What type of power are women looking for? In the context of seat reservations, there is an implication of "empowerment" in politics, but are women actually attaining power? It is necessary, then, to look into why the above factors impose limits on women holding positions on the panchayat.

Seat Reservations

Women have held positions in politics since independence, although their presence has been marginal. Throughout the 1950s and 1960s especially, talk of reserving seats for women was limited and almost non existent. Laws that promised improved conditions for women were passed, but little change was seen. However, in 1973 at the All India Panchayat Parishad's Sixth National Conference, discussion of seat reservations for women was brought to the table. While many showed support for a 30% seat reservation for women at the local level throughout much of the 1980s, women's groups opposed this move, stressing the importance of women's participation at all governing levels, not just at the local level. According to many women's activists at the time, representation at the local and district levels would prove to be a limited change for women.

The debate over the necessity of seat reservation becomes difficult when the gender relations and other factors that oppress women within the governmental structure are not identified. Kumud Sharma looks at the growing importance of women's political representation and the problems and issues that have resulted from the years of debate and eventual modifications of the Constitution that have taken place. However, Sharma fails to realize many of the assumptions he makes about the type of power women have achieved and the ability of this power to translate into other realms of women's lives. While he alludes to the importance of outside factors, he never develops their importance and centrality to the issue of implementation of seat reservation. It is often assumed that women will universally feel accountable for women's oppression and make attempts to change women's status in society. However, this is not always the case and Sharma does not account for this. He believes that "arguments relating to [the under-representation of women] revolve around two broad issues: the representative character of democratic institutions and their public accountability on women's issues." This highlights one of the greatest assumptions about the effectiveness of this amendment. The assumption is that although women are given positions in government, the system does not allow them the freedom to enact change on the community. Women are often held back from creating gender conscious programmes. Part of the reason that women have trouble implementing their ideas is that the other members of the panchayat lack motivation to implement new policies. Lilaben Laljibhai Jotaniya explained that her panchayat members were lazy and were reluctant to travel to Amreli to take care of their minor responsibilities. Another issue addressed above is that women do not also always feel personally responsible for women's problems and therefore do not always directly try to change women's status and create programmes that specifically help women.

Sharma's argument largely focuses on the democratic nature of seat reservations and systems of affirmative action along with whether or not these are fair mechanisms for change. He alludes to the contradiction in democracy by pointing out that the, "the persistent paradox of liberal democracy has been the tension between the notion of political equality and pre-existing social and economic inequalities." It is unclear, however, whether this statement presupposes that political equality will lift the laws of oppression governing women's lives in the social and economic realm or whether he acknowledges that changing the laws in a patriarchal system does not translate into the social and economic realm.

Seat reservations were implemented because women lack governmental representation. Sharma states that according to many political theorists, the lack of female representation is a failure of democracy, and an implementation of seat reservations will establish equality between men and women over time. He also defines equality as equal opportunity. But equal opportunity in which environment? In what context? To do what? Without changing the structural basis of the government, women are simply gaining equal opportunity to support a structure of principles that reproduce their repression. Peterson and Runyan insist that proportional representation "is insufficient. For the potential of [Panchayat Raj] to be realised, it must be embedded in a political culture committed to equality.... And it requires strong political leadership and social pressure, which are less likely where conservative (traditional, patriarchal) forces are strong." Sharma fails to acknowledge that in order for women to effectively become gender conscious and initiate relevant programmes, there must be a different type of equality established. The equality must go well beyond just critical numbers, especially just at the local level. But Sharma does assert that, "The biggest hurdles to transformative politics are the party system, electoral politics, and the polarisation between ideological positions and the reality of women's oppression." The problem lies in the lack of understanding of the reality of women's oppression and the main sources and reasons behind women's power or lack of power. Sharma talks about how women are beginning to understand how increased representation is necessary "to influence the redistribution of power and resources." This is an excellent example of an assumption about the type of power women need in order to be empowered: that the simple act of reserving seats will establish women with that power.

Role of Political Parties

The Bharatiya Janata Party (BJP) is the ruling party in Gujarat and also holds the majority in Parliament under the leadership of Prime Minister Vajpayee. The BJP is an outgrowth of the Rashtriya Swayamsevak Sangh (RSS) and the Vishwa Hindu Parishad (VHP). Jana Sangh was officially the precursor to the BJP, but was largely supported by the RSS and VHP and has continued to share members since its beginnings in the early days of independence. Jana Sangh came to Gujarat in the 1950s and, along with RSS and VHP, and at that time had a reputation for being fanatical Hindu fundamentalists. The political basis of the party was to establish unity among Hindus in order to marginalize Muslims and other non-Hindus, namely Christians and Jains. As a result they strongly supported the inclusion of all castes and the break down of negative caste relations. Presently the BJP still stands strongly behind its anti-Muslim pro-Hindu stance and still holds caste unity as one of its greatest goals. Ghanshyam Shah argues that the reason behind the BJP's great effort towards caste unity is that "despite the fact that the Hindu samaj is several times more powerful than that of the Muslims, it suffers humiliation and discredit because of its lack of internal cohesion, community feelings and faith in religion among its members."In an effort to gain more support from the Hindu community, the BJP has been very supportive of women and their involvement in local politics. Most of the women interviewed were either backed by the BJP or were party supporters. No one commented on the party as an inhibiting factor for advancement. In fact, part of the reason the party rose to power in the recent years is "due to a widespread disillusionment with the other parties and the common feeling that the BJP is an organisation led by people of integrity and discipline."

However, the Party does present some contradictions, which leads to questions about its record on the issue of women. The first and most important issue is that, while the amendment reserving seats for women at the local level passed easily, the efforts to apply it to the national level have been met with much resistance. Even today it has not been passed by parliament. All political parties, in fact, seem to be hesitant about passing the reservation programme at the national level. Sharma compares people's outward support of seat reservations with the actuality of seat reservations in parliament. He explains: "Seventy five per cent men and seventy nine per cent women favored reservations in legislative bodies...[but] as the predominantly male Parliament developed cold feet and did not pass [81st amendment reserving seats for women at the national level], because opposing a move towards women's political empowerment is regarded as politically incorrect, while supporting the Bill is seen as political suicide." Why does the BJP support seat reservations at the local level, but not at the national level? What does that say about the amount of "power" local politicians hold?

The BJP seems hypocritical in its views towards women's representation in government. It supports seat reservations for women at low level governmental positions where women will have very little political decision-making power, but are very hesitant on supporting women's participation at levels where they will hypothetically have more influence. Interestingly, the BJP was originally known for its support of centralizing power, which would mean limiting the state's power to some extent, and drastically limiting the power of the panchayats, placing more power in the hands of the national government. Limiting the power of the panchayats places huge constraints on the amount of developmental and social work that can take place in villages and towns. Panchayats are, in fact, under strict control of the state government and encounter much difficulty in attaining approval for simple tasks, such as road work or water systems. As regards the issue of state control, all the women interviewed responded that they would support giving more power to the panchayat members and that, if this occurred, it would be much easier to implement developmental programmes and create positive changes in their community. Also, M.S. John discovered during her study of political parties in Kerala that "the highly patriarchal nature of the party remains an impediment to the programmatic inclusion of gender issues."

This discrepancy between outward support of women's power and position within society and actual action is reflected in the BJP's treatment of caste unity. Shah finds the BJP support of caste unity hypocritical because the BJP still strongly supports the varna system, which is the official division of caste or social order in the Hindu religion. The varna system specifically refers to the privileging of some castes at the expense of others. Also, the BJP members support the everyday practices that are typically caste-specific. He goes on to say that the leaders openly show this by going to festivals and events that are open only to members of elite castes. It is difficult to establish unity among Hindus when the lines between castes are drawn so clearly.

The BJP's extensive support of Hindu tradition has had a negative effect on women. The issue that has caused the greatest controversy has been the practice of sati, or widow burning. The practice of sati dates back to as early as the thirteenth century. It was performed by women of particular castes in particular regions of India in honor of the goddess Rani Sati. She represents both religious commitment and a form of community involvement and identity. The practice was never common or widely practiced. Satis are typically performed by members of the upper castes and are extremely sacred events. Those who witness the transformation of the widow into a goddess through the burning of her body are said to receive a high blessing. Therefore, usually thousands attend a sati ceremony. Although many regimes that have ruled India since the thirteenth century have attempted to bring an end to this practice, they have failed to due so. According to Anne Hardgrove, attempting to bring an end to this practice was one of the greatest difficulties the British encountered during their more than two century rule over India, since they were continuously met with strong opposition from conservative Hindus who were starch defenders of the practice. Finally in 1829, the Supreme Court passed the Sati Abolition Act abolishing the practice altogether. This act was a result of a movement, led by Raja Rammohan Roy, against the practice of sati.

Although the practice had officially been abolished, instances of sati still occurred. The most famous case was performed on a woman by the name of Roop Kanwar in 1987. Hardgrove describes the situation that followed the actual death and its purpose below:

> Twelve days after the immolation took place, Deorala villagers persisted in glorifying Roop Kanwar's *sati* by conducting the ceremony of the *chunari mahotsav (mahotsav* literally means a 'great festival') in which women offer their *chunari* (wedding veils) on the site of the *sati* in order to obtain the blessings of the *sati* goddess.

The case caused much controversy and served as an opportunity for women and men to strongly assert their disgust over the practice. Although the case was brought to court, there was a huge resurgence from the religious male community of Jaipur, causing riots between the conservative marching men and the feminist protestors. The BJP politicians, perhaps under the fear of losing Hindu support, went along with Hindu tradition of visiting the site where the sati took place to receive the blessing as well as attended the ceremony described above.Radha Kumar comments that "...almost all the major centre to right wing political parties went to the site, not to enquire into what had happened but to stake their own claim to 'tradition'." Sati is one of the most serious issues that women in India have to face. If the male members of a political party truly support women, why, then, would they allow some women to be sacrificed for the sake of tradition, therefore implying that women hold a secondary position within the party? The BJP often supports the most widespread type of male dominance in Hindu society that takes place under the redeployment of tradition. Along with sati, dowry deaths, inheritance rights and widow's inability to remarry are other examples of assertion of tradition as a mode of oppression for women.

M.S. John argues that like the political structure, the party is also based on a patriarchal structure. John suggests "the local party committees of leftist parties, dominated by males, alternated as institutionalised sites of patriarchal power." She elaborates that the women who are successful in gaining support from political parties are those who are already "socialised" into the patriarchal political system and therefore are able to assimilate more easily into the patriarchal set up of the party structure. Personal relationships and connections in general play an important role in attaining and maintaining a position in politics. Outside of the state structure there is a system of connections usually between men that dictates much of the power relationships within government. It is extremely difficult for women to enter this network given the history and "pattern of administrative coordination within state structures." Also, when women give into this structure and series of relationship, they are often forced to give up their views and ideals to please the head members of the party. John argues the party structure and its procedures are so strong that it "makes the abilities and talents of individual women members worthless."

Re-election

Once women attain a position within government, they encounter a variety of different inhibiting factors. One of the most influential factors over women's political involvement is the difficulty of reelection. If women are to create change within the political structure and assert their own ideas, they need to remain in politics well beyond one term. Women, individually, have difficulty remaining in politics for a few reasons. These reasons include lack of outside training, the rate at which seats come up as reserved as well as the discontinuity in the specific seats that are reserved for women, and the lack of support from family and community members.

When a reserved seat opens up, many women are initially encouraged to enter politics by family and friends. However, they often are unable to remain in politics beyond this one term. Recently, seats have been coming up for reelection more frequently. While a seat may be reserved once for a woman, it is highly likely that it will not be reserved when the next election comes around and the woman in the position will be put up for reelection against men. Since the women were supported by their families and parties to run for a reserved seat, they are less likely to maintain the same support for a non-reserved seat. The husband and political party members are likely to return to their original motives and ideals, and are less inclined to support a long-term political career for their wife or fellow female panchayat member. Rasilaben Mansukhbhai Patolia, presently the president of the district panchayat of Amreli district, was originally encouraged to enter politics by her husband. Her husband had been involved in politics for over twenty years and had planned to run for the position of district panchayat president in the next election. However, when the seat came up as reserved, he encouraged his wife to run for the position. But when the next election occurs, the seat will most likely return to the general election and he expressed his desire to run for the position himself. Therefore, his wife, Rasilaben will lose her political support and would be very unlikely to run for the position again, making her experience in politics very short lived.

Through her research on women's involvement in local politics in the state of Kerala, M.S. John found difficulty in reelection to be one of the largest problems that women faced. John claims that 85% of the women she interviewed were not likely to run again for reelection and 30% would only attempt reelection if they were strongly supported by their friends, family and political party. As stated above, in Kerala the greatest limiting factor for women was lack of support from political parties, and in Gujarat the greatest limiting factor for women was the overbearing influence of the family, more specifically the husband. Although the factors are different the effect is the same. John asserts that, "Consequently, the experience of the incumbent women representatives will be lost and some of them may disappear from public life altogether, while inexperienced women members elected in the next round will have to start from scratch." Although most women come into politics with limited educational training to prepare them for the job, they can learn to succeed in their positions through experience. However, the fact that most of the women have difficulty gaining reelection negates the positive impact on gender issues of their participation in local governance to a certain extent.

Creating training programmes and support groups are helpful solutions to women's ability to remain in politics. The argument is often made by feminists and non feminists alike that one of the main reasons women struggle initially in politics is their lack of experience working outside the household.

However, training programmes are more important, because in order for there to be a change in the inheritance structure and practices of government as a whole, women must bring in gender conscious training and ideas of how their own ideals of power can be imprinted on the already existing structure. In her evaluation of women's participation in government and how this relates to democratic theory, Carole Pateman argues that while there is some basis for the connection between previous work experience and success in the political realm, there are some questions that should in fact be addressed first. She found that many political theorists believe that "experience of participation in some way leaves the individual better psychologically equipped to undertake further participation in the future." This supports the argument that women's inability to gain reelection could be one of the greatest obstacles in the success of the seat reservation in forwarding women's position within the political realm.

WOMEN'S MOVEMENT AND POLITICS

History of the Women's Movement

The women's movement has played a vital role in changing Indian society over the past 30 years. While women first began to become involved under Mahatma Gandhi during the freedom movement in the early part of the twentieth century, the movement was not solidified until the 1970s. Alongside the mass nationalist movement (1920-1947), M.K. Gandhi and his followers encouraged women to become actively involved in politics. This was monumental in that women had previously not drawn women out of the home and especially had not been directly involved in politics. Sujata Patel believes Gandhi "builds a new model of an Indian woman, dedicated to the service of the nation. However, she can perform this role only if she turns her back on sex, reproduction and family life." For the first time, women were asked to take part in the movement, albeit in restrictive ways, including the spinning of khadi and maintaining the home. Previous to this time, women had played a role in the Social Reform Movement of the 1800s, but never before had they been present in a movement in such a public way. However, the nationalists tended to ignore the importance of class, caste and religion, and as a result many women felt confined to an ideal image in which many of the same barriers were still in place. But, women were able to express themselves during the All India Women's Conference in 1924 which grew "to become the single largest national voice of the divergent groups and political tendencies, [and] infused all its old and new demands with an equal rights perspective." The demand in 1924 was focused on equal rights for women under the law. Women began to fight for better education opportunities, and coeducational environments as well as marriage, divorce, and inheritance rights. Following independence from Great Britain, women's issues were lost due to the issues of poverty, health and education. Not until the 1970s did a women's movement begin to fully evolve in India as an autonomous movement. During the years following independence, women remained prevalent in socialist activities but began to move more towards the direct confrontation of laws and seeking methods of change through the political realm. As a result, the movement that began in the 1970s differed from the previous attempts by Gandhi and his followers to mobilize women in that it was backed largely by women and was a more direct attack on the system, with women's rights at the head of the movement.

Approaches to Change: Centralised vs. Decentralised Structures

The feminist and women's movement now is composed of both activity through political parties and through non-governmental organisations. Given the variety of members that make up the movement, it is often argued that the movement is decentralised. Often the centralised efforts did not come from women. However, Nandita Gandhi and Nandita Shah argue that the origins are not as important as the outcomes because "the leadership, circumstances and manner of involvement of women was mainly initiated by men and political parties; nonetheless, it helped women become aware of their militancy and collective strength." But, there are both national and non-national organisations headed by women working for a variety of causes ranging from basic human rights to the combating of oppressive societal values to simple policy change, such as the inclusion of women's seat reservation under the 73 amendment. The women's movement is composed of women from all castes as well as women who live in both rural and urban settings. While centralised government supporters see this as a downfall to the movement because it contributes to the movement's inability to solidify and inability to easily assign roles to implement effective change, others argue differently. Radha Kumar believes the 33% seat reservation for women is a limited form of change for many women participating in the women's movement because "...amongst large sections of the contemporary [women's] movement there is the feeling that singling out individual women not only leads to a biased and partial view of the movements they were or are engaged in, but also reaffirms hierarchical leadership structures and hides from history the majority which makes up the movement." Not only does Kumar reaffirm the points made earlier by Connell concerning the patriarchal structure of the government, but she brings up an interesting point about how legislative changes overshadow the other, often times more effective work that is being done by women not involved in the government.

Leslie J. Calman assesses the role of the women's movement in political participation by emphasizing the importance of outside support in conjunction with policy change and centralised structure. The purpose of the decentralised structure of the Indian women's movement is to create change in the long run. Calman argues that "centralised movement organisations are thought to be more successful in the short run at influencing established institutions of government.... On the other hand, a decentralised movement, while less effective in moving government, seems better suited to organizing and expanding participation at the grassroots and to generating new ideas and strategies." She argues that creating consciousness about the limitations women face in society as well as exposing the implications of women's position in the relative structures is the central element necessary to create change. She follows by asserting that a decentralised structure is necessary to implement this consciousness. Calman recognises the importance of consciousness raising efforts and its role in empowerment and argues that:

> It is the quest for empowerment "through consciousness raising about the place and capacity of women and the poor, through schemes designed to generate economic self-reliance, and through the facilitating of decision making by participants in movement organisations" that most marks movement activity as distinct from politics-as-usual within the electoral system.

While raising gender consciousness would most likely make the seat reservation a more positive change for women, it is not necessarily a solution to the problem. Calman believes the "...success for the women's movement will not be measured in laws passed, but rather in the establishment of access to economic and political power." It is certainly important that women are able to achieve positions in which they are able to make decisions themselves, whether it is in political decisions or in simple everyday life decisions. Her argument that "the state alone does not have the capacity (even if it had the will) to reform the myriad of social structures that perpetuate women's secondary status..." is a strong one, however by stating this in conjunction with her support of gender consciousness training and women's self empowered decision making, Calman creates her own assumptions. She gives the impression that economic self-reliance and political decision making power will create equality for women in India. There is no question that this will have a positive effect on many women's lives, however there is little reason to believe that this will completely solve the problem for women as her argument implies. For example, can these changes cause a person set in old patriarchal way of thought to think and act in non-patriarchal ways? Certainly attempting to create change at the community level has proven to be more effective than starting from a higher position and trying to implement change from the top downward. But, the organisations that are supporting the decentralised women's movement are limited themselves. To what extent can these organisations and their programmes have an effect on the male community even at the local levels?

There is also a division within the women's movement over the most important obstacle that women face and how to go about breaking down the barriers in women's lives. Calman identifies two types of women in the feminist movement: those who focus on human rights and equality under the law and those who focus on empowerment through the dismantling of social norms and family control brought about by prevailing ideological ways of thought. The limitations of the former lie largely in the failure of governments and law officials to implement these policies. However those who focus on the latter method have proven to be more effective in creating change. Without the dismantling of these social norms, it is virtually impossible for women to attain power in the public sector. A more effective method would be for women to work from the bottom up.

Once they attain power within the home and within the social and economic realms of society it seems that only then will they have a better chance at being able to fully utilize power in the political sphere. Creating a space for women in the political sphere often seemed to have little effect on the women outside of politics. This shows that women's representation did not translate well into the other realms of women's lives. Calman articulates that,

> Women cannot hope to exercise public power so long as they are powerless over their own lives because of forced subservience to fathers, husbands, and in-laws; violence within the family; and limited educational opportunity. Nor can they

exercise power over their own lives or public life if they are consumed with poverty, ill-health, and a lack of adequate food and clean drinking water.

The latter point is also extremely important to observe. It is difficult for women to focus on change and gain power in the community when they lack basic necessities. Political equality and basic rights are difficult to achieve when the women must first focus on attaining water for basic chores for sustainability. Alternatively, even though these difficulties provide barriers, often it is the most oppressed people who recognize the urgency of their situation.

Environmental factors affect the daily lives of the women and men in Babapur and the surrounding villages in the Amreli District. The main issue for the people is access to water. A few years back a dam was built about thirty miles away, causing the rivers nearby to dry up, leaving the people with a massive water shortage. The Indian Census states that Babapur has one hand pump, one well and one tap but no tank, tube well, river, fountain, canal, lake or spring. Babapur serves as an example for all the other surrounding villages in this assessment of its water amenities. Some of the other surrounding villages have access to a tank or other modes of water distribution. A village's access to water depends largely on the ability of the panchayat members to demand water delivery and begin water programmes under the tight control of the state government. Therefore the main agenda on all local legislation is water. Most villages are reliant on water delivery by a tank which is then stored in the village center. There are typically no pipeline systems in place to equally distribute the water among the households, so this often leads to minor inter-household disputes. The water shortage especially affects women because they use water to perform most of their daily chores, including cooking meals, washing clothes, and cleaning the house. If the tank is not delivered or if the tank is stationed in an area of the village which is a great distance from their household, the women have to bear most of this burden. Ramuban Dayabhai Mor, a village sarpanch, explained that she was very dedicated to the issue of water shortage because she felt the water situation affected women the most. According to her, women should not have to leave their houses to wash clothes, get water for cooking and other such household chores that require water.

Along with the removal of social, economic and political burdens, the women's movement has also focused on empowering women through basic self-esteem building and knowledge on self-reliance. Originally, the women's movement had been more focused on gaining equality with men rather than recognizing women as different from men yet still complementary. Kumar notes that the women's movement in India transitioned from the fight for equality to a focus on self reliance and economic independence. She believes "that over the last one hundred and eighty years, the focus of campaigns for an improvement in women's lives has changed from needs to rights and within this from restricted right to parity in selected areas to the larger right of self determination."An example of an effort to increase women's self confidence and ability to become self reliant is a workshop put together by the Purohit family. About a year ago they hosted a workshop at their ashram to teach women basic self-reliance techniques. Over 1,000 women participated in learning self-defense mechanisms, basic fire safety rules, and other confidence-building skills. Although the skills taught seem simple and limited, they could actually provide women with a sense of self-worth and self-reliance that can potentially translate into confidence that will be useful in the political realm.

The role of administrative decentralisation of the political structure over the long-term is also necessary in government structure itself. The function of the Panchayat Raj initially was to "establish a linkage between local leaderships enjoying the confidence of local people and the government, and translate the policies of the government into action." Therefore, the most important function of this political body is to provide a bridge between the needs of the local people and the government officials in order to create long-term developmental change within the community. However, Hoshiar Singh argues that the panchayats have failed to be effective in implementing developmental change in both the agricultural and social realm of local communities. Singh also "attributes the limited success of *panchayat raj* to lack of money, lack of cooperation from government departments, half-hearted policies overly penetrated by state authorities from above, and the defective structure of PR institutions." It has also been argued that the panchayats are not only ineffective but have become hurtful to the rural poor, the population it had initially been created to help through misuse of power and corruption in government. This raises the question of whether or not women will be able to even gain political empowerment, let alone empowerment in other realms of life.

FAMILY AND RELIGIOUS STRUCTURE

Family Influence

Family members heavily influence women's involvement in politics. While male family members support their wives and daughters by attempting to create an environment where women can have not only a presence but a long-term involvement in politics, there are numerous cases in which the women become overpowered by their husbands. Husbands of appointed female political officials often make most the political decisions for their wives. This limits the woman's position to the equivalent of a seat-filler rather than a decision maker. As stated earlier, it is often patriarchal nature of the political structure itself that is oppressing women rather than the individual men who are themselves members of it. However, often men outwardly support the seat reservation for women and even encourage their wives to participate, but situations show that sometimes men support their wives' participation just so they can control the seat that she fills. M.S. John, who did similar research in Kerala, found that the main constraint there was political parties. However, she acknowledges that "instances of proxy rule and back-seat driving by male family members of female representatives, common in some parts of Northern India, were not found in the area of the study."

While political parties were not the major constraint in the study I conducted, as John stated, "back-seat driving" was. This was the case with Rasilaben Mansukhbhai Patolia, the district panchayat president of Amreli district. She became involved in politics because her husband had been an active member for over twenty years. He had planned to run for Mrs. Patolia's position, but once he found out that the seat had been reserved for a woman, encouraged his wife to run instead. Although she expressed ideas of her own, her husband tended to handle most of the responsibilities and attended most of the meetings without her. During the interview itself, he answered many of the questions addressed to Rasilaben. When Rasilaben did answer a question, although her answers were brief, they were very telling. But the overshadowing of the husband remained a huge obstacle in the research. Even if the husband was not present, women were often still hesitant to relay too much information to an outsider without an adequate amount of trust. However, the presence of Mini Purohit was helpful in establishing trust with the interviewees.

When analysing political theory, it is clear that there is a separation between public and private spheres. Although they are divided they each influence the other greatly. Carole Pateman explains why situations such as the one described above emerge when women enter politics. She examines John Stuart Mill's argument which claims

> ... that the relation between men and women, or more specifically between husbands and wives, forms an unjustified and unjustifiable exception to the liberal principles of individual freedom and equality, free choice, equality of opportunity and allocation of occupations by merit that (he believes) govern other social and political institutions in nineteenth-century Britain.

While Mill's argument, according to Pateman, is flawed, it emphasises the point that marriage impinges on liberal democratic possibilities. Pateman also argues that the "individual," on whom liberal theory is based, is in fact a male individual. Man and individual are interchangeable and women are thus omitted. This confirms that democracy does not necessarily translate the same way for both genders. So for women entering the political realm through a reserved seat, contradictions between cultural practices and political theory have serious implications for the way in which women exist in politics.

Community Response

While in general, the women interviewed spoke positively about the community reaction to the implementation of seat reservation in the panchayat system, there were some cases in which women were faced with very strong negative responses. Kamalaben Shanilal Bodar is the president of the Taluka Panchayat in Kahambha. It is important to note that no men were present during this interview. She originally became interested in politics over twenty years ago because of her husband's involvement in government. He encouraged her to partake in this election, and since then she has not only involved herself as a member of the district panchayat but is vice chairman of the education committee as well as a member of the women's security and safety commission for the last six years. Presently, the men in her village, who are members of the same caste as Januben Champrojbhai Dhal, are trying to force her out of office. She explained that the community as a whole has been trying to force her to resign or leave everything. They have been mentally harassing her for years by spreading rumors and trying to make her lose face within the community. They even misguided her husband and caused him to leave her with her son one year ago. Presently the men are even harassing her daughter and criticizing her attempts at raising her daughter to be independent and educated. Kamalaben is caught in an extremely difficult situation. She has remained in her position and continued to make all the decisions herself. She is reluctant to leave the position since she has already lost so much, however she is also tired of the constant harassment and effect it may have on her daughter. Kamalaben did emphasize that her party (BJP), staff and her parental side of the family have been very supportive of her throughout her involvement in the panchayat. She emphasised that in the future she would like to see more independence and equal rights for women. Even though she does not want to break up the family, she feels women deserve equal respect. Although she herself would like to fight for women's rights she feels her situation is difficult because of the constant harassers who claim that she is only fighting that battle because she is unhappy in her own family situation and is therefore looking to break up other families. One of the most important points she makes is that "as bad as my situation is, other women in politics have to struggle even more than me."

Caste and Class

Caste plays an important role in Hindu society, particularly in rural communities over which panchayats have authority. Thus it may have the largest effect on women's involvement in politics. Women of higher caste suffer different consequences and are subject to different standards than women of lower castes. However, certain characteristics extend across all castes in the Hindu religion. Joanna Liddle and Rama Joshi discuss the importance of purity for women, especially women of the Brahmin caste. In order to remain in one's caste status, according to Liddle and Joshi, karma is one of the most important elements for maintaining this status. Furthermore, "this ritual purity is in the nature of a religious status, but it usually coincides with economic wealth and social esteem. Three of the major signs of purity are vegetarianism, teetotalism and tight constraints on women, indicating that a significant degree of ritual purity comes through domestic activities." Since the Brahmin caste is held in the highest esteem, women who are members of this caste are held to the highest standard of purity. The most serious expression of this is through the practice of purdah, which is still widely spread in Gujarat today. Purdah is defined by Liddle and Joshi as the seclusion of women. The practice of purdah is extremely restrictive on every aspect of high-caste women's lives. This is the case because "high-caste women's work in a patriarchal caste society is confined to the domestic sphere, and a return to employment marks a significant rejection of the male control over female sexual and economic independence." So while women of the highest caste are the more privileged and have arguably more power in society, in general they are also subject to the highest standards.

There were several examples of women's religious confinement during my research in Amreli. Januben Champrojbhai Dhal is a village sarpanch who is subject to the practice of purdah. While she was present at the interview, along with fifteen male family members, previous visitors to the house informed me that they had never seen her come out before. Subsequently the interview was largely dominated by the husband, whose responses often had little to do with the questions asked. When asked about the community response to women's involvement in local politics, the husband responded that the village had been very supportive of this change for women. At first they had been opposed, then remained silent and then finally accepted it and gave their support. However, I was informed by Mini Purohit that this family comes from a very strict Brahmin caste that still strongly believes in the practice of purdah. She explained that other women in the village in reality did not have a voice in the social and family issues and that Januben was in fact the only one, although technically her husband took over most of the sarpanch responsibilities.

Although purdah is still practiced in many communities around Babapur, there is a movement away from the seclusion of women and a relaxation among the educated middle class. Ursula Sharma observes that Liddle and Joshi believe this change is due to a movement "from caste-oriented to class-oriented strategies for maintaining power and status." Although it has economic implications, caste is largely based on the religious structure, whereas class is solely based on the position of one's family economically. One allows for social mobility while the other does not. Since the rigidity of the caste structure, along with the strict religious practices, limits women's power in politics, a movement towards a "class-oriented" society could increase women's independence and power status in the political and economic realm. If the societal structure increasingly becomes based on class, women are less likely to be held to this image of purity. With this flexibility women may be able to achieve higher status in the public sphere. Sharma presents an interesting argument as to why Indian society is making this shift from a caste-based structure to a class-based structure. She highlights that "this exit from seclusion is not part of some inevitable march towards emancipation resulting from 'modernisation,' nor is it a result of contact with Western culture, as many would like to believe. It is rather a part of the logic of the emerging class structure." In turn, she argues, women are then subject to a different form of male control under a class society than under a caste-based society. Therefore, while this movement towards class-based societal structure could provide women with more access to politics, women may still face oppression, just a new form of oppression derived from the new class-based society.

The assumption that women have begun to emerge from their homes into the public sphere as a result of Westernisation and modernisation is further refuted by the argument that women's subordination is a result of western imperialism and financial influence. For example, Liddle and Joshi argue, "male domination does not occur on its own, but...it is crucially tied up with social hierarchy," which supports the influence of caste. However they go on to state, "these two systems of power occur within a third system, the international capitalist order under which the Indian economy is subordinate to Western financial interests." This emphasises the point made earlier by Mohanty that there are multiple types of male dominance and not one universal controlling concept. Carole Pateman recognises that there is a dichotomy between the private and the public spheres and attributes this largely to the recent influence of capitalism. She believes that although, as capitalism and its specific form of sexual as well as class division of labour developed, however, wives were pushed into a few, low status areas of employment or kept out of economic life all together, relegated to their 'natural,' dependent, place in the private familial sphere.

However, since the caste system has been in place since close to 1500 years, and still remains a strong base for Hindu social structure, it is difficult to attribute women's confinement in the private sphere mainly to capitalism. Liddle and Joshi discuss a number of impacts that caste has on women's status. They assign women's inability to inherit property as the most influential factor that caste laws project. Unlike Pateman, they believe that this is the main reason why women have been excluded from the economy and public sphere. The second impact of caste on women Liddle and Joshi say is the "control exercised by men over women's sexuality, through arranged marriage, the prohibition of divorce, and the strict monogamy for women, leading to sati and a ban on widow remarriage, including infant and child widows." All of the restraints on women in the private sphere inhibit their ability to assert power in politics. However, it is important to reassert Connell's earlier assertion that patriarchy is not a surface problem composed solely of controlling men, but rather a system in place that every member of society is a part of.

Often the issues the government chooses to focus on are themselves a hindrance to women. State policy tends to dwell on economic and capitalist endeavors. Connell analyses Burton's conceptions of the relationship between femininity and masculinity by stating that the origin of many concepts of gender stem from schools and families. By neglecting the social sphere, the state is in a poor position to attack gender ideology and effect change on gendered oppression, which it aims to change with the implementation of reserved seats for women. This argument does have some validity. If policy changes are made without a clear understanding of women's roles in society, the change could end up hurting women or even lessening their already confined position.

In Anjali Bagwe's analysis of gender in rural India, she addresses the impact of Ester Boserup's study on the effects of developmental policy on women and poverty. Bagwe insists "what made governments around the developing world sit up and take notice was her clear thesis that the lack of understanding and consequent neglect of women's role by economists and development planners had itself led to the marginalisation and pauperisation of women and their families." So if developmental programmes under colonisation and economic adjustments in the recent past are reasons for women's domestication, then it seems obvious why a policy change in government would not necessarily get to the root of the problem. Likewise, however, a reversal of policy in the economic sphere may also not prove to be an effective method of change, given the extent to which women's roles in society and gendered assumptions have been institutionalised within Indian society. Robert Connell also argues that although class and economic situations play an important role in determining women's roles in society and as a result contribute to their oppression, one cannot attribute this as the cause. He believes "we cannot continue to see class dynamics as the ultimate cause of gender dynamics in the state.

These social dynamics constantly interact, but one cannot be dissolved into the other." However, an even stronger argument that Connell makes is that by claiming that a focus on economics excludes women is in actuality discounting the importance of women's role in the economy. Although women are excluded from the public sphere to an extent, and have become more removed in the past few hundred years according to Bagwe, their roles are still extremely important.

In fact, "feminist historians have traced the nineteenth-century construction of a feminised 'domestic' realm, increasingly seen as the exclusive sphere of women... [the husband/father] was the economic actor....Though powerful as ideology...it drastically underestimated women's economic activity, and ignored women's role as cultural producers (for example novelists) and lobbyists in church and politics."

Many female elected members of the panchayat feel limited when the panchayat council deals with local economic or financial issues. While many involved argue it is women's lack of understanding of public issues that cause them to be less effective in dealing with economic or financial issues, it may rather be their lack of experience and more importantly their lack of experience with the language used to deal with these issues. Connell asserts that "the language of finance and 'economic rationalism' has been the vehicle for an attack on welfare ideology, and a downgrading of women's interests on a very broad front." Women are often blamed for financial mistakes while they are in office, but this is largely due to their lack of training by their surrounding members. Lila Laljibhai Jotaniya, a previous sarpanch of Babapur, encountered this type of situation during her term. She was handed an unsigned check for money owed to the village, and was not trained to check for details.

Consequently the village did not receive the money it was owed and suffered a setback financially. Although she dealt with the consequences, she was still unjustly taken advantage of by a corrupt member of the government.

Another major issue that limits women's power in politics is the large amount of corruption that takes place in government. Usually the corrupt members are from a high caste or class and are more focused on earning money than providing socially beneficial programmes to the community. Arundhati Roy presents a particularly negative perspective on the democratic system that has evolved in India, which largely refers to the panchayat system. She argues, every 'democratic' institution in [India] has shown itself to be unaccountable, inaccessible to the ordinary citizen, and either unwilling or incapable of acting in the interests of genuine social justice. *Every* strategy for real social change -land reform, education, public health, the equitable distribution of natural resources, the implementation of positive discrimination - has been cleverly, cunningly and consistently scuttled and rendered ineffectual by those castes and that class of people who have a stronghold on the political process.

While her perspective is strong, she highlights a very important problem. In order for women to promote empowerment, they have to be able to effectively implement programmes they feel will benefit the community in which they are governing. This type of corruption within government provides an added barrier for women's advancement.

CONCLUSION

In this study, I examined the effects of seat reservations in panchayats on the status of women in Hindu society in India. Society is composed of numerous forms of power and power relationships. These relationships have different implications in the political, economical, social and religious spheres. In the political environment, many who support legislative changes such as seat reservations often fail to realize that women's position of lesser power in society is not reducible to a single opportunity or even a single power relationship. By examining the different areas in society where women face limitations, the importance of the various relationships and the way in which they affect one another become evident.

This study further analyses the role of political parties in women's participation in politics and the limitations that arise from the lack of solid support women receive from their political parties. The BJP in particular supports giving women the opportunity to be in politics but restricts their ability to remain in politics over a long period of time. Therefore it is difficult for women to gain experience and thus achieve a type of power within the governmental structure. Women face challenges with reelection and continuous community and family support.

Furthermore, for this study, the women's movement provided an example of a decentralised effort to empower women in Indian society. Calman argued that this type of approach promoted long-term change since it was based on a wider understanding of the power relationships that women face outside of the political sphere. Centralised approaches to creating change for women are limited because they generally do not affect the moral and cultural values that have forwarded women's disempowerment.

Family, caste and class provide some of the most influential power relationships between men and women. As displayed above, the husband cannot only affect women's decisions in politics, but also he can control her political position altogether. Likewise, women of higher castes are subjected to higher standards of purity and tradition within the private realm and as a result are unable to exercise other forms of power freely.

The liberal democratic perspective acknowledges that Peterson and Runyan's "power-over" type relationship does exist in government between men and women and that this situation should be rectified. But often the preconceptions of this type of power are irrelevant and lack a degree of understanding necessary to recognize the implications of such a relationship. The problem of women's status is not merely reducible to the fact that there are more men in politics than women. Rather, the basic system itself benefits men over women. This suggests that there must be structural changes that go much further than surface adjustments. Robert Connell argued that state reforms are often deceptive in nature because they operate under the assumption that they are providing an influential change for women, when in reality they are just further supporting the already existing patriarchal structure.

Liberal feminists have frequently argued for law reversals as a method of gaining equality for women in the greater society. However, the liberal feminist ideology supports this assumption that is largely dominant in the West, which assumes power relationships can be dictated by a clarified procedure. By assuming that power is constituted in the body of the state, the liberal democratic perspective ignores the very important and influential relationships that exist between men and women outside of the political realm. The relationships between husbands and wives as well as the relationship between single women and both married and unmarried men also have significant implications on the power status of women in society. Often men will support the political participation of unmarried educated women in their community, but will not support their wives' and daughters' political participation. This particular situation results from Hindu men's preconceived notions about women's place in the private sphere and assumption of purity associated with religious ideals.

When analyzing power relationships across cultures from a Western perspective, there is a tendency among liberals to examine oppressive forces in a two-dimensional manner. Often these assessments made by Westerners about power in developing societies are based on foreign concepts of power. Chandra Talpade Mohanty, as explained earlier, criticised feminists for assuming that male dominance was a "singular, monolithic notion of patriarchy." The same argument can be used in regards to the assumptions about power in politics across cultures. The implementation of seat reservations is a good example. This once again ignores very important power relationships in the cultural, economic and social spheres by focusing on a simple "singular" power relationship in the political sphere.

Mohanty also emphasises the importance of culturally situating the study in order to gain a stronger understanding of the power relationships that exist in the different realms of society. There is also an assumption among some Western liberals that democracy not only is effective in all societies but works in similar ways. However, differences in culture and in economic and religious practice play a major role in forming the way in which democratic governments function in each society.

There is a preconceived notion in the liberal democratic perspective as to how power is constituted. It is widely believed that power is achieved through the designation of roles set up by a constitution or a written document. This process involves a clear procedure that suggests the reversal of a law set up by a constitutional structure has the ability to reverse or change the power relationships supported by the law. However, power and power relationships are not simply written practices but in actuality extend much deeper than the written laws that seem to promote these relationships. Therefore, we cannot look at the state, or governmental structure in general, as a surface patriarchal structure that contains laws that must be overturned in order for women to gain empowerment in society. Rather, we must look beyond the laws to how the system functions and what type of relationships exist outside the political structure that affect women's status in society.

REFERENCES

Bagwe, Anjali, *Of Woman Caste: The Experience of Gender in Rural India*. Calcutta: Zed Books, 1995.

Barry, Jim, Trudie Honour and Sneha Palnitkar, "Gender and Urban Governance in Mumbai and London." *International Review of Women and Leadership*, 4.2, 1998.

Basu, Amrita, *The Challenge of Local Feminisms: Women's Movements in Global Perspective.* Boulder: Westview Press, 1995.

Basu, Amrita, and Atul Kohli, *Community Conflicts and the State in India.* Delhi: Oxford University Press, 1998.

Basu, Zenab, *Tribal Women Empowerment and Gender Issues.* New Delhi: Kanishka, 2001.

Bhatnagar, S., "Grass Roots Politics in India: A Case Study of the Kangra Valley." *Asian Survey,* 15.5 (1975), 440-452.

Billings, Dwight B., and Shaunna L. Scott, "Religion and Political Legitimation." *Annual Review of Sociology,* 20(1994), 173-202.

Calman, Leslie J. "Women and Movement in Politics in India." *Asian Survey* 29.10 (1989), 940-958.

Caplan, Patricia, *Class and Gender in India: Women and their Organisations in a South Indian City.* New York: Tavistock Publications, 1985.

Connell, R.W., *Gender and Power: Society, the Person and Sexual Politics.* Stanford: Stanford University Press, 1987.

—, "The State, Gender, and Sexual Politics: Theory and Appraisal." *Theory and Society* 19.5 (1990): 507–544.

Datta, Rekha, and Judith e. Kornberg, *Women in Developing Countries: Assessing Strategies for Empowerment.* London: Lynne Rienner Publishers, 2002.

Dhal, Januben Champrajbhai, Interview with author, Amreli District, Gujarat, May 2, 2003.

Dhar, Aarti, "India: Local Initiatives work wonders in Kerala." *The Hindu* June 5,2000

Douglas, Carole A., "Daughters of Independence: Gender, Caste and Class in India." *Off Our Backs: A Women's Newsjournal* 17.3 (1987): 21.

Dugger, Celia W., "A Woman's Place: A special report; Lower-caste Women Turn Village Rule Upside Down." *The New York Times* May 3,1999, sec. A: 1; Column 3.

Farrington, John, *Participatory Watershed Development: Challenges for the Twenty First Century.* New York: Oxford University Press, 1999.

Foucault, Michel, *The History of Sexuality: Volume 1: An Introduction.* New York: Vintage Books, 1990.

Franzway, Suzanne, Dianne Court and R.W. Connell, *Staking a Claim: Feminism, Bureaucracy and the State.* Sydney: Allen and Unwin, 1989.

Gandhi, Nandita, and Nandita Shah, *The Issues at Stake: Theory and Practice in the Contemporary Women's Movement in India.* New Delhi: Kali for Women, 1991.

Ghorpade, M.Y., "Panchayat Raj in Karnataka - II." *The Hindu* October 4, 2001 — "Panchayat Raj in Karnataka-I." *The Hindu* October 3, 2001 "Government Grades Panchayats." *The Times of India* December 27, 2001.

Hansen, Thomas Blom, and Christophe Jaffrelot, Ed. *The BJP and the Compulsion of Politics in India.* Delhi: Oxford University Press, 1998.

Hardgrove, Anne, "Sati Worship and Marwari Public Identity in India." *The Journal of Asian Studies* 58.3 (1999): 723-752.

Hiebert, Paul, *Konduru: Structure and Integration in South Indian Village.* Minneapolis: University of Minnesota Press, 1971.

Jaffrelot, Christophe, "Communal Riots in Gujarat: The State at Risk?" *South Asian Institute, Department of Political Science, University of Heidelberg.* 17 (2003): 1-20.

John, M.S., "Empowerment of Women Panchayat Members: Learning from Kerala (India)." *Asian Journal of Women's Studies* 6.4: 66–82.

Jotaniya, Lilaben Laljibhai, Interview with author. Babapur, Gujarat, May 8,2003.

Kaplan, Caren, and Inderpal Grewal, Ed. *Scattered Hegemonies: Postmodernity and Transnational Feminist Practice.* Minneapolis: University of Minnesota Press, 1994.

Kasturi, Leela, "Greater Political Representation for Women: The Case of India." *Asian Journal of Women's Studies* 4.4 (1998): 9.

Khullar, Mala, "Women's Caring in India: The Intersecting Public and Private Sphere." *Asian Journal of Women's Studies* 5.3 (1999): 64.

Kumar, Radha, *The History of Doing: An Illustrated Account of Movements for Women's Rights and Feminism in India, 1800-1990.* New Delhi: Kali for Women, 1993.

Liddle, Joanna, and Rama Joshi, *Daughters of Independence: Gender, Caste and Class in India.* New Delhi: Zed Books, 1986.

Mahmood, Cynthia K., "Rethinking Indian Communalism: Culture and Counter-Culture." *Asian Survey* 33.7 (1993): 722–737.

Malhotra, Anshu, *Gender, Caste and Religious Identities: Restructuring Class in Colonial Punjab.* New Delhi: Oxford University Press, 2002.

Marriott, McKim, *Village India: Studies in the Little Communty.* Chicago: The University of Chicago Press, 1955.

McGee, Leslie, *Invented Identities.* New York: Oxford University Press, 2000.

Mendelsohn, Oliver, "The Transformation of Authority in Rural India." *Modern Asian Studies* 27.4 (1993): 805-842.

Mor, Ramuban Dayabhai, Interview with author. Amreli, Gujarat, May 9,2003. Nair, C.G. "Mahila Samakhya Caught in Spat." *The Hindu* June 30, 2002.

Pateman, Carole, and Elizabethe Gross, *Feminist Challenges: Social and Politcal Theory.* Boston: Northeastern University Press, 1986.

Pateman, Carole, *The Disorder of Women: Democracy, Feminism and Political Theory.* Stanford: Stanford University Press, 1989.

—, *Participation and Democratic Theory.* New York: Cambridge at the University Press, 1970.

—, *The Sexual Contract.* Stanford: Stanford University Press, 1988. Patolia, Rasilaben Mansukhbhai. Interview with author. Amreli, Gujarat, May 2, 2003. Peterson, V.S., and Anne S. Runyan. *Global Gender Issues.* Oxford: Westview Press, 1999.

Raman, Vasanthi, "The Women's Question in Contemporary Indian Politics." *Asian Journal of Women's Studies* 7.2 (2001): 39.

Ray, Bharati, and Aparna Basu Ed. *From Independence Towards Freedom: Indian Women Since 1947.* Oxford: Oxford University Press, 1999.

Root, Hilton L., "What Democracy can do for East Asia." *Journal of Democracy* 13.1:113-126. Roy, Arundhati. *The Algebra of Infinite Justice.* New Delhi: Penguin Books, 2002.

Sangari, Kumkum, and Sudesh E. Vaid, *Recasting Women: Essays in Indian Colonial History.* New Brunswick: Rutgers University Press, 1989.

Sapiro, Virginia, "Research Frontier Essay: When Are Interests Interesting? The Problem of Political Representation of Women." *The American Political Science Review* 75.3 (1981): 701-716.

"Sensitise Officials to People's Problems." *The Times of India* May 26, 2002.

"Sensitive Officials to People's Problems." *The Times of India* May 26, 2002.

Sharma, Kumud, "Power and Representation: Reservation for Women in India." *Asian Journal of Women's Studies* 6.1 (2000): 47.

Singh, Hoshiar, "Constitutional Base for Panchayati Raj in India: The 73rd Amendment Act." *Asian Survey* 34.9 (1994): 818-827.

Singh, Khushwant, *The End of India.* New Delhi: Penguin Books, 2003.

Staff Reporter, "India: Citizen's Group Appeal for Violence-Free Panchayat Poll." *The Hindu* June 4,2001.

Upadhyaya, Prakash C., "The Politics of Indian Secularism." *Modern Asian Studies* 26.4 (1992): 815-853.

Venkatesan, J., "India: Panel for more powers to the Panchayat Raj Institutions." *The Hindu* October 8, 2001.

Visweswaran, Kamala, *Fictions of Feminist Ethnography.* Minneapolis: University of Minnesota Press, 1994.

Wolpert, Stanley, *A New History of India*. Oxford: Oxford University Press, 2000.

5

Panchayati Raj and Gram Sabha

The Constitution (73rd Amendment) Act, 1992 has added a new part IX consisting of 16 Articles and the Eleventh Schedule to the Constitution. The 73rd Amendment envisages the Gram Sabha as the foundation of the Panchayat Raj System to perform functions and powers entrusted to it by the State Legislatures. The amendment provides for a three tier Panchayat Raj System at the village, intermediate and district levels. Articles 243A provides that the Gram Sabha may exercise such powers and perform such functions at the village level as the Legislature of a state may by law provide. The 73rd amendment thus envisages the Gram Sabha as the foundation of Panchayat Raj System. "Gram Sabha" means a body consisting of persons registered in the electoral rolls comprised within the area of Panchayat at the village level. In the Panchayat Raj system Gram Sabha is the only permanent unit. Duration of Panchayat i.e. Mukhiyas and other members of Panchayat continue for 5 years only from the date appointed for the first meeting, but the villagers do not change.

Empowerment of Gram Sabha means strengthening of the Panchayat Raj Institution (PRIs). Success or failure of this system depends upon the strength of the Gram Sabha. The eleventh scheduled of the constitution created by the 73rd Amendment contains 29 subjects on which the Panchayats shall have administrative Control, Articles 243H empowers State Legislature to make by law provision for imposing taxes etc. by the panchayat. Obviously, these panchayats before imposing any levy or tax in the village would be required to get clearance from the respective Gram Sabha.

Drafting and implementation of development plans for the uplift of the villages would be vetted and monitored by the Gram Sabhas.

Panchayat Raj Institutions (PRIs)

Panchayat Institutions are the vehicles of political empowerment of people at the grassroot level for shaping their own destiny. A vast majority of people are living at the grassroot level in the rural and remote areas without any touch of modern day. A large section of such deprived people belong to Scheduled castes, Scheduled tribes and other Backward casts as also women in general at the grassroot level.

In Bihar, election of PRIs could not be held after the Constitution (Seventy third) Amendment Act, 1992 which became effective from 24th April 1993.

The state of Bihar had well organised and efficiently functional Panchayat Raj Institutions. The Mukhiya (Chairman) of the Gram Panchayat, which is the lowest unit of the PRI at the village level, is the kingpin at the grassroot level. The District Magistrates, Sub Divisional Officers and Block Development Officers had often noted with surprise and at times with embarrassment that before any government machinery could move to provide relief to the people in the rural areas affected by natural calamities like flood, fire etc, the Mukhiya of the local gram panchayat was already there by the side of the affected people. Though most of the Mukhiyas generally represented the feudal elements in the villages, nevertheless, their apparent benevolent gesture and prompt response to the need of the affected people had made the institution of Mukhiya very popular among the rural people. The previous election to the PRIs in Bihar was held during May-June 1978 and thereafter the PRIs did not have any popular mandate.

The three tier Panchayat Institutions in Bihar consist of a Gram Panchayat at the lowest level, Panchayat samiti at the Block level and Zila Parishad of the Dist ict level. The chairman of the Gram Panchayat is called Mukhiya, the chairperson of the Panchayat Samiti is called Pramukh and the Chairperson of the Zila Parishad is called Adhyaksha.

Bihar after 73rd amendment of the constitution encated Bihar Panchayat Raj Act, 1993 making provisions regarding reservation for the Scheduled Castes, the Scheduled Tribes, Women, and Backward class of citizens. These reservation provisions invited writ petitions before Hon'ble High Court Patna (CWGC No. 3351 of 1994- Krishan Kumar Mishra and others). The Hon'ble High Court vide its order dated 19th March 1996 in CWJC no. 3351 of 1994 with eleven other CWJCs quashed certain provisions of the Bihar Panchayat Raj, 1993 regarding reservation. The net results of the above judgement was that seats can be reserved for the Scheduled Castes, the Scheduled Tribes and Women and the offices of Chairpersons cannot be reserved as these posts are to be treated as single post. As regards reservation for Backward class of citizens, the Hon'ble High Court quashed Schedule of the Act with a direction to revise the list of Backward class of citizens. In other words, until a new Schedule containing the list of Backward class of citizens is in position no reservation can be given to such class of citizens.

The state Government filed a SLP vide Special Leave Petition (Civil) no. 9724-9728 and 9819-25 of 1996. The Hon'ble Supreme Court passed an interim order on 22. 7. 97 with the observation that the matter should be placed before the Hon'ble Chief Justice of India for constitution of the appropriate Bench for the disposal of these matters. The State Government came to the conclusion that elections to Panchayats has been stayed by the Apex Court and accordingly the proposal to hold the election was shelved. There was another public interest litigation in the Patna High Court bearing CWJC no. 8765/1998 (Nand Kishore Singh versus

Union of India and others). It was heard by the Chief Justice Ravi S.Dhawan and Justice Aftab Alam. When the Court asked the Advocate General why the election was not held, the Court was told that there was a stay order as an injunction from the Supreme Court. The Court sought the order from the State Counsel, but the order as was claimed could not be produced. The High Court in its order of 13. 4. 2000 stated that the order of Supreme Court order "was being interpreted by tearing a phrase out of its context virtually by misinterpreting the Supreme Court order." The High Court further observed "the mystery of a non-existent injunction which was declared to exist, but is conspicuous by its absence. This is chicanery of legal engineering." The court also observed that "..... not to hold election (of Gram panchayats) would be a clear abnormality and against the mandate of the Constitution." Hon'ble High while concluding its order observed: "The court hopes that this furtherance of running a government not in keeping with the Constitution of India will cease. Local government without elected representatives is an insult to the Constitution of India". Again the State Government went before Hon'ble Supreme Court for clarification of its order dated 22. 7. 1997. Apex court in its judgement on 29. 8. 2000 held that "there is no bar for holding elections to different Panchayats in accordance with law, as it stands today, which will be subject to the final decision in pending appeals."

Accordingly process of election to PRIs started in October 2000 and actual election was held in April 2001. That elections to PRI would be held in Bihar was a surprise even to District Magistrates. The State Election Commission has observed in his report that it was shocked to find that "district administration (meeting of District Magistrates and Divisional Commissioners on 16th January 2001) was still doubtful about the intention of the Government and the Commission to conduct the election."

The 2001 election to PRIs has for the first time elected 44815 female representations in the PRI of which 9266 are SC females. Altogether 29962 S.C citizens have been elected in various units of PRIs. This has exhibited the establishment of grassroot democracy in Bihar.

However, full powers as assigned to the Panchayat Raj Institutions under the 73rd Amendment of Constitution or even under Bihar Panchayat Raj Act 1993 notified vide L.G.-1.020/93-274 Leg dated 28th October 1994, have not been delegated. Rules are yet to be notified empowering functioning of the PRIs. Hon'ble High Court Patna in various writ applications have been observing against the state government on this abnormal delay in transferring actual power to PRIs. This has affected the moral of the elected representatives. Absence of any training facilities to these representatives have made them ignorant about their role as agents for ensuring economic development of their constituents and for establishing participative and accountable grassroot administration.

Gram Sabha

Bihar Panchayat Raj Act 1993 (Bihar Act 19 of 1993) enunciates powers and functions of the Gram Sabha. The following functions of the Gram Sabha.

- *(a)* Rendering assistance in the implementation of developmental scheme pertaining to villages;
- *(b)* Identification of beneficiaries for the implementation of development schemes pertaining to the village. Provided that in case the Gram Sabha fails to identify the beneficiaries within a reasonable time the Gram Panchayat shall identify the beneficiaries;
- *(c)* Procuring voluntary labour and contributions in kind or in cash or both, for community welfare programmes;
- *(d)* Programmes of adult education and family welfare within the village;
- *(e)* Promotion of unity and harmony among all sections of society in the village;

(*f*) Seeking clarifications from the Mukhiya and members of the Gram Panchayat about any particular activity, scheme, income and expenditure; and

(*g*) Reports of the vigilance committee.

(*h*) Such other matter as may be prescribed.

Section 7 of this Chapter, Bihar Act 19, 1993 also provides that the Gram Sabha shall consider following:

(*a*) The annual statement of accounts of the Gram Panchayat, the report of the administration of the preceding financial year and the last audit note and replies, if any, made thereto;

(*b*) The budget of the Gram Panchayat for the next financial year;

(*c*) The report in respect of development programmes of the Gram Panchayat relating to the preceding year and development programmes proposed to be undertaken during the current year;

(*d*) Reports of the vigilance committee.

The above functions can be effective and meaningful only after a model plan of development of the village is before the Gram Sabha. Such development plan should be based upon economic requirements of the village for the villagers, through use of locally available resources, necessity of augmenting such resources (physical and financial) and methods through which the end result of task of socio-economic development can be achieved.

Preparation of model development plan for villages is basically to help the villages/Gram Sabha in accomplishing the target of development of the socio-economic conditions of the village. It is the most necessary vital tool in empowering Gram Sabhas to discharge their functions effectively and efficiently.

REFERENCES

Bhadouria, B.P.S., *Panchayati Raj and Rural Development*, Commonwealth Publishers, New Delhi, 1981.

Kanango, Suhla Deh, "Panchayati Raj and Emerging Women Leadership", *An Overview, Social Action*, Jan.-March, 1996.

Kaushik, Susheela, *Women and Panchayati Raj*, Haranand Publications, New Delhi, 1993.

Mehta, A., "Report on Panchayati Raj Institutions", GOI, Ministry of Rural Development, New Delhi, 1978 .

Thakkar, Usha and Rohini Gawankar "Women in Panchayat: March towards Empowerment", One India, One People-Special Number on *Women in Politics*, March, 2004.

6

Women's Participation in Panchayats in Scheduled Areas

Introduction

The presence and participation of tribal women in panchayati raj institutions have brought about a formidable change in their position within the tribal social organisation, as well as in the overall hierarchical structure of the Indian society leading towards their empowerment. This has been the result of the enactment of Panchayati Raj Act (1992), which provided for one-third representation to women in panchayats including those belonging to the Scheduled Tribes. The extension of the Act to the Scheduled Areas (1996) has further increased the representation of tribals as well as women giving them more powers.

The Scheduled Tribes (S.T.) constitute 8.08 per cent (1991 census) of the total population of India and are spread unevenly to different parts of the country, 92.61 per cent of the total tribal population lives in the rural areas. The Constitution of India in its Articles 244(1) and (2) in part X has listed the 'Scheduled Areas' and 'Tribal Areas' under the Fifth and Sixth Schedule respectively. The Tribal Areas in the Sixth Schedule are the states of north-east whereas eight states outside the north-east, which are tribal dominated regions, are in the Fifth Schedule. These are—Andhra Pradesh (6.31

per cent tribal population, 1991 census), Bihar (7.66 per cent), Gujarat (14.92 per cent), Himachal Pradesh (4.22 per cent), Madhya Pradesh (23.27 per cent), Maharashtra (9.27), Orissa (22.21 per cent) and Rajasthan (12.44 per cent tribal population). The Constitution envisages a special system of administration for these areas so that their rights in land and forest are protected and the development takes place in the context of their culture and environment.

The history of tribal people suggests their continuous exploitation and marginalisation. The tribal people remained at the periphery of the wider political system and kept their women marginal to their own tribal polity. In certain places, especially where the tribals were in a majority, as in the north-east or even in parts of Central India, they established their authority and rule. But women played a limited role in the tribal political institutions. In other regions, where their strength was less and their interaction with the non-tribals greater, they adopted ways and means to improve their status. *Sanskritisation* was one such process, which resulted in the formation of several sub-castes and sub-tribes. The *Bhilalas* for instance, are a product of the union of the *Rajputs* and the *Bhils*. Though called tribals, the *Bhilalas* consider themselves higher than *Bhils* in the local hierarchy.

The process of *sanskritisation* has slowed down but not completely dissipated where economic asset and political position, more easily accessible now, provide mechanisms for improving social status. This, on the whole means also adopting various features restrictive to women's freedom. In places where the communities have taken advantage of their collective strength, attempts are being made to revive the traditional identity and culture. This has brought the tribal question into the national as well as international political arena. The 1980s in particular, have seen the emerging conflicts between the tribals and the non-tribals, the critique of development programmes and the issues of human rights and self-governance. The dichotomy between the environmentalists and economists and between the self-determinists and integrationists has its roots in the colonial period, which has only exacerbated in the recent past. The provisions of the Fifth and the Sixth Schedules of the Constitution though provided autonomous political structure did not help much as the majority of tribals remained at the periphery of the wider socio-economic and political system. The extension of Panchayati raj to the Scheduled Areas is an attempt towards providing self-rule to the tribal people through their own panchayats.

Unlike in many other communities, tribal women are considered indispensable, especially for the role they play in the socio-economic life. There is a difference of values related to morality regarding sex and sexuality and much lesser degree of stigma attached among the tribals. A woman's entry into panchayat is similarly not opposed, at least not for the similar reasons. Among the tribals, besides the difference in value system, there is an additional factor, that it brings their family and community a status and respect, of which they were ling denied. The men belonging to the higher castes, on the other hand may perceive women's entry by 'allowing' them to keep the seats safe for them. This paper shows that in cases where tribal women are dependent on their husbands for support and assistance in panchayat work, it is mainly due to women's lack of awareness and experience, and less because of the social norms.

Even this support, which is extended not so much with the idea of 'keeping seats safe', is also of a different nature. It is this difference in the value system and experience that makes the situation of tribal women different. Not only they are able to remove the tag of 'namesake' or 'proxy' members quicker given the right opportunities, they begin to learn and take initiatives much faster and earlier. In this sense this paper emphasises the significance of 'gender' as well as 'tribal' in the context of tribal women.

It must however be stated here that the status of women in tribal societies and their egalitarianism has often been over emphasised. Freedom of economic activity or participation does not always speak of their better status, as it is often done out of compulsion or necessity. Not only women are burdened with work, or given the responsibilities of children and arranging for food, fuel and water, they are considered fit only for certain specific works and not the important ones of political-jural nature. This has been demonstrated culturally and symbolically in various ritual aspects among them.

Not only do women's presence in the tribal councils or panchayats has been low but within the tribal community itself there has existed a loose form of social stratification giving more power to certain families, and to men among these families. And this has intensified with the introduction of private property in the names of males to be passed down in the male line unlike the earlier situation of collective use-rights on land and forest in which women played a significant role. The men and certain families have often dominated the panchayats on the tribal areas.

On the other hand, the tribals on the whole have been usually looked down upon as 'backward' ignorant and illiterate people who should be 'developed', so as to make them a part of the 'mainstream'. It is well known by now that the tribals are not only the preservations of natural resources and knowledge base, but are also placed higher on what are regarded as the indicators of development like the sex-ratio and the age at marriage. On the contrary, the in-roads made by the process of development have led to their exploitation and harassment. Introduction of alien culture, values and perception not accompanied by awareness, knowledge or education has added. The process of modernisation has done no less harm or good for the tribals as the earlier process of *sanskritisation*. Both processes tend to add on their hierarchies —caste or class and have their own gender implications. (Chauhan, Abha, 1996).

Such an outlook is reflected in the views and working of several government officials or local elite who think tribals can never change, no matter what is done for them. Some sympathetic people have paternalistic attitude towards 'poor ignorant tribals' for whom something must be done. This can be seen in the reaction of the people to the 1996 Extension Act. The Act increases tribals representation and gives them immense power and recognises the customary role of the Gram Sabhas, but there are many outsiders who control resources and positions and too much exploitation and harassment has already taken place. Even with the earlier reservation for the Scheduled tribes, the activities of the panchayats were manipulated, like other laws, by either outsiders or local elite. Then, the Government and the State machinery always have power to exploit the resources for the 'public interest or the 'national cause'.

This control of the situation by the non-tribals over the years, and the constant increase in their numbers has left the tribals ignorant and unaware, except the very few ones. The extension Act therefore, could generate a backlash on the one hand, and give opportunity to find a loophole by the outsiders. The postponement of panchayat elections in June 1999 (later held in Jan –Feb, 2000) due to cases filed in the High Court against the reservation for tribals was a clear indication of what the future beholds for the tribals. On the other hand, as long as tribals lack education, awareness and information and specific training, things will not change much for them.

The observations made in this paper are based on the study of 75 tribal women representatives (1994 Panchayat elections) from different districts of Madhya Pradesh conducted in the year 1999 when the state was not divided. The districts covered the Scheduled Areas of the State like Bastar, Jhabua, Mandla and Khargone (some of which are now in Chattisgarh) representing various tribes as Baiga, Bhilala, Bhil, Gond, Halba, Kanwar, Muria, Oraon, Pradhan and Raria. The tribal women in the sample were from all the levels of Panchayat like Sarpanch (17), Panch (34), Janpad Panchayat (block) member (13), janpad Panchayat Chairperson (3), Zilla Panchayat member (7) and Zilla panhayat Chairperson (1). A detailed *structured interview schedule* was prepared for this purpose consisting of several questions that provided quantified data, but most of them were open-ended which allowed for a more open discussion.

The study focuses on the profile, performance, problems, needs and perceptions of tribal women representatives as different from their men as well as other women. It also brings out the need to understand and analyse the situation of tribals vis-à-vis the non-tribals and the wider issues like self-governance in tribal areas, the election process and the question of women's reservation as a method of ensuring their political participation. Emphasizing on the applicability of a different and alternative model in the extension of panchayats to the Fifth Schedule Area, this paper tries to bring out the usefulness of such a model.

Panchayati Raj in the Scheduled Areas

The local self-government has been in existence in India for a long time. The prevalence of *Gram Sabhas* or rural communities is found in the *Vedas,* in *Ramayan,* in the *Sabhaparva* of *Mahabharat,* in the *Arthshastra* of *Kautilya* and in the Buddhist and Jain literature. The Mughals interfered very little with the villages and incorporated them into its administration as a unit for revenue and police purpose. The establishment of British in India resulted in altogether a different kind of change as Lord Rippon's famous Resolution of 1882 recommended the starting of local self-government. (Sharma, Shakuntla, 1994:89-90). Through the Government of India Acts of 1919 and 1935, village panchayats came to be established more systematically with defined powers and functions. The Constitution of India further dealt with the issue of taking steps to organize village panchayat and this became more firmly entrenched with the creation of Panchayati Raj in India in 1959 when the authority and responsibility for rural development was entrusted on the people.

A large part of tribal India under British rule remained unexplored and untouched though, various Acts, particularly related to land and forests were promulgated. The British economic policies favouring individual titles to property and creating a market for land and forest products escalated the exploitation of the tribals at the hands of money-lenders, contractors and other subordinate officials. The repercussions of this could be seen in various tribal revolts that took place in British India between 1820 an 1890 and even later which were crushed by the Britishers and gave them the reason to introduce laws and regulations to isolate tribals to the restricted area at the pretext of their special protection.

The Government of India Act 1919 provided that the Governor-General in Council may declare any territory in British India to 'Backward Tract' and that any Act of the Indian legislature should apply to such tracts only if the Governor-General so directed. *The Government of India Act 1935* further classified the areas into the 'excluded' (north-east region) and the 'partially excluded' areas. These areas were to be insulated from the control of the Indian legislature and ministries, and left in direct charge of the Governor of the Province who was always a British and usually an ICS officer.

What were known as 'excluded' and 'partially excluded' areas during the British rule came to be known as the 'Sixth' and the 'Fifth' Scheduled Areas in the Constitution that came to force (1950) in India after independence (1947). The Fifth Schedule [244 (1)] contains provisions regarding the administration and control of the Scheduled Areas and Scheduled Tribes. In the Constitution the 'expression "Scheduled Areas" means such areas as the President may by order declare to be Scheduled Areas'. In reference to the Scheduled Tribes, the Constitution says that, 'the president may with respect to any State or Union Territory and where it is State, after consultation with the Governor thereof, by public notification specify the Tribes or tribal communities or parts of or groups within tribes or tribal communities shall for the purpose of their constitution be deemed to be scheduled tribes in relation to that state or union territory, as the case may be'.

The tribals were spread over in most parts of the different sub-divisions of what became the state of Madhya Pradesh in 1956 (these were – Madhya Bharat, Bhopal, Vindhya Pradesh and Sironj Sub- division). Of all these sub-divisions, most of the tribal areas were found in the Central Provinces and Berar regions where the beginning of panchayat system was made in 1920 through the *Local- Self Government Act.*

The Central Provinces and Berar Panchayat Act of 1946 had taken note of the special needs of tribal areas and section 156 of this Act stipulated that if the state government was of the opinion that if the standard 3-tier panchayat structure was unsuitable for any tribal majority area, it could apply chapter 6 of the Act which provided for setting up Tribal and Pargana Panchayats in the predominantly tribal areas. The State used this provision by the notification of 21st January 1955, when 57 tribal panchayats and 17 *pargana* panchayats were established in Bastar and Jashpur sub-division of Raigarh district and were notified for a special tribal panchayat structure in 1956. (Buch, Nirmala, 1996: 28). The Act of 1962 followed the similar provisions for the panchayats in the tribal majority areas. Even panchayat elections held in 1965 and 1970, were not held in these areas of tribal concentration. Later this provision was reversed and those prevalent in other regions were made applicable in 1972 in tribal areas as well.

Incidentally, *The State Panchayat Acts of 1981, 1990 and 1993* (as originally enacted) in Madhya Pradesh made no exception for tribal areas or retain the possibility of such exception. While on the one hand, the state did not made any special provision for the panchayat structure in the scheduled Areas as provided in the 73 Amendment Act, it made a move simultaneously on the other hand, for inclusion of certain Schedule V areas of the State in Schedule VI recommending the need for different autonomous self-government institutions in these areas. The government also applied pressure on the Union Government to frame a law to facilitate the setting up of District Councils in the four tribal dominated areas of 17 other districts under the Sixth Schedule. A large number of people mostly non-tribals, but also tribals expressed their disapproval of the Schedule VI structure in the tribal areas of M.P., mainly for their own interest but also because of the vast magnitude of change that has come in these areas over the years creating diversity and heterogeneity. But opposition to the provision of application of the 73rd Amendment Act to the Schedule Areas of Madhya Pradesh came from very few quarters and similar provisions were applied throughout in the whole of the State. The panchayat elections were also held uniformly throughout Madhya Pradesh in June 1994. The state law was finally mended in 1997 to conform to *The provisions of the Panchayat (Extension to the Scheduled Areas) Act, 1996* by which the 73rd Constitutional Amendment was extended to these areas with some modifications.

Article 243 M of the Panchayati Raj Act, 1992 questions the uniform applicability of the Act and calls for special measures for the governance for Scheduled Areas. The Article, 243 M (1) states that 'nothing in this part shall apply to the Scheduled Areas referred to in clause (1), and the tribal areas referred to in clause (2) of Article 244'. However, according to Article 243M4 (b), 'Parliament may, by law extend the provisions of this part to the scheduled areas and the tribal areas referred to in clause (1) subject to such exceptions and modifications as may be specified in such law. But, in most of the states with scheduled Areas, including Madhya Pradesh, panchayat elections were held uniformly. In some states like in Andhra Pradesh, Orissa and Maharashtra holding elections were withheld as they were challenged in the various High Courts. (Mukul, EPW, 3-9 may 1997: 928). The courts viewed the extension as unlawful and according to them the Pachayati Raj could be extended to the scheduled Areas only through an Act of Parliament. Consequently, to look into these matters and making recommendations for extending the provisions of the 73rd Amendment to the Scheduled Areas, a Committee under the Chairmanship of Dileep Singh Bhuria (then the Member of Parliament) was constituted in June 1994.

The Bhuria Committee submitted its report in February 1995 with far reaching recommendations on the law to extend the provisions of Part IX of the Constitution to the Scheduled Areas. It dealt with the issues of village governance and participatory democracy, effectiveness of customary laws, community control over resources and appropriate administrative framework for Scheduled Areas. The Committee felt that while sharing the new panchayati raj structure in tribal areas, it is desirable to blend the traditional with the modern by treating the traditional institutions as the foundation on which the modern super structure should be built and taking cognizance of their indigenous institutions and ethos while considering democratic decentralisation in tribal areas.

The important recommendations of the Bhuria Committee included wide-ranging powers to the Gram Sabha, reservation of seats as members and chairpersons and the formation of district and sub-district councils in tribal districts with powers (administrative and legislative) identical with those in the Sixth Schedule Areas.

There were some criticisms of the Bhuria Committee Report. The recommendation (para 1[2]) of the report suggests that all tribal sub-plan areas and other smaller tribal concentrations, not already notified as Scheduled Areas, should be done so under the Fifth Schedule of the Constitution. According to B.K. Roy Burman, the relevance of this recommendation for framing legislation for operationalizing the 73rd Amendment of the constitution in the existing Scheduled Areas is not clear (Burman, B. K., Roy, 1997: 19). It will pose two problems according to him. One while it will strengthen the upper layer of the bureaucracy, it will cause misgivings among the non-tribal peoples in those areas and sour tribal and non-tribal relations; and second, the people in this area would be vulnerable to be ruled by regulation promulgated by the Governor as the Fifth Schedule does not stipulate any devolution of power at the local level but provides for its centralisation (p. 19-20). The recommendation in fact ignores the ground reality and diverts attention from the real reason for not very satisfactory functioning of the tribal Sub-plan approach as admitted in the Seventh and Eighth-plan. If the tribal Sub-plan has anything to do with the Fifth Schedule, the report should have explained , says Burman, why the condition is equally bad in the States like Orissa, Madhya pradesh and Maharashtra where bulk of the tribal predominant areas of a State like West Bengal, which are not covered by the Fifth Schedule, the conditions are more or less the same if not slightly better in some cases.

Apart from the criticism of the paternalistic design of the Fifth Schedule, other points of debate focused on – the reorganisation of the administrative boundaries based on ethnic and demographic considerations, composition of the four tier structure and the relationship between each, the role of the MPs and MLAs in the panchayat bodies and the replication of the Sixth Schedule provisions to the Fifth Schedule Areas which would invite a non-tribal political backlash.

Finally, after some delay on the part of the Government and protest by certain individuals and organisations, the Act namely *The Provisions of the Panchayats (Extension to the Scheduled Areas) Act, 1996* came into force on 24th December, 1996. The objectives of this Act were to extend the provisions of Part IX to the Scheduled Areas with certain modifications, to provide self-rule to the tribals, to ensure participatory democracy, to evolve a suitable administrative framework, to safeguard and preserve the traditions and customs of tribal communities and to prevent outside interference and exploitation of the tribal people. This Act is to be applicable in the Scheduled Areas referred to in clause (1) of Article 244 of the constitution. The States in the Scheduled Areas were required to amend their own Panchayat State Acts before the expiry of one year, i.e. by December 23, 1997. All States except

Bihar and Rajasthan (which did later through an Ordinance) amended their Panchayat Acts to give effect to the provision contained in the Extension Act, 1996.

The Act directs the legislature of a state not to make any law, which is inconsistent with the customary law, social and religious practices and traditional management practices of community resources. The Act also recognises the important role of village community and give wide-ranging power to the Gram Sabha for safeguarding and preserving traditions and customs of the people, approve the plans, programmes and projects for social and economic development of the village and several other powers to protect and regulate the natural resources as well as its misuse by the outsiders. Besides these, the other important points the Act envisages are - the reservation of one half of the total seats for the scheduled tribes in the Scheduled Areas and the post of Chairperson at all levels of panchayat and the pattern of the Sixth Schedule of the Constitution to be maintained while designing the administrative arrangements for the district level panchayat.

Thus the Extension Act, 1996 though diluted some of the recommendations of the Bhuria Committee Report, has accepted most of them, particularly the provisions relating to the power of the Gram Sabha. B.K. Roy Burman while appreciating these points is critical of some of these. According to him as the Act is for extension of the provisions of part IX of the Constitution in the Scheduled Areas, it is presumed that where it does not make specific provision on any matter the relevant provision in IX will operate. He raises problems regarding the use of certain concepts in the Act like 'community' or 'customary law', which would pose confusion and ambiguity at the operational level. There is a need as envisaged in the Act, to extend the sixth Schedule to all tribal dominate areas of the country and later to even non-tribal areas, according to B.K. Roy Burman.

B.D. Sharma (also the member of Bhuria Committee) considers the 1996 Act as an important step in the direction of tribal self-rule. He however, feels that the agenda must include – areas totally left out from consideration like the Sixth Schedule areas, Urban Areas in Scheduled Areas not covered, some States with substantial tribal population totally left out like West Bengal, Kerala, Tamilnadu and Karnataka, and Tribal Areas in the Fifth Scheduled states but outside these areas. (Sharma, B.D., 1998: 31-40). Some people feel that the positive aspects of the Act are meant to ensure an easy access to land for industry. Given the fact that 80-85 per cent natural resources are found in the tribal areas, it is going to affect them the most. (Pinto, Ambrose, EPW, Vol. 33. No. 49, Dec. 5-11, 1998). With the processes of economic liberalisation and globalisation gaining strength, a destructive development is likely to be initiated legitimised by public interest. This would be at the cost of tribal way of life and culture, of their knowledge, resources and production skills, in fact at the cost of the human survival and the preservation of environmental and ecological balance.

Besides these some important points are related to the customary laws and practices of the tribals, which vary among and within all tribes in different states. It may not be possible to have different laws for each tribe within a district or state. And, the customary laws are not properly codified and documented. The 'village' as described in the Act, which may be a 'hamlet', will pose a situation in which the revenue village may not be coterminous with the social village. The term 'community' is not defined in the Act clearly, and therefore, it would be difficult to delimit a village. The reservation, especially for all chairpersons to be members of scheduled tribes, especially at the block and zilla levels will create problems, particularly in those districts where tribals do not constitute more than 50 per cent of the total population of the district. In such places there will be a general resentment. Then there will be structural and administrative complications in the scheme. In Madhya Pradesh, a special section has been added to the *Madhya Pradesh Panchayati Raj Adhiniyam, 1993* (chapter XIV A) by way of an amendment known as '*Special*

Provision for Panchayats in Scheduled Area', Madhya Pradesh. This came into force on 5th December 1997 and provide for the extension of the provisions of part IX of the Constitution relating to the Panchayats in the Scheduled Areas of the State. It has incorporated most of the provisions of the Extension Act, 1996. These provisions ensure ample and significant representation of the tribals in the Scheduled Areas of Madhya Pradesh. The implementation of the provisions of the Extension Act, 1996 in Madhya Pradesh started with the amendment of certain other important laws, like the Excise Act, the Land Revenue Code, the Mining and Mineral Rules, the *Gram Nyayalaya Adhiniyam* and the Panchayat Act itself.

As far as the acquisition of land is concerned, the M.P. Amendment Act made a provision with the Extension Act that before making the acquisition of land in the Scheduled Areas for development of projects and before rehabilitating persons affected by such projects in the Scheduled Areas, the Gram Sabha or the panchayat at the appropriate level shall be consulted. The actual planning and implementation of the projects in the scheduled Areas shall be co-coordinated at the state level. Similar is the case with the grant of prospecting license or mining lease for minor minerals or for grant of concession for the exploitation of minor minerals by auction. (Sharma, B.D., 1998: 21-22). The powers have been devolved to the Gram Sabha in matters of planning and management of water bodies, enforcement of prohibition or regulation or restriction of the sale and consumption or manufacture of any intoxicant, and management of village markets. The issue of Minor Forest Produce and that dealing with the move against money lending are however, still to be taken care of. (Singh, S.K., 2000:31). But, in actual practice not all of them are implemented and there are still gaps and problems in their execution.

Reservation and Election – Madhya Pradesh

The 1962 Act as well as 1981 Act provided for cooption by the elected members, of upto two women as members of gram panchayats and janpad panchayats if they did not figure, or were less than two, amongst the elected members. In the zilla panchayats it included cooption of one woman member. An Amendment in 1988 introduced 20 per cent of seats for gram panchayat and janpad panchayat, as well as 10 per cent for the posts of sarpanchs of gram panchayats, and members of janpad panchayat and zilla panchayat. The 1990 Act followed the same provision but included a reservation of 10 per cent for the first time, in the district panchayat pradhans with at least one each for a member of these posts to be reserved for SC and ST women in the total parts for each category. The reservation of a particular seat was to be made by draw of lots and by rotation.

As far as reservation of seats for SC/ST is concerned, in Madhya Pradesh (as created in 1956) the *Panchayat Act of 1962* included through an amendment in 1973 for reservation of seats in Gram Panchayats for SC/ST in proportion to their population in the Gram Sabha area. If no reservation was possible due to their small population co-option was to be made of SC or ST member as the case may be. The Madhya Pradesh Panchayat Act of 1981, section 1 (4) provided for reservation for SC/ST in each village Panchayat proportionate to their population in the Gram Panchayat and for co-option in case no SC/ST member was elected. Section 15 stipulated that in a Gram Panchayat where more than 50 per cent seats are reserved for SC/ST or both together, the Sarpanch or Up-sarpanch, if Sarpanch was not found had to be from these categories.

In the Janpad panchayat also, section 19 provided for co-option of a SC/ST member if no such member was elected to the Janpad Panchayat. Under section 23, reservation was provided for SC/ST in the posts of Janpad Panchayat presidents in proportion to their respective population in the State. In addition, if more than 50 per cent members of a Janpad Panchayat were SC/ST, the President or the vice-President as the case may be, was to be elected from amongst SC/ST. In the zilla panchayat, section 26 stipulated co-option of a member of the Scheduled Caste or Scheduled Tribe or one each from both if the elected members in the zilla panchayat did not include SC, ST or both of them. Where more than 50 per cent members belonged to the SC or ST, the President has to be elected from amongst them as per section 27 of the Act. If the President was not an SC or ST, the Vice-President had to be SC or ST.

Madhya Pradesh Act of 1990 include section 13 (4) for reservation for SC/ST in gram panchayat seats proportionate to their population in the gram panchayat area. Section 17 provides for reservation of posts of Sarpanch for SC and ST in proportion to their population in the block. If the gram panchayat sarpanch was not a SC or ST the Up-sarpanch had to be elected from SC/ST members. In the Janpad Panchayats, section 22 provide for reservation of posts of Chairpersons of Janpad Panchayat for SC and ST proportionate to their population in the district. If the Chairman of the Janpad Panchayat was not from SC/ST, the vice-chairman had to be from SC/ST in proportion for their respective population in the State. If the Pradhan of zilla parishad was not SC/ST, the Up-Pradhan had to be SC or ST.

The Constitutional 73rd Amendment provided for members to be elected and co-opted or nominated as ex-officio members. The reservation of one-third seats for women (including those of SC/ST), and for SC/ST according to the proportion of their population has been provided. This has enabled a large number of women to be in panchayat bodies. The reservation as finally provided at the time of the 1994 panchayat elections for the seats of chairpersons and members in the panchayats at three levels, show that 14.86 per cent was reserved for scheduled castes, 29.88 per cent for scheduled tribes and 17.03 per cent for other backward classes. A little over 33.87 per cent seats were reserved for women, of which 14.84 per cent were for women of scheduled castes, 28.86 per cent for women from scheduled tribes and 17.51 per cent women from OBCs leaving 37.79 per cent for women in general category.

The Panchayat (Extension to the Scheduled Areas) Act, 1996, has further extended the reservation for the scheduled tribes in the Scheduled Areas. The reservations made in 1999 for the second Panchayat elections in Madhya Pradesh saw an increase for S.T category , i.e. 31.83 per cent, but a marginal decrease in other categories like 14.51 per cent (S.C.), 16.84 per cent (OBC) and 33.71 per cent (women). For the reservations made for total women, 14. 52 per cent were for S.C. women, 32.61 per cent for S.T. women and 17.23 per cent were for OBC women. (Buch, Nirmala, 2000: 177-178). The increase in the reservation in percentage of S.T. category as well as women belonging to Scheduled Tribe category is the reflection of the reservation for scheduled tribes in Fifth Scheduled Areas being of all chairpersons and not less than 50 per cent of members besides being proportionate to their population.

The above data show enhanced increase in the participation of tribal women in the panchayats in the Vth Scheduled Areas since the passing of Panchayat Extension to the Scheduled Areas Act, 1996.

The state government constituted the State Election Commission in February 1994. The constitution of 30,922 gram panchayats, 459 panchayats at the block level and 45 zilla panchayats at the district level was notified in March 1994. The delimitation of wards/constituencies was completed in April and the elections were held in May-June 1994. Of the total members of gram panchayats 63.12 per cent were elected without contest and 8.38 per cent sarpanches of gram panchayats, 13.60 per cent janpad panchayat members, and 7.50 per cent zilla panchayat members were elected unopposed. There were also cases of women and reserved category candidates contesting and getting elected on unreserved seats. Seventeen women became presidents of zilla panchayats against 15 posts reserved for them and 23 women were elected as presidents of janpad panchayats on unreserved positions.

Concluding Remarks

The following points emerged from the above analysis:

First, tribal women must be looked as a part of the tribal community, which has suffered at the hands of the non-tribals and marginalised in the process of development. During the study, it was noticed at many places that the non-tribals dominated the panchayats. As a result, the scheduled tribes are given special provisions constitutionally and now with extension of panchayati raj in the Scheduled Areas, they have been given power of self-governance. Tribal women suffered as much, in fact more by virtue of their belonging to the tribal community. It is therefore, now a time to involve tribal women equally in the process of development and governance in the Scheduled Areas where Constitutional powers have been given to the tribals for self-governance.

Second, tribal women must also be seen as women, and not just 'tribal'. This is because they have been always deprived from power and decision making positions, as well as from control over natural resources. It is shown in the study that the important positions in the traditional panchayats were always held by males that were passed on more or less in a hereditary manner. Today when the seats are reserved for tribal women, men of such families still dominate the panchayat through them. The women sarpanchs of *Salkhera* and *Barbel* gram panchayats in Khargone district are wives of men who have dominated the traditional panchayats since more than 20 years.

Third, it is important to keep in mind that tribal women are tribal as well as women, i.e. they are 'tribal women'. In this sense, their situation is different from both, and must always be dealt with exclusively, analytically and substantively. The need is to look at their situation from the holistic perspective without loosing the gender dimension. Tribal women have similarities and differences with the other women on the basis of their community/tribe and with tribal men on the basis of their gender. The study on tribal women in panchayati raj in Madhya Pradesh has tried to bring out such similarities and differences for the reason that tribal women are clubbed with tribals when people talk about them, or simply as 'women' when the women are being studied. Their background, awareness, participation, performance and perceptions are analysed on this premise by focusing on various aspects of panchayati raj institutions. The findings are accordingly drawn.

Background

The study reveals that panchayati raj institutions in tribal areas of Madhya Pradesh comprised of young and educated women, as against the prevalent view. Seventy per cent of them are below 49 years of age and 30 per cent are educated (plus there are nearly another 30 per cent who call themselves 'literates', i.e. who can sign their names). Agriculture is the main occupation of the people and though some of them are from economically influential families, a large number are from middle and lower class households. Most of their family's annual income is less than Rs. 25,000 and they own between 1-9 acres of land. The political background of the respondent's support the point that most women, compared to other groups have such links. The tribals have often been used as vote bank where every woman count more as a vote with not so much effort made to involve women in political decision-making bodies.

The background of the respondents clearly suggests a shift in the power structure at the grassroots level. The reason that it happened in tribal areas shows that such shifts are not confined to the rural areas alone. Like in the rural areas, this study shows that even among the tribals there were always certain families who controlled the political-economy and the social life of the tribal community. Such families were the first to take advantage of the panchayati raj Act when their women came out to contest election on the seats reserved for women. Though this dominance is still continuing, as some respondents expressed while talking about the changes in the political institution at the village level, a large number of women and men have also been elected from poorer families.

It is clear from the study that most of the support came from the respondents' families, followed by those from the community and caste people and the other villagers. This support extends right from the decision to stand in election till the end of the five-year tenure. It is however, significant to note that nearly half the respondents acknowledged the support of some or the other political party. The Congress and the BJP are the two main parties and most of Panchayat representatives are Congress members or supported the party, though the BJP has made some dent. However, during the field-work it was found that the candidates standing for the post of panch or sarpanch of gram panchayat were either not affiliated to any party, or was found to belong to the same party. Here the post and not so much the party was the concern.

From this brief analysis of their background, certain points can be summarised:

First, women are dependent to a large extent on the support of their husbands and other family members. They mainly took the decision to contest, campaign and other decisions. Of those who said they do not go alone to attend meetings (44%), 75 per cent said their husbands or some adult male member of the family accompany them, while the rest said their husbands actually represent them.

Second, the domain of certain influential families is still continuing and has been further entrenched, though the provisions of the 73rd amendment Act has given space to much larger and diverse people, including women and members of Scheduled Castes and Scheduled Tribes. As the elections are becoming more political and expensive with increasing use of money and muscle power, only a certain section of the society has taken the advantage of this. The number of contestants, including women increased for the second round of election. In Madhya Pradesh, the number of contestants in 1994 panchayat elections was 488394, which increased in the 2000 elections. Also there has been a decline in the overall percentage of those who are elected unopposed in the two elections from 23.14 to 15.55 per cent (*Panchaika,* January, 2000).

Third, reservation of seats for women in panchayats or even in other political bodies is the most viable and appropriate method in the given circumstances, to ensure women's representation. Not only women's entry into panchayats could have been made possible without reservation, nor it could be sustained without it, at least for the time being. Many people opposed reservation initially on different grounds like it will disturb the family life, women will become targets of attacks by anti-social elements, not many of them will be available etc. The data in the CWDS study (1999) have exploded several myths about women's entry, their participation and performance. This study too has shown the presence of a large number of women from poor families and who have no political connections. The reservation is therefore, a necessary condition for ensuring their political participation.

This study shows that, though in many cases women (40%) were asked or even persuaded to contest elections at the first instance, majority of them fought and won (60%). About 50 per cent did not seem to be very keen to contest elections, as they did not make any effort in this direction. In this study, all tribal women respondents contested panchayat elections on the reserved seat, and all but four contested for the first time. Nearly 95 per cent stated they would never come to occupy positions in panhayats, if there was no reservation of seats for women. Though majority of them (77 per cent) were willing to contest again, a large number (62 per cent) said they would do so only if the seat is reserved for them. Even then, most of them had some idea as to why seats are reserved for women, and were also aware of the provision of the Constitutional 73rd Amendment, especially that of reservation for women and scheduled castes and scheduled tribes.

The above analysis shows the positive points in regard to women entry in panchayats. However, there are certain problematic areas as well which need to be identified to work on them and strengthen the panchayati raj system. By and large, the dominance of men still continues to a great extent. They do not want their wives or other female family members to contest and get elected if the seat is not reserved for women. They do not want to give away their own chance and express dissatisfaction in case if the seat is re-reserved. A male member belonging to the family of a woman Janpad panchayat member of Udaipur block in Sarguja district (village *Sontarai*) was extremely upset that all the four-panchayat seats in the constituency were reserved for women.

It is not surprising that though most of the women respondents want to stand again for elections, majority of them (more than 60 per cent) said they would do so only if the seat is reserved for them. Some of them who were not sure said that they would recontest elections if their husbands, or other family members or the villagers decide so. In a few cases, especially for zilla panchayat elections, some respondents said that they would re- contest only if their political party wants them to do so. Thus, there are many factors which influence women's choice to re-contest which range from general, like party's decision to the personal ones, like if the seat is unreserved.

Awareness and Participation in Panchayat Activities

The analysis of women's awareness, participation and performance in panchayat activities showed that given the background and degree of participation can be regarded as satisfactory, though some people expressed their opinion that there has not been much change as the power has remained in the hands of the few people.

The most positive thing in this regard is an improvement in all-overall awareness of women in panchayat's work and its activities. As many as 73 per cent women were aware of the development programmes undertaken by the panchayats. Seventy – seven per cent were aware about the timings and agenda of the panchayat meetings and equal number knew about the powers of panchayat. Implementation of the government policies and undertaking of the development programmes were regarded as the two main powers of panchayat. Seventy three per cent of the respondents replied the question regarding their awareness about the issues undertaken in their panchayats.

Most of these were stated to be related to the housing under *Indira Awas Yojana* or construction work mainly under *Jawahar Rajgar Yojana* or those related to pension schemes, maternity benefits etc. Sixtythree per cent also identified the source of income of their panchayats, which came mainly from either government funds, panchayat property, collection of taxes and through politicians. The participation and performance in panchayat has brought about a positive change in tribal women's image and the respect they receive from other as expressed by more than half the respondents. People come to them with problems and they are called by them on important occasions. Many respondents expressed that people have started believing that women can perform well as panchayat representatives.

Some of the areas, which required more attention, were lack of women regular attendance in meetings, raising of the issue and the dominance of the male members of the family in the panchayat work. Nearly 63 per cent of them said that they do not raise any issue and those few who did were mainly confined to health, women and child welfare or drinking water. About 62 per cent of them attend meetings regularly where as 48 per cent either do not attend meetings at all or attend at times. Fifty per cent of those who were not attending meetings regularly said that their husbands 'manage' the affair.

Some or the other person help most of these women respondents (nearly 55 per cent) in their work. Of these, a considerable number of them take the help of Sarpanch, (36 per cent), other colleagues in panchayat (23 per cent), and the husbands (25 per cent), while some are helped by the villagers, the government officials, political parties or to an extent by the non-governmental organisations. They serve as support structures for women and are very useful. However, many times these support mechanisms do not become useful when women are completely dependent on their husbands and Sarpanch and do not at all attend meetings or participate in the panchayat activities. In the section on the 'Problems and Solutions', 25 per cent respondents said that they are helped by their family members, mainly the husbands and 38 per cent said that when people come to them with their problems, they send them the Sarpanch. Nearly half the respondents still feel that there has not been much change in their image, they cannot work independently and lack required information and knowledge.

It is necessary that women come out of this domination and subordination for which they need to be educated and trained. Though these two are not sufficient conditions in themselves, their dearth prevents women from taking important decisions. Besides lack of awareness, education and training, the respondents also expressed their opinions regarding other problems. Lack of financial or economic resources was considered as the most important one. Interference by government officials and their non-cooperative attitude, groupism, besides family problems and traditional values, were other problems.

Thus, both the negative as well as the positive features of women's participation and performance must be kept in mind to reduce their problems and strengthen their capacity to perform functions and roles in the panchayati raj panchayats. It can be said that compared to the non-tribals, the tribals need more education, awareness and training in panchayats works, and tribal women require these even more than tribal men or other women.

These hierarchical relationships need to be broken, if the self-rule and autonomy to the tribals has to become a reality in the Scheduled Areas as envisaged in the Extension Act, 1996. Simultaneously, more networks and linkages with various people and agencies on an equal footing are required to be developed. Since women constitute one-third of the panchayat representatives and also since, at least one-third of the Gram Sabha members in the meeting are to be women, it is important that they emerge as new leaders to take up the challenging role in tribal politics. Reservation of seats for women, especially for tribal women is essential for some more years, but efforts are required to ensure that women's political participation go beyond it which will help to foster new image of women who can come in politics on their own and perform independently.

REFERENCES

Banerjee, Summanta, *India's Simmering Revolution: The Naxalite Uprising,* Select Book Service Syndicate, New Delhi, 1984.

Bathla, Har Bhagwan, *Panchayati Raj and Political Parties: An Empirical Study at Grass- roots Level in Haryana,* Nirmal Book Agency, Kurukshetra, 1994.

Batliwala, Srilatha, 'Concept of Women's Empowerment-A Framework', *Women in Panchayati Raj: Perspectives from Different States,* National Seminar on Women in Panchayati Raj, Uma Resource Center, ISST, Bangalore, 27-29 April, 1995.

Buch, Nirmala, *Panchayats after the 73rd Amendment: A Study of the Panchayati Raj Instituations in Madhya Pradesh,* Mahila Chetna Manch, Bhopal, 1996.

—, *Women Experience in New Panchayats: The Emerging Leadership of Rural Women, CWDS* Occasional Paper, No. 35, New Delhi, 2000

—, *Madhya Pradesh* in *Status of Panchayati Raj in the States and Union Territories,* Concept Publishing Co., 2000, New Delhi.

Burman, B. K. Roy, *Bhuria Committee Report: A Critique, Panchayati Raj Update,* Institute of Social Science, New Delhi, May- June, 1995.

Center for Women's Development Studies, *Partners in Grassroots Democracy,* Report of the Workshop on Panchayati Raj and Women, New Delhi, 24-25 August, 1989.

—, *Women and Panchayati Raj* Report of the Workshop at IIC, New Delhi, 24-25 August, 1989.

—, *From Oppression to Assertion: A Study of Panchayats and Women in M. P., Rajasthan and U. P.,* CWDS, New Delhi, 1999.

Chauhan, Abha, 'The Status of Tribal Women in India', *Trends in Social Science Research,* Vol. 3 , No. 2, December 1996.

—, *Tribal Women and Panchayati Raj in the Scheduled Areas of Madhya Pradesh,* Women's Link, July September, 1999.

Desai, A.R. (ed), *Rural Sociology in India,* Popular Prakashan , Bombay , 1969.

Dutta, N.K., *Madhya Pradesh* in *Status of Panchayati Raj in the States of India 1994,* ISS, Concept Publishing Company, New Delhi, 1995.

Friedrich Ebert Stiftung (FES) *Women in Politics,* New Delhi, 1992.

Furer-Haimendorf, C., *Tribal India: The Struggle for Survival,* Oxford University Press, Delhli.1992.

Gopalan, Sarla, *Women in Panchayati Raj,* Advisory Planning Commission, New Delhi, 1993.

Government of India, *Towards Equality: Report of the Committee on the Status of Women in India,* Ministry of Social Welfare, Government of India, New Delhi, 1975.

Government of India, *Panchayati Raj at a Glance: Status of Panchayati Raj Institutions in India 1987-1988,* Ministry of Agriculture, GOI, New Delhi, 1989

—, *Report of the Working Group on Development and Welfare of Scheduled Tribes during 8th Five Year Plan, 1990-1995,* Ministry of Welfare, P-1.

Guha, Ramchandra, *Savaging the Civilised: Verrier Elwin and Tribal Question in Late Colonial India, Economic and Political Weekly* , Vol,XX1, Nos. 35, 36, and 37 Special Number, 1996.

Institute of Social Sciences, *Status of Panchayati Raj in the States of India 1994,* Concept Publishing Company, New Delhi, 1995.

—, *Panchayati Raj Update,* Issues of 1995, 1996 and 1997.

Jain, L.C. *et.al. Grass Without Roots: Rural Development Under Government Auspices,* Sage Publications, New Delhi,1985.

Kaushik, Susheela *Women and Panchyati Raj,* Friedrich Ebert Stiftung, (FES) Har Anand Publication, New Delhi, 1993.

Kumud, Sharma, *Transformative Politics: Dimensions of Women's Participation in Panchayati Raj',* Indian Journal of Gender Studies, New Delhi, Vol. 5, No. 1, January- June 1998.

Mahipal, *Madhya Pradesh Pnnchayati Raj Adhiniyam 1993* in *State Panchayat Acts: A Critical Review* VANI, New Delhi, 1995.

Muzumdar Veena, *Key Note Address* in Seminar on *Women in PanchayatI Raj,* Uma Resource Centre, ISST, Bangalore, 27 – 29th April 1995.

—, *Reservation for Women in Panchayats: A Reply, Economic and Political Weekly,* June,10 1989.

Mukul,, *Tribal Areas: Transition to Self- governance,* Economic and Political Weekly, May 3, 1997.

Multiple Action Research Group (MARG) *They Call Me Member Saab: Women in Haryana Panchyati Raj,* New Delhi, 1997.

Pinto, Ambrose, *Fillip to Land Transfers: Land Acquisition Bill 1998,* Economic and Political Weekly, December 5-11, 1998.

Savyasaachi, *Tribal Forest dwellers and Self- rule: The Constituent Assembly Debates on the Fifth and Sixth Schedule,* Indian Social Institute, New Delhi, 1998.

Sharma, B.D., *Tide Turned,* Sahyog Pustak Kuteer Trust, New Delhi.

—, Tribal Self- rule: Madhya Pradesh (Garm Sabha), Sahyog Pustak Kuteer Trust, New Delhi,1998.

Singh, S.K., Panchayats in Scheduled Areas, Status of Panchayati Raj in States and Union Territories, Concept Publishing Company, New Delhi, 2000.

Singh, S.S. and Suresh Mishra, *Legislative Frame Work of Panchayati Raj, in India,* Intellectual Publishing House, New Delhi, 1993.

Srivastava, K.B. *Panchayats in Scheduled Areas,* Centre for Panchayati Raj, National.

7

Emancipation of Dalit Women in Changing India

Among the many changes that have occured in India during the last two decades, the social dynamics of self-assertion of the so-called lower castes is one of the most significant. The new economic policy that has opened India to global market forces, to a degree unprecedented since 1947, the rise of the Hindu nationalism that has brought the BJP to power, not to mention the open nuclearisation of the subcontinent are, of course, major events transforming India in decisive ways.

But, there are more profound social changes taking place that affect the very core of Indian society. Its most fundamental and specific character, the caste system, is under tremendous pressure, which can be ascertained in two different ways.

Firstly, the caste sytem of regulated hierarchical relationships—the old *jajmani* system—has been virtually destroyed by a series of far-reaching developments: the family/caste relationships which ordered status and professional occupations, the mode of production and the ideological basis on which it has developed for long are now strongly affected by the widespread market relations and by the political manoeuving nurtured by fifty years of universal franchise.

Secondly, the decline of caste boundaries—as a system governing and ordering the patterns of relations between the dominant and the dominated, between high status and low status groups, between patrons and clients—has not necessarily weakened the caste *per se*, revealing a specifically Indian social paradox: to a large extent the struggle against the ideological and material hierarchies of the caste system attacks the system, not caste. To dismantle the prevalent order of power, the so-called low castes—the OBCs, Other Backward Classes in administrative terminology—have fought for caste-based reservations of college seats and government jobs.

The OBCs have also used castes as vote banks favoring either national parties dedicated to their cause (such as the Janata Dal led by Prime Minister V.P. Singh who launched the Mandal crusade for extended reservations in 1990), or political formations which address OBCs' interests in specific states, such as the Samajwadi Party of Mulayam Singh Yadav in Uttar Pradesh, or the Bihar Unit of the Janata Dal (now Rashtriya Janata Dal) run by Laloo Prasad Yadav.

In this context, the changes could not but affect the worst endowed Indians, those traditionally called the Untouchables, whom Mahatma Gandhi called Harijans (the sons—and daughters—of Hari, one of Vishnu's names), and whom the Administration calls the Scheduled Castes. They may also be labeled in metaphoric and generic Regional denominations, as the First Dravidians—Adi Dravidar—in Tamilnadu. They are the Dalits in today parlance. Dalits was first a self-coined militant denomination which appeared in Maharashtra in 1972, and means, in the Marathi language, the trampled down, the oppressed. It is now the acknowledged and politically correct form all over India and emphasises the most dominant characteristic of their social and political existence.

The key question is simple to formulate but very difficult to answer: how could those who have been for millenia placed beyond the pale of the *varnas* which order the "touchable" majority castes of the Hindu society emancipate themselves? They have been oppressed not just economically or even physically, but also ideologically. Presumed to be impure by the twice-born castes who believe that they pay in their present reincarnation for the bad *karma* of their previous lives, the Dalits have traditionally been relegated to the extreme margins of society, not only socially but also geographically, in much of rural India they have to live in separate hamlets, away from the main villages whose temples they cannot enter.

In this paper, we shall address the issue of oppression and emancipation by paying attention to the Dalits from Tamilnadu, the southeastern Indian state known for its vigorous identity politics articulated by the Dravidian movement. We shall begin at the grassroot level by exploring the legacies of the past through the life-story of a female agricultural laborer, Viramma; she expresses perfectly, yet without extraordinary drama or cheap self-pity, the perceptions of those who have internalised the logic of caste oppression and hope for an improvement in their life through the largesse of the upper castes. We shall thereafter provide a larger perspective, on the dynamics of change which pervade, from a Dalit standpoint, their position in society. These changes raise an intricate but decisive question: which new identity will sustain the emancipation process? Must it evolve through integration into the mainstream, or must it acknowledge a very specific and traumatic experience, untouchability and its stigma, which calls for a struggle against the mainstream? The issues at stake are not only social and economic, but also cultural and political.

Certainly, we do not pretend to provide a comprehensive picture of Tamil Dalits. Our purpose is to call attention to a few noticeable patterns and to raise a few significant questions relevant to an all-India perspective.

Strength and Submission: Viramma's Life-Story

Before considering the Dalit movement in Tamilnadu in the 1990s, it would be useful to draw from the narrative of an humble illiterate Tamil woman—let us call her Viramma—who, through the 1980s, once mutual trust was established, narrated her life story and philosophy in great detail using the most vivid and simple words. Her story is of great interest not only for its vividness and frankness, but also for its gusto. It certainly provides a first-hand account of what was and still is, to a large extent, the daily life, the joys and sorrow, beliefs and the psyche of millions who share the life and the views of this mother of twelve children—only three of whom have survived—residing in a village amongst paddy fields, in an enclave of former French Pondicherry territory hemmed in by Tamilnadu, a four-hour coach drive from Chennai (formerly Madras). But Viramma's story also sheds light on what is discussed here: the dialectics of oppression and emancipation of those who for ages have been subjected to the scourge of untouchability.

She conveys the views of the older generation, and offers an image of those sometimes labeled "the Subalterns," not always in line with the "subaltern" school of historians of India—who emphasize that behind the established history, there is another history to decipher: the mute or the open struggles of the dominated classes. They are right: there is a mute history to discover and recover, but it is not always a history of protest. Like Viramma, most of the "subalterns" have probably had to balance an aspiration for a better life with the strong consciousness of what their *dharma* of submission is supposed to be, all the while experiencing the full force of the dominant classes and the state power machinery eager to crush even the most incipient forms of protest. This does not prevent struggles, but it does reduce their occurence.

Let us forget for a moment the new vocabulary—in 1996 Viramma was still ignoring the word "dalit"—and call Viramma by the caste name she uses for herself: Paraiyar, the caste of funeral drummers who play the *parai* drum and whose name, in a slightly altered form, was diffused throughout the world by the French and the British during the time of the East India Company. From the most numerous local "untouchable" caste name, Paraiyar, they coined a generic word: pariah.

Viramma is a Paraiyar whose daily life revolves around her family, hard work and caste culture. But as "one has to fill one's belly," Viramma's life also centers on the patronage of the main local landlord to whom she has become attached under the traditional bondage link between the master and his *adimai.* Viramma sees this status as one combining dependence and a degree of protection, for the master is her usual recourse in case of necessity, particularly when money has to be borrowed to meet the costs of important social occasions: funerals, weddings or other ceremonies in the family. This pattern of personal relations between the dominant and the dominated is extremely important, for it acts as a considerable obstacle preventing Viramma and others like her from joining a caste or class line of struggle to better their situation. Like many older Untouchables, Viramma appreciates the few improvements she has seen in her lifetime. Still she clings to the traditional perception of what the Pariah's *dharma* is: a sense of submission combined with a sense of duty. The internalisation of the dominant paradigm of submission does not, however, prevent her from either joking about Brahmins (for she depends on Reddiars landlords, not on Brahmin masters) or from identifying herself completely with the Paraiyar culture, which distinguishes itself from upper caste norms in numerous ways, including a much freer speech, a much greater non-religious inspiration, and a strong sense of humor. Though not blind to the domination she faces, lamenting and complaining occasionally, she does not dwell on her misery. Her strength, her capacity to face terrible hardships, the way her culture sustains her moorings, she is a singer with a large repertoire and a born storyteller — are impressive.

Few of the theoretical interpretations by foreign scholars on Dalits in Tamilnadu fully highlight the complexity of Viramma's life. She shares, as Michael Moffatt underlines, the consensus that places the Dalits at the bottom of the caste hierarchy and accepts the rationale of a system based on "purity," a system that orders the hierarchy among the different Dalit castes as much as it does between them and the rest of Hindu society. However, Viramma also illustrates the view of Katherine Gough, who stressed the distinctive features of the Dalit sociocultural world, freer than the inhibited Brahminical model, and based on an admixture of less authoritarian family structure and a greater caste solidarity. Contrary to Mencher's analysis, Viramma does not basically challenge the dominant values. She accepts the concepts of *karma* and *dharma.* Mencher's finding is, however, much more prevalent amongst the younger generation, which Viramma finds disturbing. She thus tries to calm her son who questions the rationality of God's discriminations, and condemns the exploitation of Dalits by the dominant castes. Believing that things are better "when everyone is in his own place," Viramma, like many elders, is afraid of the militancy of the younger generation, which dismisses the legitimacy of the ritual duties of the Paraiyars and which silently asserts itself in such aspects of daily life as the way to dress after fieldwork, the way to walk in the main village street, or the manner in which to speak. While Viramma takes pride in adhering to the Pariah's *dharma,* her son, exposed to the modern reformist political discourses, wishes to uphold his self-respect. Viramma fears this aspiration to full emancipation and believes that controversy and protest are risky because power remains in the hands of the dominant castes.

A Twin Legacy: Dominance and Protest

Bare statistics might underline the size of the problem of untouchability. Scheduled Castes accounted for almost 11 million people in Tamilnadu—19 per cent of the state's population—and in several districts these castes account for as much as 25 per cent, higher than the all-India average of 16.5 per cent (in 1991, there were 138 million Dalits in India). Such figures, however, give no indication of the extent to which untouchability is still practiced. While some change is noticeable in this regard, traditional patterns of contempt and submission have not disappeared. In Tamilnadu, the old *paraceri* where the Paraiyars have to live has always been built away from the *ur,* the main quarter of the village where high castes as well as "backward castes" (another denomination for OBCs) reside. Worse, even the new "colonies" (the local modern euphemism for Dalit quarters) built up by the government for Scheduled Castes are still generally erected apart. Temple entry is still prohibited in the *ur* for the *ceri* dwellers, and the age-old compulsions concerning funerals and rituals calling for the *paraimelam* (the "Pariah orchestra") are still expected to be fulfilled. Tea stalls and arak shops do serve Dalit patrons, but usually keep two sets of glasses so that Untouchables may not "pollute" the glasses used by others. Despite recent changes, the usual perception of Dalits amongst high castes and even backward classes remains derogatory: village Paraiyars continue to be stereotyped as ritually impure, "uncivilised," uncultured, unsophisticated and quarrelsome. Mixed marriages of Dalits with other castes are rare in town. They would not be accepted in the villages.

The socioeconomic status of most Dalits is still very depressed. Most of them (72 per cent) are landless agricultural laborers. Dalits account for 23 per cent of the rural population in Tamilnadu, but own only seven per cent of the land, and even those who do own land have, for the most part, very small plots. In terms of access to amenities, they are well below the state average. Ninety per cent of rural Dalits are still illiterate; the figure for non-Dalits is 10 per cent. With the diffusion of capitalism in rural India, agricultural laborers are progressively less attached to the landlord families as *adimai,* and try to make a living as day wage laborers or contract for a specific operation such as the peanut harvest, paddy transplantation, cutting sugarcane and so on. That does not necessarily signify a total break with landlord families. But this emerging proletariat has to pay for its relative freedom by losing whatever protection the master previously bestowed on his attached laborers. The extent of this "protection" varied according to the master's benevolence, but was also, for the most part, a result of two non-competing rationales: on the one hand the "established wisdom" ruled by the *swadharma* paradigm, defining the duty of everyone according to his/her caste (the dharmic landlord thus has a duty vis -à-vis his *adimai);* and on the other hand, what there is has been called the iron law of wages, such as granting the workers only just enough to reproduce the workforce or making loans to impoverished laborers thereby strengthening the bond of dependancy on their creditor.

Dalits are not only experiencing poverty; they are also victims of violence. The official registries of violence do not tell the whole story, for all acts of violence are not reported to the courts. If murders are somewhat difficult to conceal, rapes and beatings (including in police stations) are clearly underestimated. The press covers and comments on big events, but not all acts of violence are reported. On the other hand, the increased number of reports and registrations does not necessarily express an aggravation of the situation: they may testify to the fact that more and more victims, or more and more concerned militants and support groups, make public what was previously concealed. For each tragedy that draws national attention, such as the burning alive in 1969 in Kilvenmani (Thanjavur district) of 42 Dalits, including children, as a response to a strike for better wages, how many cases are forgotten, or ignored? Besides raw brutality and open murders, one must not forget the silent violence of everyday life, the violence of poverty, debt and bondage, the violence of discrimination, the humiliation on Dalit men, women, and children experience. Even if practices associated with untouchability recede to some extent, the "change of hearts" that Gandhi called for is still largely unrealised.

Must we conclude that radical thought and social reform movements have had no impact on the traditional mindset? Such a question does not have an easy and definite answer. The *bhakti* movement launched in South India around the VIIIth century A.D. personalised the relationship between God and the devotee, beyond the hierachy of castes and without the esoteric knowlegde and the ritualistic intercession of Brahmin priests. However, the movement quickly became part of mainstream Hinduism, and did not result in the disappearance of untouchability. In the ranks of the Saivite Nayanmar saints we find an "untouchable,"

Nandanar, just as we find Tiruppanalvar in the ranks of the Vaishnava Alvars. Both could approach God, but only after a purifying ordeal: the *bhakti* movement, after all, gave everyone an avenue to approach God personally, whatever his or her rank in the caste hierarchy. Its goal was not to dismantle the caste system.

From the 19th century onwards, a number of social reformers emerged in Tamilnadu, as in other parts of India, with a discourse against caste prejudices. Different trends can be noted in this connection: the *siddhar* mystico-ascetic tradition as rejunevated by Ramalingaswami (1823-1874), the nationalist humanism represented by Subramanian Bharati (1882-1921) and Bharatidasan (1891-1964), and the Marxist approaches of novelists such as Jayakanthan or Pavannan.

Tamilnadu, like other parts of India, has a neglected history of petitioning by the most oppressed, starting with a petition sent to the British in 1799 by Untouchables facing eviction from their huts close to Fort Saint George in Madras. More significant was the creation of the Adi-Dravida Mahajana Sabha in 1857. Petitions for using the term Adi-dravida and prohibiting the word "paraiah," for reservations in scholarships, government jobs, seats in village panchayats and municipal councils started in the last decades of the 19th century. Journals and magazines multiplied, including *Tamilan* in 1907, whose editor, Ayoti Das, converted to Buddhism in 1898 and founded the Indian Buddhist Association in Madras two years later.

But, much larger moves against the impact of a rigid caste system were brewing at that time. They were launched not by the Panchamas, but by those who would call themselves the non-Brahmins, a designation which could well have been complemented by an additional attribute: non-Dalits. The Non-Brahmin Movement, founded in 1916, fought against the disproportionate Brahmin hegemony in administrative services and professional circles. Soon after, its political arm, the Justice Party, gained provincial power in the Madras Presidency under British rule. But this awakening of the well-off Non-Brahmins was mainly the surge of a bourgeois group of rich entrepreneurs, lawyers, bankers and *zamindars,* most of them from castes of "fair" status, for the expansion of their economic interests, better social recognition and a due share in political power. The fate of the "depressed classes" in general, and of the "Untouchables" in particular, was not their concern. On the other hand, the Self-Respect Movement, founded in 1925 by E.V. Ramaswami Naicker, had a much stronger impact. Periyar ("The Great One" as Naicker was later named) explicitely combined his struggle for the Dravidians (an ethnic concept excluding the Brahmins supposedly from the Aryan North from the rest of the South Indian population) with a frontal attack against Hinduism and its ideological justification for the caste system and gender inequality. To a large extent, the Self-Respect Movement was an immediate consequence of the 1924 Vaikom agitation in Travancore that Naicker had been drawn into. Naicker was by then a prominent Congress leader, but had become utterly disappointed by the response of the Congress to the Vaikom agitation. Naicker left the Congress Party, presaging a radicalisation of his sociopolitical views, which discarded the viability of a democratic electoral process in fighting either untouchability or, more generally, "the evil of caste."

To summarise, the 1920s and the 1930s saw three distinct trends in the ideological attack on untouchability: the first embodied in Gandhi, a Hindu not opposed to caste, but actively condemning untouchability as a shameful perversion of Hinduism; the second in Ambedkar, a Dalit struggling for political rights of the Untouchables through reservation and already thinking about taking the Dalits away from the clutches of Hinduism through conversion to Buddhism; and the third in Periyar, who simultaneously attacked caste and religion, linking the liberation of man—and woman—with a militant atheism. In the 1940s Periyar assumed the mantle of the ailing Justice Party, and transformed it into the Dravidar Kazhagam (the Association of Dravidians). His aim was to use the D.K. as a platform for waging an ideological struggle against Brahminical views and for mobilizing thinkers and agitators who opposed in the stultifying effects of religion and brahminical paradigms on the otherwise great Tamil culture and society.

In 1949, the D.K. experienced a split when C.N. An-nadurai broke away to launch the Dravida Munnetra Kazhagam (Association for the Emancipation of the Dravidians). Annadurai's main point of departure from Periyar was his acceptance of the electoral process. He thus, discarded the extremist atheist militancy of the D.K. while keeping many of its goals. The Dravidian movement cannot thus be reduced to a mere chauvinist anti-Hindi, anti-Brahmin, anti-North regionalism, driven by ethnic secessionism. In its early years the DMK, under the leadership of C.N. Annadurai and M. Karunanidhi, had a strong social reformist dimension. It is precisely this combination of a social agenda with an ethnic card which pushed the DMK to power in 1967. Since then, the Dravidian parties, either the DMK, which split in 1972 or its Anna DMK rival, have been continually in power in Tamilnadu.

Dravidian parties have consistently implemented a strong reservation policy in favor of the Scheduled Castes. In addition to positive discrimination, they have strongly contributed (particularly the DMK in its pre-electoral speeches) to the dissemination of an anti-caste discourse calling for equality down to the remotest village. We must not underestimate the impact of what some might discard as mere rhetoric: words, even if not always followed by acts, are not innocuous, and help to change the mindset, particularly of the young generations born under the DMK or the Anna DMK rules.

But this rhetoric was neither adequate for improving dramatically the socio-economic status of most of the Dalits, nor did it prevent the Dravidian parties from using the caste labels for gaining electoral constituencies. Despite Periyar and the atheist Dravida Kazhagam, religion is as alive in Tamilnadu as it is in the rest of India.

This does not mean, however, that nothing has changed in the life of the Dalits since the 1940s. As in other states, a set of policies has slightly improved the fate of the Scheduled Castes, especially through the distribution of housing sites, street water taps and electricity, access to schools, specific subsidies or benefits in the implementation of rural development programmes. However, land reforms and poverty alleviation programmes have not made a breakthrough, which perhaps explains why there was no radical change in the status of most of the rural Scheduled Castes landless agricultural laborers who constitute most of the Tamil Dalits.

Dalits today are certainly more aware of their rights than before. But, the weight of the Dravidian parties whose resilience was founded on a large sociopolitical base encompassing the Scheduled Castes and the Backward Classes (all supposed to benefit from the 69 per cent reservation of seats in colleges, universities and government jobs) did not leave much space for an autonomous Dalit political party until recently. One has also to appreciate how, after the ADMK assumed power in 1977, the Dravidian movement came to be linked with the extraordinary charisma of the two successive film stars turned chief ministers, M.G. Ramachandran and J. Jayalalitha, whose politics banked on populism to win elections and foreclosed any radical move.

Limited emancipation was therefore perceived by many Dalits—and by Viramma—as the result of two processes, quite often linked together: the benevolence of the masters on one hand and, on the other, the result of decisions taken at the State level and implemented within the existing structure of political power relations from the top to the bottom through the dual network of the bureaucracy and party representatives.

Beyond Improvement: The Need for Emancipation

The emancipation of Dalits of course requires much more than their material progress, no matter how necessary this first step may be. The social and developmental policies of the Central or state governments, despite their limitations and shortcomings, have brought changes in the Dalit "colonies," and quite a number of higher castes people are apprehensive about the implications. Such resentful villagers can be both high caste landlords who think that decidely too much is being given to those "Untouchables," as well as people of modest means and status who feel grieved that the Scheduled Castes can receive government loans at better rates than themselves or stipends for going to college. Rural Dalits now also have access to symbolic and practical sites, although village temples where other castes go are still barred to them. They can, however, enter the village school, a decisive change, notwithstanding the continuing prejudice of some teachers and a high dropout rate. For some OBCs living a difficult life, those below them, though stigmatised, are still seen as unwanted competitors. We must therefore distinguish two, not necessarily mutually exclusive, types of reactions inside and outside the Dalit fold. On the one hand, attention is simply directed towards the material improvement of Dalit life. On the other, physical destitution and ideological submission have been so linked together for so long that any material improvement is interpreted as triggering a new emancipative thinking amongst the Dalit. In a world where everything is a sign, to wear a fashionable nylon sari, to smoke a cigarette in the village street, to take a request to the bureaucracy is to testify to changing attitudes.

This is a key issue. For the Virammas, any sign of material improvement confirms their views that positive changes can be obtained from within the existing social structure. Maintaining the traditional humility while accepting whatever benefits come from the government is thus seen as the best path to follow, since it does not directly oppose the powerful and thus reduces the risk of reprisal. Many Dalits from the younger generation, however, assert themselves and object, even publicly, to the rationale behind the discrimination. They are better aware of their rights, and keener to use their vote and the political process for articulating their aspirations, their sense of self-respect and their dignity.

Emancipation is thus, firstly an internal process. It involves a process of liberation of the self from the old internalised prejudices. But what are the goals? Generally, the model for emancipation is set (even if unwillingly) by the upper castes themselves. For many Dalits, emancipation is tantamount to an adoption of mainstream behaviour. The ultimate goal, in this process, is a dissolution of the "pariahhood" or "dalitness." To free oneself from the traditional bonds and enter a free labour market is just a first step. To speak and wear clothes as others do, to have access to what they enjoy, whether in the village space, in the sphere of power, in the professions, or in the religious world—these are the many tests of the real possibilities of not just improving one's material life but more generally, and as importantly, breaking the old discrimination barriers enclosing Dalits in their multi-faceted submissive status. Such a model of successful emancipation implies integration of at least some Dalits in the mainstream society. Confirmation of emancipation through assimilation comes when honors are bestowed upon a Dalit by members of upper castes themselves. This is true all over India when a Dalit is elected or nominated at a post of high responsibility. The most significant case in this regard was the almost unanimous election in 1997 of the first Dalit Indian President, K.R. Narayanan.

In Tamil Nadu, where, as in other states, no government is formed without at least one or two Dalit ministers. One case, at least, illustrates that such recognition is not limited to politics but can also occur in the mainstream cultural sphere:

Ilayaraja, the music composer, is enjoying success not only in the film world but is also donating money for the renovation of the prestigious Ranganathaswami temple at Srirangam, one of the most sacred of Hindu sites in South India, and has even won the blessings of the senior *jagad-guru* of Kanchipuram, the most eminent Brahmin pontif of Tamil Nadu.

This is only one side of the picture. To enjoy the same rights of justice and equality—concepts embodied in the preamble of the Indian Constitution—is of paramount importance. But, the question remains for the Dalits: are they just ideally free to do as others do, or do they have other ways open to them for charting the route to emancipation? There is now an assertive trend among the Dalits which refuses to incorporate the dominant cultural values as a modus operandi of emancipation. Dalit cultural associations, groups such as the Forum for Dalit Culture *(Dalit panpattu peravai)* and Dalit journals are trying to open new ways in this regard. A new Tamil Dalit literature—varied in style and ideological content—portrays Dalit life and denounces the existing order. While the beginnings of this literature can be traced to the Christian Sri Lankan novelist Daniel, its major exponents today are the novelist Poomani, the short-story writers Idhayavendan and Devibharati, the writer Bama and the playwright Gunasekharan, to mention only the most prominent examples. The rejection of the dominant cultural values is multifaceted, and of course does draw on outside influence such as other Dalit literary or political experiences (leading Marathi Dalit author Arjun Dangle, for example, has been translated into Tamil), or the works of revolutionary Marxist intellectuals. On a much larger scale, the influence of Ambedkar, whose writings have been extensively translated in Tamil recently, is beginning to rival that of Marx and Periyar. Symbolically, the three of them appear on the cover of K. Manokaran's *Varalarrup por,* where they are portrayed as being attacked by a Brahmin and an orthodox Marwari (a regional group of merchant castes from Rajasthan, whose members have established themselves in bazaars all over India, many also being moneylenders).

At a more theoretical level, the writings of Raj Gautamam reassess completely the cultural history of Tamil Nadu. Gautamam traces the roots of the age-old oppression afflicting the Dalits to the perverted values of the caste system "imported" from the North. In such a radical analysis, the cultural values of the high castes are no longer a recognised model to adopt for joining the mainstream: they are the definite sources of inhumanity. Dalitness may sometimes join hands with those pleading for the greatness of the Tamils. With Gautamam, however, Dalitness defies established Tamilness, calling for a new culture on which freedom may be based. Emancipation, then, is not only a liberation from social bondage but also a construction of cultural tools required for alternative modes of thinking. Amongst such tools, urban Dalit intellectuals have created, beyond the established publishing houses, numerous small literary and ideological journals and poetry magazines. Although often with modest circulations and short-lived, such publications have repeatedly reappeared. These *ciruppattirikai* have long been a resource for hundreds of groups moving new ideas, and not just in Dalit circles in Tamilnadu.

In addition to words, images also convey a part of the new message. It could be plain drawings, such as those adorning some recent publications. Some of them are explicitly militant, and contest the dominant Hindu paradigm: on the cover of *Yuttam Totarum,* a collection of Subbaiya's revolutionary poems, Ambedkar is seen trampling a copy of Manu's laws, the ancient Hindu code. There are also unusual cover photographs which go one step further by showing objects that refer, either directly or indirectly, to what the Hindu purity criteria derogatorily associate with the "Untouchables": a large bloody piece of beef hanging at a butcher's stall on the cover of Kurusu Sacrats' *Nav-val,* or a rotten mummy in a fetal position on the cover of a collective "metafictional novel." Such images are not just a pale copy of western surrealism, although in both instances their deliberate intent was to shock the conformists. More deeply, those images of beef and blood, of birth and death, express strongly the reappropriation by authors of the symbols of pollution, and hence untouchability. The use of such symbols clearly sends a new message: Dalits are not to be ashamed of the "polluted" images traditionally ascribed to them.

For the moment, those images on book covers have a limited circulation, even amongst literate Dalits. There is, however, a much more prevalent symbol around which Dalit identity is expressing itself: the portraits and the statues of Ambedkar. The Ambedkarite Republican Party and the Ambedkar People Movement are still not very widespread, but they are now much more visible than before. Ambedkar's statues are to be seen in large numbers, blue flags flutter in towns and villages. Ambedkar is very much present these days in intellectual debates, bookshops, newspaper columns, academic conferences and so on. He is now regularly referred to in political discourses of all shades, even by B JP politicians. This sudden importance of a hitherto-neglected political personality who died in 1956 is an apt testimony to the growing strength of Dalit consciousness. Skeptics might contend that sheer opportunism drives all sorts of orators and politicians to pay tribute to the new hero as a means of cornering the Dalit vote. Yet, empty though it might be, the rhetoric is itself both a testimony to and an instrument of change among those without voice. It shows that, like other groups, they have a figure revered by the establishment, a highly educated Dalit, a key reactor of the Indian Constitution who rejected Hindu domination and converted to Buddhism, a modern-day Dalit saint complete with his suit and tie. An attack on a statue of Ambedkar, a not uncommon occurrence, is seen as a desecration.

It is not by chance that Bhim Rao Ambedkar has become an icon. His contribution to the emancipation of the Dalits — combining theoretical work and official responsibility in the service of the nation with a constant concern for the emancipation of his brethren—is unparalleled. The Republican

Party he founded has not met with his expectations, but his example and his motto, "Educate, organize and agitate," is still the guideline for many NGOs who believe that dignity and justice are not just bestowed from above but have to be gained through struggle.

Rise of Dalit Militancy

Dalit liberation movement today pursues three main lines of action. The first seems to equip the Dalits with confidence; the second resorts to militant action; and the third raises the issue of the appropriate political tools.

The first two lines of action can be combined to a certain extent. The example of the Dalit Liberation Education Trust is significant. As the name suggests, this Madras NGO, run by Christian Dalits, identifies education as a powerful tool for social change, though without denying the need for action. It helps to rethink the conditions for liberation and, like other NGOs, tries to place the traditional oppression and the quest for justice in a broader framework with large implications in the field of civil and human rights. This helps both to question the limitation of Indian democracy, tainted by untouchability, and to raise the Dalit liberation issue in international forums. To equip Dalits with a better knowledge of their rights helps to bridge the gap between theory and practice.

A second line of struggle resorts to spectacular militant action. Sometimes the goal is symbolic—important for recognition, pride, confidence—and the figure of Ambedkar as an icon of Dalit emancipation is often privileged in such actions. The best known has been the long struggle by Dalit groups from Maharashtra to have the Marathwada University renamed Dr. Babasaheb Ambedkar University.Protest or revindicative marches, or celebrations of Ambedkar's anniversary, not to mention the collective reaction to attacks on Ambedkar statues, offer opportunities for public expressions of Dalit identity and aspirations which are sometimes serious enough to attract national attention. Such was the case with the protest agitation in suburban Bombay in July 1997, a protest marked by the killing of 10 Dalits.

But action can also have economic goals, taking the protest beyond identity symbols, as the agitation for *pancham* lands shows. *Panchami* is a very old term for those beyond the pale of the four varnas *(panch* in sanskrit means five), i.e., those defined by the Laws of Manu as Untouchables, barred both from education and landownership. In 1890 the British regime in the then Madras Presidency passed a law assigning land to the Dalits. It took more than 50 years for 650 acres of uncultivated land to be distributed to about 500 Dalits families in seven villages of Chingleput district, south of Madras. Despite the law prohibiting the sale of such lands to non-Dalits, other castes were able to gain control of them in the 1950s. In 1989, a movement for the reappropriation of these lands began in Chingleput. It expanded in 1994, when village police fired on a crowd in Karanai protesting the forcible removal of a statue of Ambedkar installed just hours earlier on claimed lands. The incident, in which two Dalits died, had a profound impact in the state, and resulted in the consolidation of the Panchami Land Committee. In 1996 the Committee, with the support of 127 Dalit organisations, launched a march of about 100,000 claiming their land rights.

The emergence of such large movements raises two distinct issues. The first relates to the structure of the Dalit movement itself, which is riven by internal divisions. The more radical groups are close to the Communist Party of India (Marxist-Leninist), which is marginal politically but plays an important ideological role. Other radical Dalit groups combine an ultra-left ideology with a concern for Tamilness as articulated by the Liberation Panthers, a Southern Dalit group supporting the Tamil Tigers in nearby Sri Lanka. Christian Dalits are much more important in struggle than their small numbers might suggest, and include Protestants like Rt. Rev. M. Azariah, Bishop of Madras, Church of South India, and Catholics. A number of Dalit priests complain about the persistence of caste prejudices in the community and the Church hierarchy. The most militant follow Liberation theology, which finds in Dalit emancipation an obvious field of action and theorisation. Militant groups can sometimes bridge religious and philosophical differences. At other times, differences result from competition between concurrent groups, and more fundamentally from disagreements about strategies and perceptions of the transformed Dalit identity.

The second issue is political. Before independence, Gandhi persuaded Ambedkar to renounce the separate Dalit electorate the British were ready to concede (a good opportunity to weaken the National Congress, as the British saw it). After 1947, for decades the Dalit vote was not autonomous. Most rural Dalits have, for long, "voted for the master," *i.e.*, for the landlord. The rise of the DMK introduced, as already noted, a new rhetoric and progressive actions. But Dalits were not seen as a special entity needing more than specific reservations and development programmes offered to the Scheduled Castes. Like the Congress Party at the national level, the DMK saw itself as an umbrella organisation, able to muster votes from everybody (with the exception of the Brahmin in the early stages), from the Dalit agricultural laborer to his landlord. The Communist parties have certainly had an impact in some areas, particularly with labour movements among agricultural laborers. But the established communists of the CPI and CPI-M, faithful to the doctrine, could not emphasize caste differences in their organizing. The Marxist-Leninists of the CPI-ML are certainly much more engaged in the Dalit struggle for land, and may even believe in the revolutionary potential of a Dalit mass movement, but they are a very small minority. The major parties in the state—the DMK and Anna DMK—are now perceived by many Dalit groups and NGOs as mainstream structures, paying mere lip service to the Dalits without offering them sufficient room in the leadership or adequate support to make a real difference. Hence the renewed quest for the best political instrument: should the Dalits conduct political struggle in larger formations, or should they set up their own parties?

The caste movement reappeared in Tamilnadu with a bang in 1987 when the Vanniyars—a numerous caste of small peasants, classified as OBCs—launched an agitation in the northern districts to highlight their problems, at the cost of numerous lives. Shortly thereafter, their organisation, the Vanniyar Sangam, set up a political party, the Pattali Makkal Katchi (PMK), the Workers Party, which failed in successive elections to attract sufficient Vanniyar votes to elect representatives who could air their grievances in the Legislature. Subsequently the PMK, under its Vanniar founder leader C. Ramadoss, developed a new and inclusive strategy, presenting itself as the party of the OBCs, Muslims and Dalits, and adopting the North Indian concept of *bahujan* —the masses—which extends the definition of the oppressed far beyond the Scheduled Castes. This strategy seeks to overcome the fact that, in the field, OBCs have been as violent adversaries of the Dalits as the high castes, exemplified by the history of clashes between the Vanniyars and the Paraiyars in Northern Tamilnadu and even more so by the violent confrontations between Pallars, a Dalit caste renamed Devendra Kular Velalar (Velalar is a high caste of landlord origin) and Thevars. Alliance building and the arithmetic of electoral politics may help Dalits and OBCs gain access to power, through coalition if necessary. This is the story of the Bahujan Samaj Party in Uttar Pradesh, the most populous Indian state, where Mayawati had the distinction of being, albeit briefly, the first Dalit Chief Minister in India, first with the support of the Samajwadi Party, backed largely by OBCs, and then paradoxically with the support of the Bharatiya Janata Party, which, whatever its present policy of wooing Dalit voters and offering party seats to Dalits and Tribals, still has a high caste image.

Having learned from the tactics of the Bahujan Samaj Party, the PMK leader, not without some debate in the party, decided to back the apparently disgraced leader of the Anna DMK,

Jayalalitha, who had allied herself with the BJP during the 1998 general election. The Anna DMK made an unexpected comeback (partly due to the weak support extended to the DMK by disappointed Dalits), and for the first time the PMK won four seats to the Indian Parliament. In the fluid political situation prevailing in an uncertain coalition, the PMK even got one ministerial appointment in the BJP-led Vajpayee Government. The happy nominee, it must be noted, was not a Vanniyar, but a Dalit, publicizing his identity in his very name: Dalit Ezhilmalai.

Neither in Tamilnadu nor in Uttar Pradesh is the alliance between Dalits and the BJP fortuitous. It may sound strange that Dalits should ally with the political arm of the hard core Rashtriya Swayamsevak Sangh, whose religious sister organisation, the Vishva Hindu Parishad, pretends to embody the eternal values of Hinduism. Two observations might explain this unexpected alliance. First, despite a high caste leadership, the strategy of the Sangh Parivar, the coalition of organisations that propagate Hindutva, is to try to accommodate all Hindus in its fold, including Dalits and Tribals (and the BJP plays the same card). Second, in the very fluid situation that has followed the decline of the Congress Party, political risks, including odd and unstable alliances, are sometimes the necessary precondition for political power. Dalit political parties are caught in this general predicament. Caught between this drift and the bane of division which has so weakened the Ambedkarite Republican Party, the road is not an easy one. Clearly enough, new formations will emerge, the last one in Tamilnadu being the "New Tamil Country" (Pudiya Tamilagam) founded in 1998 by a noted Dalit militant, K. Krishnasami, Chairman of the Devendra Kula Velalar Federation, the association of the main Dalit caste of South Tamilnadu. Whether such Dalit parties succeed or fail is not the issue; their very appearance is significant. Certainly, the progress of the PMK and the appearence of a Tamil Dalit party point to the fragmentation of the established Tamil polity: caste parties are now challenging the traditional hegemony of the Dravidian non-Brahmin parties, but they are also unwilling to portray themselves as exclusively Dalit for fear of losing the electoral support of other castes.

As a matter of fact, the Pudiya Tamilagam appears in a context marked by deep conflicts. In 1997 the relationship between the OBC Thevar caste and the Devendra Kula Velalars (DKV) took a turn for the worse. With the higher castes migrating to urban areas, the Thevars have become land-owners, and rely upon the DKV for agricultural labour. But the social equation has changed, and the Dalits aspire to more than mere survival. They are not satisfied with whatever little (and poor) land the state has given them. While elders like Viramma point out that their situation has improved in the last fifty years, the younger generation expects a lot more, including jobs and respect.

As V.S. Sam-badan has observed, the sparks of violence which disturbed the southern districts in 1997 have been symbolic: desecrations of Ambedkar statues, changes in the names of districts or public transport corporations. But, behind the sparks basic issues continue to divide "backward caste" like the Thevars from the Dalit Pallars: based on economic competition, social assertion and political access to power. Politics and symbols met unfortunately in the gruesome murder of six Dalits from Melavalavu village, in Madurai district, on June 30, 1997.

This included Murugesan, the new president, and Mookan, the new vice-president of the village *panchayat,* that had for the first time a constituency reserved for Dalit candidates. In a number of reserved constituencies, no Dalit had dared to contest. Murugesan was convinced to do so, despite severe obstruction by the local dominant castes to "reversed" constituencies. He was elected, but prevented from taking office, and finally murdered, and even beheaded. Two weeks later, far from Melavalavu, the Indian Parliament and Members of the States Assemblies chose another Dalit as President of India.

The divergent fates of the two Presidents is not just paradoxical. It emphasises that much is still to change, and that what is possible and even celebrated at the national level is not necessarily accepted at the ground level of the village. George Matthew, Director of the Institute of Social Sciences, has rightly pointed out that the Melavalavu murders are not just "one more instance of caste tension. It was a serious attack on the institution of the *panchayati raj* (the village government) which has the potential of changing the powerful rural groups." Since the recent administrative reforms, the *panchayat* is not just an honorable body of elected villagers, without much say on real issues. It now has control of local resources, and its president enjoys both status and power. Hence the reluctance of many established castes—including OBCs, which may be locally dominant—to accept a Dalit leadership, which offends them on both accounts, status and power. The necessary change of mind is not just a matter of Dalit consciousness. Change is needed as well among those high castes or OBCs who believe they are born leaders. As Mathew notes, the murders call into question the kind of political and social education that has taken place in Indian villages since Independence: "while empowerment of the weaker sections, organizing them to fight for their rights, was happening as a natural reaction to oppression, there was no concomitant move to educate the dominant caste about the changing times, the values of democracy, social justice and equity."

While all tensions do not result in murder, the difficulties faced in expanding democracy and the slow pace of real change at the local level have resulted in a feeling of "broken promises" among the Dalits. Could a Dalit political party offer a way out? Several choices are open to Pudiya Tamilagam. The first would be the way it plans its expansion. Will it become not just the party of the Devendra Kula Velalar but also encompass the Dalit castes from northern Tamilnadu? But should it stop there? If it succeeds in attracting most of the Dalit vote in Tamilnadu (and not just the two per cent it got during its first electoral test in 1998), it may hope to play a major role in the political life of the state, and be strong enough to join a governing coalition. It could follow the PMK's lead and try to build an alliance with OBCs and Muslims. The PMK and the new Dalit party would therefore compete on the same field. Once a party chooses to contest elections, this must sooner or later result in dialogue with other groups and parties. The very names of the two formations open perspectives larger than caste: workers, in the case of the PMK, and a renovated Tamilness in the case of the Pudiya Tamilagam. The key question remains: Is the concept of *bahujan* a myth, or a hopeful anticipation? Or does such a hope result from a simplistic reading of the power distribution in Indian society, separating the "high caste oppressors" from all the other groups? In the field, to say the least, "other backward classes" and Dalits do not necessarily share the same views or the same interests, and the union with the Muslims supposes that Dalits do not fall prey to the strategy of Hindu communalists who have attempted with some success to subordinate the Dalit caste identity to a larger "Hinduness" affiliation.

This brings us to the basic question of caste. Faced with "broken promises," Dalits have to consider conducting their struggle in a specific caste frame—either as a group of Scheduled Castes or through their own political party—to implement specific actions linked with reservation and human and civil rights. But, how to reconcile such a choice with the Ambedkarite concept of the annihilation of caste? What is needed is not just the political tool of a caste party, and even the hypothetical all-India confederation of Dalit regional parties, however necessary that might be at this moment. The need of the times is also to carry on a cultural revolution.

Culture, Identity and Empowerment in Changing India

Whatever interpretation is given to the interaction between castes of different status in the old *jajmani* relationship, caste culture is hierarchical and divisive. With the weakening of the caste *system,* the interplay of unequal but regulated relations between castes is bound to collapse, except on the new level of political alliances. But neither political tools nor the new National Human Rights Commission and its state counterparts that help to implement the existing legislation are enough. Many Dalit groups and intellectuals believe that an alternative culture has to emerge as well, culture being understood broadly. In most cases, the goal is to free the Dalits from the dominant Hindu paradigm.

Conversion has sometimes been seen as the best opportunity, be it to Buddhism (particularly in Maharashtra after Ambedkar), Christianity or Islam. But, conversion does not solve all problems on the ground or in the larger social context: converts may also be discriminated against, in or/and outside their new community. Furthermore many Dalits are not ready to convert, and conversion can hardly be a precondition for change. The problem is therefore to be able to go beyond the filter of religious persuasions. The programme for action published in Madras by Katti Padma Rao, a Dalit leader from Andhra Pradesh, is an attempt to address the challenge of emancipation in all fields. A mix of strong anti-Hinduism, socialism and radical opposition to the caste logic, it is certainly not credible and practical on all points. But it illustrates the difficulties faced by militants who believe that the overarching reality of untouchability calls for an equally overarching emancipation strategy, one that is attentive not only to socioeconomic contexts and political tools but also emphasises a radical rethinking of attitudes, ideas, daily practices. Trying to build an alternative culture is a process which asks for constant efforts at rejecting the legacy of the dominant past.

Padma Rao's first point is certainly too radical to be implemented. Impracticable and as much of a restraint on freedom as the old system, though in different ways, it goes to the core of the caste problem, that is, endogamy: "intra-caste marriage must be banned. Inter-caste marriage must become mandatory." A second line of action recommends alternatives to the dominant culture in terms of names (dropping the caste titles, giving to children or to houses names choosen outside the Hindu fold) and celebrating festivals honoring Dalit leaders instead of Hindu gods. A third line of action addresses the "reconstruction of rural culture," banning caste titles from villages names or village streets, stopping construction of specific Dalit "colonies" in favor of mixed settlements, in addition to eliminating illiteracy, establishing health centers and rural libraries and opening community halls for meetings. The fourth proposal calls for the propagation of people's art and culture through a revalorisation of popular art forms and, simultaneously, new creations celebrating Dalit life and Dalit heroes. The fifth proposal addresses the spread of education and calls for the multiplication of village schools, educational institutions and research centers, not to mention the revision of curriculum and text books. The sixth recommendation focuses on the necessity to spread alternative culture among women in order "to encourage them to resist the pressure of patriarcal domination" brought by Hindu culture. Padma Rao also calls for economic reorganisation (on socialist lines) and political reorganisation (building a political organisation for all the oppressed classes, with the goal of Dalit rule in mind).

The radicalism of such a programme limits its practicability, but the attempt to build up a detailed line of action at least identifies clearly the fields where change is needed and defines one line of thinking. The resolute denunciation of the dominant Hindu culture supposes profound changes in the daily life and in the "empire of signs" which governs its semiology. Politically and socially, Padma Rao suggests a blue and red perspective where the blue (the Dalit color) emancipation calls for a class (red) alliance with "backward and minority classes" against the upper castes Hindu ruling classes.

The question remains whether an alternative Dalit culture and Dalit activism is enough, or does Dalit emancipation also require a change in the mainstream culture? S.K. Thorat, in a paper on "Dalit and Human Rights" has seen the Dalits today as "a part of the whole, but a part apart." One can hardly find a better formulation of the present dilemma facing Dalit militants and all those struggling for Dalit emancipation. "A part apart" could be the motto of some Dalit intellectuals who believe that only Dalits can emancipate themselves, and that non-Dalits cannot really understand the Dalit experience, nor be fully trusted. "A part apart" could also convey the mixed feelings of a large part of the 80 per cent non-Dalit Indians who do not see themselves as oppressors but still believe that the former "Untouchables" are not really fit for integration into the mainstream.

Let us consider the thoughts of a noted fellow-traveler of the Dalit movement, D.N. Nagaraj, on the dialectics of Dalit oppression and emancipation in a small but very dense book: *The Flaming Feet.* His experience is largely drawn from the Dalit movement in Karnataka, and combines themes in cultural politics with motifs and metaphors in literature. But Nagaraj offers clues and raises issues which are of much larger value, in space as well as in content. His parallel between Gandhi and Ambedkar brings us back to the point raised earlier: the need for a change in the self-perception of the Dalits, but also in the self-perception of the non-Dalits. What history shows in this regard is that what is needed is not the Gandhian emphasis on Dalit quest for self-purification as a precondition for the eradication of untouchability. Against Gandhi's self-purification need, Ambedkar posits a quest for Dalit self-respect, which raises immediately the question of identity and the need for the emergence of an alternative culture which could eliminate the stigma of untouchability and stand in opposition to the established logic and psychology of the caste system. Ambedkar went so far as to leave the Hindu fold in his quest for a new collective identity. But while his neo-Buddhists followers and a number of intellectuals would define themselves today as non-Hindus, it is still doubtful that the Dalit masses would follow suit.

Is Indian democracy able to help Dalit emancipation, not just through reservation by law but also through the diffusion of new perceptions among Dalits and non-Dalits alike? The question centers partly on the place given to the individual, and partly on accepted norms. Nagaraj, addressing the problem of violence against Dalits, notes rightly that the village, as Ambedkar saw it, cannot be the basic unit for justice, for traditionally "the structure of justice rests on the consensus of the entire village, which could also mean the unchallenged rule of the upper castes." Here again, the caste ethos has to be rightly assessed: as Nagaraj notes, if an upper caste Hindu misbehaves in the village, this will be considered as an individual act, involving individual RE-sponsibility. But if a Dalit break the norms, he will be perceived first as a member of his group, and the entire Dalit community could suffer retaliation. A narrow path is thus open to Dalit militants who seek a way to attack oppression by combining ideology and material domination (hence the importance of the struggles for rights *and* land, which address these two fields), but also by trying to respect the "code of conduct," in the process gaining greater legitimacy in the "traditional" society, which is vital for the success of the Movement. In the meantime, the Dalit activist, "in a paradoxical position," has to recognize that "on him or her is the larger responsibility of creating a new sense of ethics for both the conflicting communities." More to the point, the success of the Dalit movement cannot be delinked from that of other social movements, be they the women's movement, the farmers' movement or the ecological movement. With the latter two, the relationship is not an easy one.

Looking at the bleak picture of untouchability in rural India, must we believe, as some Dalit militants do, that emancipation in the villages will be impossible against so many odds, however resolute the struggles, and that migration to town is the only way to free oneself? True, the rule of caste is not so rigid in large cities. But are Indian towns really such an attractive promised land? Urban India might also bring up much more acutely the problem of cultural memory, a memory already challenged either because it is lost in a silent history or because of the contempt it raises not just among non-Dalits but also sometimes among Dalits as well. The fact that some urban Dalit intellectuals who try to theorize Dalitness and emancipation do not always have an intimate knowledge of the psyche and culture of rural Dalits suggest the continued importance of rural movements, rural perceptions and rural memories.

Last but not the least stands the Dalits' "rights to cultural space." In Dalit writing in the Kannada language, Nagaraj finds two schools. The "school of social rage" "concentrates basically on the experiences of anger, agony and revolutionary hope." The "school of spiritual quest" transmutes the social rage "into a spiritual vision of equality." Why "spiritual quest?" Not necessarily because of an attachment to a defined religious line, but because this school "tries to understand the world of poverty and untouchability in terms of metaphysical dismay over the nature of human relationship. The ethos of the portrayal of life is not informed by anger and agony, but by a celebration of the joys of life and its possibilities, which also includes the will to change."

Beyond the sphere of literature, these two schools can also suggest a model, a metaphor for the choices offered to the Dalit society at large, or for the types of action open to militants. Those animated by an intimate or spectacular social rage might feel that no middle ground exist between nihilist or desparate intellectual marginality and strident revolutionary advocacy and militancy. But how to build from this anger a moving and intimate connection with the entire Dalit community? Can this rage sustain a durable way, beyond minority extremism, for the political, cultural and social emancipation of the Dalit masses? There is an unavoidable contradiction between activist groupings and larger party politics, the former being generally prone to isolation and/or repression, the latter bringing quickly enough, after the first electoral successes, the need for compromise. On the other hand, the spiritual quest—or may we say the humanistic path—is more prone to being coopted by the system. The real challenge for the second path is to resist this coopration while transforming the system. Nagaraj pleads "for a radical reconstruction of villages from a critical-modernist perspective which can also mean a radical revision of existing values along the lines of Indian religious reformers." Some Dalit militants or leftist radicals would call for a complete break with religion, reformed or not. Others would follow Nagaraj in opting for a middle-of-the-road line. A third group might find that this complex goal offers a path of change more acceptable to Indian society, because it is less disconnected from the legacy of a past not entirely encapsulated in upper caste orthodoxy. Whatever paths are chosen, Dalits intellectuals and militants know very well that deconstructing the prevailing Indian social order and constructing a new one will not be an easy process. It will involve Dalits and non-Dalits, the past and the present, the community as a whole and its fragments, and the self. It is a total enterprise, with innumerable implications. But it is clearly a process in which Indian Dalits are engaged today.

The Colors of Change: Blue, Red, Saffron, Rainbow?

At the end of this century, we are on the whole observing a rather confused situation. Indian society is in a state of flux. Castes are very much a part of the political game, but the caste system as such is condemned. The OBCs are asserting themselves everywhere, including in the decisive circles of power. One finds more and more Dalits in positions of responsibility and power, largely through the reservation system, while most of the community is still subject to various sorts of overt or covert discrimination. But there will be no scaling back of expectations now, despite the atrocities still perpetrated against Dalits and the setbacks to protest struggles or revendication campaigns. Promises have neither been fulfilled or forgotten. But the Dalit aspiration for change has become too strong in the minds of millions for backing down. Myriads of daily struggles, spectacular or not, sustain this aspiration, which has now gained access to the media and the political field.

The present state of uncertainty is in itself a victory and suggests that the past cannot perpetuate itself indefinitely. But Dalit emancipation remains a challenge for it raises formidable issues pertaining not just to the fate of the Dalits but also to Hinduism and to the Indian society as a whole. Seven points might call for answers, that only the future will provide:

- The first addresses Dalit identity itself: must the Dalits place themselves behind the blue standard and, faithful to Ambedkar, find a place in the larger society without abandoning their sense of belonging? But how to reconcile the legitimate revendications of a caste (or "macro-caste" if we put all Scheduled Castes together) so oppressed for centuries with the goal of "annihilation of caste?" This goal supposes that members of other castes, both the oppressed and oppressor will let castes be annihilated. Could it be the historical mission of the Dalits to constantly harass the dominant para digm and shake the old oppressive order?
- The second point is a correlate of the first one: how to preserve Dalit memories? Can the experiences, the his tory of millions of Dalits simply be abandoned for the sake of joining the mainstream? This could be a temptation for urban intellectuals. But how can the past and the present of more than 150 million people be ignored for long? The urban-rural divide between Dalits becomes an additional challenge. Will the political and the NGOs activists bridge a potential gap between a growing corps of urban Dalit intellectuals and the mass of rural illiterates? The answer varies from place to place, and depends on the types of links preserved by the Dalit intelligentsia with rural Dalits.

This relationship will have a decisive impact on the way in which a genuine and practicable emancipation is theorised.

- A third point relates to the nature and the real extent of the "mainstream" Hindu identity. Is there only one Hindu ideality set by the *shastras* of the Brahminical tradition? Is there not also a legacy of other traditions on which to build the future, a large and diverse cultural space which encompasses not just the Dalits but also the Tribals, the reformist movements formulating a new Hinduism where the individual has a place, the secular democratic ideal, not to mention eventually other faiths not based officially on caste? Where do
- The OBCs stand in this landscape? The fourth varna, the Shudras, were also excluded from knowledge and power by the dominant classical paradigm. Are the survivals of such exclusions strong enough to make possible an alliance between OBCs and Dalits, or is that just wishful thinking? Is Melavalanu an anachronism or a sign that the OBCs, gradually empowered overthe past 100 years, are not yet ready to share the cake to which they have just gained access?
- The fourth point takes us to the impact of regional parameters. In the Tamil case, the legacy of the Dravidian movement is decisive. Even if the fragmentation of the Dravidian parties' vote banks opens the field to more autonomous formations, the question of competing identities remains, unavoidably perhaps, a challenge. Dalit or Tamil? It is not by chance that the new Dalit party calls itself "New Tamilnadu." The Dravidian ideology offers a way out of the dilemma of Dalitness/Tamilness, for it offers a seducive interpretation of history: by putting the blame for the scourge of caste and untouchability upon "the Brahmins

who came from the North," one may link the future Dalit emancipation to the more egalitarian and secular values attributed to the old Tamil civilisation. Beyond the specificity of this case, the question of regional affiliations remains important: will they obstruct a possible pan-Indian union of Dalit movements, or will the circulation of activists and ideas facilitate the incorporation of regional figures from other parts of India, helping to build a new and richly diverse national legacy? As an example, Periyar has now become an icon for the Bahujan Samaj Party in Uttar Pradesh.

- The fifth point queries the possibility of the union of the Red (the Left) and the Blue (the color of the Dalits). The established Left has always tried to circumscribe the challenge of caste, without really addressing it, and simply denounced caste as a mask for class. With the Dalit issue gaining momentum, it will be more and more difficult for the Left to ignore this challenge for long, partly because Dalit sensibilities on this issue can no longer be ignored and the concept of "oppressed" requires urgent theorizing. For the time being, the Communist Parties have not been a part of *bahujan* strate gies. There are also substantial differences between the parliamentary Left, which has definitely to answer the challenge of caste parties, and the ultra-Left, for whom the Dalits are the potentially revolutionary subjects par excellence?
- The sixth point is about alliances between the Dalit and other social movements. The alliance between Dalits and OBCs is not simply a matter of political conven ience and electoral arithmetic. Politics is not just a matter of power: it is more basically a question of goals, policy and change. What are the forces that are bring ing changes to the daily life of millions of Dalits? Will they transform the socioeconomic fundamentals of Dalit life and, indeed, affect the entire social balance?

Dalit emancipation requires the imperative need for fresh thinking amongst non-Dalits about untouchability. On a wider level, how to connect the Dalit movement with the women's movement? Could Dalit women, more and more visible in the present struggles, help transcend caste barriers through gender commonality? And to what extent will an alliance with Muslims and Christians help transcend, through Dalit involvement, the instrumentalised prejudices between the minorities and the Hindu majority, knowing that the "old song" of the irreparable Hindu-Muslim divide is mostly fiction?

- The seventh point brings us back to the difficulty to forge a stronger relationship with OBCs if Dalit emancipation calls for, as many militants contend, a rupture with Hinduism? Or put differently and abstractly: how must Hinduism itself change in relation to Dalit emancipation? If the duality/dichotomy between "the Brahmin" and "the untouchable" was a foundation of the caste system, what will happen with the latter rejecting his/her status? Could we imagine that the double process of OBCs' upliftment and Dalit revendication may help a new Hinduism emerge, less preoccupied with orthodox hierarchies, more open to individual or lineage relations to deities in a much more fluid society? The dismantling of the caste system and the politicisation of caste would not hinder such an evolution. In the changing cultural and political context, Hinduism is bound to change, perhaps along the lines proposed by some of 19th and 20th century reformist movements, paying less attention to castes and probably also by inventing new ways of accommodating Dalits.

In this context, one cannot underestimate the strategy of Hindutva, which tends, despite the weight of its high caste leadership, to weaken caste differences in order to forge a pan-Indian Hindu identity. Dalits and Hindu tribals are clearly being invited to hitch their wagons to the communal project, and to let them assert an overarching Hindu identity rather than a primordial (caste or tribe) affiliation. Will the saffron hypothesis of the Sangh Parivar offer a major temptation to Dalits to join a new communal mainstream, which would also subvert more radical Dalit leanings?

All these issues, and many more, pose uncertain and difficult questions to which the answers are, as yet, inchoate. But the Dalit movement is definitely here to stay and will probably, as today, continue along diverse paths, tempted sometimes by isolation and at others opening itself to other forces. Blue, red and saffron are the predominant colors of change. In the end a rainbow might emerge from the synthesis of now-divergent paths. At minimum it will have to be a secular, democratic synthesis consistent with the Dalit movement's call for justice, respect and progress. The nature of the Indian polity is at stake as well, and so is the future of India's dominant ideologies and the nature of the social bond. This challenge is not just a matter of intellectual analysis or social theory. In thousands of Indian towns, in hundreds of thousands of Indian villages, the fate of the Dalits will largely fashion India's future, and this is not irrelevant to India's ambition for the next century. Dalits call for equality. As never before, they enter as actors, under our eyes, the field of history. Everyone must understand that, by doing so, they struggle for themselves, but not just for themselves.

REFERENCES

Anandhi, S., *Contending Identities. Dalits and Secular Politics in Madras Slums,* New Delhi: Indian Social Institute, 1995.

Gauthamam, Raj, *Talit parvaiyil tamijp panpatu* (Dalit perspectives on Tamil culture, in Tamil) Pondicherry, 1994.

Gough, Katherine, *Rural Society in Southeast India,* Cambridge, 1981.

Kannan, M. and F. Gros, "Les dalit tamouls en quête d'une littérature," *Bulletin de l'Ecole Française d Extrême-Orient,* Paris, 1996, no. 83, pp. 124-153.

Kannan, M., *Nirappirikai,* May 1996, no. 8, pp. 71-78.

Manokaran, Karuna, *Varalarrup por* (The History of the War) Samikaniti Patippakam, Tiruppur, 1993.

Mathew, George, "The meaning of Melavalavu," in *The Hindu,* September 30, 1997.

Mencher, Joan P., "Group and Self-Identification. The View from the Bottom." *ICSSR Research Abstracts Quaterly,* New Delhi, 1973, Vol. III, 2-3.

Moffatt, Michael, *An Untouchable Community in South India. Structure and Consensus,* Princeton, 1979.

Nagaraj, D.R., *The Flaming Feet. A Study of the Dalit Movement in India,* Bangalore: South Forum Press/Institute for Cultural Research and Action, 1993.

Omvedt, Gail, *Dalit Visions. The anti-caste movement and the construction of an Indian identity,* New Delhi: Orient Longman, London: Sangam, 1995.

Padmanaban, A., *Dalits at the Crossroads. Their Stuggle Past and Present,* Madras, 1996, p. 175.

Preda, Predan, Ramesh, Prem: *Putaikkappatta piratikalum ejtap-patta manitarkalum (The buried copies and the men on whom it has been written about),* Kiranam Veliyidu, Chennai, 1992.

Rao, Katti Padma, *Caste and Alternative Culture,* Madras: Centre for Research on New International Economic Order, 1995.

Sambandan, V.S., "Behind the southern sparks (I). Changing economic equations," *The Hindu,* July 31, 1997.

Thiagaraj, Henry (ed): *Human Rights from a Dalit Perspective,* Dalit Liberation Education Trust, Madras, n.d. (circ. 1994), and the *Dalit International Newsletter,* published from Water-ford, CT, USA.

Thorat, S.K., "Dalits and Human Rights. A Part of the Whole but a Part Apart," paper presented to the *National Workshop on Human Rights and Societal Changes with Reference to Scs and Sts,* Madras, August 3-4, 1996.

Webster, John C.B., *Towards Dalit Liberation. From Indian Church to Indian Theology. An Attempt at Theological Construction,* Madras Dalit Liberation Education Trust, 1992.

Zelliot, Eleanor, *From Untouchable to Dalit. Essays on the Ambedkar Movement,* Delhi: Manohar, 2nd revised edition, 1996.

8

Violence against Dalit Women in Panchayati Raj

Dalit women constitute over 80 million of the 167 million Dalit population in India, 47.96 per cent of the total Dalit population, 16.3 per cent of India's total female population and about one out of every twelve Indians. 89.5% of them are involved in economic production as an important part of the labour force in the country both in the rural and urban as well as agriculture and non-agriculture production. 94% of them are engaged in the unorganised, self employed sector, marked by over work, low wages, non payment of equal wages, absence of social security or maternity benefits. The surplus capital created by them by not accessing statutory minimum and equal wages for her labour will run into millions of rupees, contributing to the wealth and comfort of families and communities at the cost of her self-development, health and family.

Historically, Dalit women were actively involved in the anti-caste and anti-untouchability movements from the time of Babasaheb Ambedkar from the 1920s. Today they are the strongholds of the Dalit movements in thousands of Indian villages. They continue to play critical role in the movements for land rights and movements against liquor in many parts of the country. They are making their mark as independent thinkers and writers in the literary world and visionary leaders in the Panchayati Raj institutions.

We Recognise: Caste-class-gender interface in Dalit Women's lives Vulnerably positioned at the bottom of the caste, class and gender hierarchies, Dalit women experience endemic gender and caste violence as well as extreme deprivation and disabilities as the outcome of the severely imbalanced social, economic and political power equations. Development indicators between Dalit women and Dalit men on one hand and dominant caste women on the other hand show growing inequalities, which reflect the historical and continuing measure of discrimination, exclusion and exploitation specific to Dalit women. Their socio-economic vulnerability and lack of political voice when combined with being a woman and Dalit increase the incidence of voilence on them. The large numbers of crimes against Dalit women that go unreported, unregistered and unpunished strengthen the notions of impunity while committing crimes against Dalit women. In the commission of offences against Dalit women, the offenders try to establish their authority and humiliate the community as noted by the National Commission on Women.

"The number of cases of different nature of crimes committed from 1997-2001 shows that there has been an increase in the heinous crime of murder and rape committed on the members of the Scheduled castes in 2001. The number of the murder as well as rape has increased significantly comparing the quintanal average".

Violence on Dalit women continues unabated despite a number of Constitutional Provisions of equality, non-discrimination, special protective, promotional and monitoring measures, legislative measures and international obligations and commitments.

Nature of Violence Against Dalit Women

The nature and cause of violence against Dalit women range as wide as one can scan. These are firmly rooted in the caste ethos which prescribe the position and behaviour of Dalit communities in relation to dominant caste women, men and children and their material possessions. Any perceived deviation or non-compliance is enough reason. While family violence is also prevalent, the threat of violence from the dominant castes looms high in every family and community across the country. A study of 500 Dalit women survivors of violence from Bihar, Uttar Pradesh, Tamil Nadu adn Andhra Pradesh gives us in-depth insight into the different aspects and issues related to violence on Dalit Women.

Physical assault, verbal abuse, sexual harassment and assault, rape, sexual exploitation, forced prostitution, kidnaping and forced incarceration primarily by male members of the dominant castes are common experience of Dalit women. Violence is carried out in the public, in public view, in work places, in custodial institutions, in the fields, around the villages, in trains, bus stands and even in toilets. Violence in many cases tends to be regular and continuous and by persons who have some power and authority over her or the family. Sexual exploitation by promise of marriage and later desertion and even murder is not uncommon. Perhaps the most gruesome and common is rape and murder.

Certain kinds of violence seems to be reserved for Dalit women–extreme filthy verbal abuse and sexual epithets, naked parading, dismemberment, forced to drink urine and faeces, tied to a pole and beaten, branding, pulling out of teeth/tongue/nail, and violence including murder by proclaiming them witches. Forced prostitution through dedication to Goddess is reserved for Dalit women as is the fact that majority of manual scavengers are Dalit women. Child marriage is a sexual offence on young girls with serious consequences on their physical and psychological growth. Dalit girls are victims of physical and sexual violence similar to that of adult women at the hands of dominant caste men. Demands for sexual relationships, sexual exploitation, rape, mental harassment, torture by police and other administrative machinery are most often placed only on Dalit women.

Yet another cause for violence on Dalit women is any demand made by her or family and community for legitimate rights endowed by the state, which are contradictory to traditional caste and customary norms. Thus questioning of any violence or denial of access to right is considered sufficient cause for severe repercussions. So called audacity for exercising legitimate powers in choice of voting, attempts to perform roles and duties in positions of authority and responsibility in various elected or other official bodies or even demands for participation in cultural or religious functions lead to violence on Dalit community, most often with Dalit women as the victims. Supporting a couple who may want to marry across caste boundaries, preventing the performance of child marriage, demanding that an atrocity be registered, supporting victims' families or survivors of violence, simply questioning the illegal or extra legal behaviour of dominant caste members or deciding to seek justice in an atrocity can lead to fresh atrocities. Violence on Dalit women who are elected representatives in Panchayati Raj institutions are widespread preventing her from exercising her legitimate authority and responsibility.

The violence by the dominant caste communities reveals the 'worldview' of the dominant caste on Dalit women as inferior, impure, of low character, easily available and accessible. Often the perpetrators in so many words tell the woman that she can complain to whichever authority she may please, who will not anyway do anything against them. The support and the complicity of the law enforcing authorities quite often is a reason for the large scale impunity as is also seen by the fact that authorities play an active role in perpetrating violence, preventing the legal proceedings on cases and facilitating 'name-sake' punishments or compromises. The caste nature is evident in addition to the underlying gender aspects in violence by dominant caste members on Dalit women. Dominant caste women have in some instances been found to supoort and encourage their men to commit crimes against Dalit women.

Dalit women face considerable violence in the domestic front. Alcoholism and associated demands of money from men is very often associated with family violence. Other causes also are inability to bear children, not bearing male children, suspected extra-marital relationship, being good looking in some cases or ugly in others, denying sex to husband, demanding property, demanding freedom or asserting her space and rights. Patriarchal values are very evident in the violence where women are expected to be obedient, pure and keep to their place in life.

The violence on Dalit women is multi-faceted, complex and used as a weapon for the continued caste-class-gender subjugation and exploitation of Dalit women and the community as a whole.

Impact of Violence on Dalit Women

Violence causes social, physical and mental trauma to women, much of which is long-term suffering. When the perpetrators continue to hold authority over the woman or family and roam about the village without any threat of punishment, the women and even family and community experience severe fear and intimidation. Physical effect is easily understood in the injury or health complications experienced by the women. Social effects are seen in the form of social boycotts, denied work, excommunication, naming and shaming by the community, added control by the family etc. The nature of violence and their frequency is often a tool to perpetuate a culture of silence and crush the spirit. It would not be too far-fetched to see them as a planned design to continue the exploitation and prevent any assertion or progress of the community and its members.

Accessing justice is a far cry to almost all Dalit women. This study and other reports show that perpetrators are punished in less than 1% of the cases. They go scot-free in more than 99% of the crimes committed, and are even seen to further threaten and punish the same survivors. The study further reveals that in 39% of the instances of violence the survivors did not seek legal redress for fear of bringing dishonor to the family or did not trust she will get justice or for lack of human or financial support. In 27% of the instances of violence, the survivors' appeal for justice to the gram Panchayat or administration is thwarted by pressure and threat from the perpetrators. In 18% of the instances, the police thwarted justice by threatening, refusing to file the complaint, worked out an extra-legal compromise or foist false counter cases. In 2% of the instances some kind of informal justice was arrived at and in 14% of the instances the legal process is on. 4% of the cases are in court and the rate of conviction is a mere 0.1%.

The serious and large number of instances of violence on Dalit women coupled with the low access to justice, with added potential for fresh violence at every stage by state and non state actors result in a cycle of socio-economic rights denial and violence on Dalit women, denying their right to life and security, their right to freedom and choice, their right to development and participation, their very being and dignity.

Despite the gravity of the situation, there are very little efforts or mechanisms by the Indian state or other movements or organisations to protect Dalit women or support her quest for justice. The National Conference on Violence Against Dalit Women is a all to 'Crack Impunity and Initiate Action' on violence against Dalit Women.

The National Conference on Violence Against Dalit Women

The Conference is organised jointly by National Campaign on Dalit Human Rights (NCDHR) and National Federation of Dalit Women (NFDW) with the immediate objectives of bringing together Dalit women survivors, activists, academicians and political leaders to create awareness among the community and expose the failure of the state to protect and promote Dalit women's rights. The long term goal is to build effective monitoring and legal mechanism to support women who face violence, train and support Dalit women rights defenders, build alliances with other movements, enusre effective functioning of the justice and administrative systems and lead towards desired policy changes to prevent violence against Dalit women and crack the culture of impunity.

DEMAND

Identity and Recognition

- Recognise Dalit Women as a distinct social group in the Indian population, recognizing the complex and specific nature of historical and continuing prevalence of untouchability, discrimination and social exclusion and the resultant violence committed against them.
- Study the complex interfaces of caste-class-gender to inform and provide the basis of policy-strategy direction, principles and guidelines for addressing issues and concerns of Dalit women.
- Ensure that disaggregated data on Dalit women and girl children is collected and reported in all census reports, progress reports and action taken reports in the development and human rights aspects and well as when reporting to international treaty bodies.
- Recognise the contribution of Dalit women in national productivity and well-being and ensure that she has a share in the country's wealth and resources.
- Include the concerns of Dalit women in the mandates and activities of both Dalit and women's movements.

Life and Security

- Adopt the amendments recommended by the National SC/ST Commission and the National Human Rights Commission and ensure strict and effective implementation of the SC/ST (Prevention of Atrocities) Act, 1989 and Rule 1995, viz. ensure that cases are registered under this Act, expand rule 7, include social and economic boycott under offences and hold erring officials accountable and use other sections currently unused in the Act.

- Enact a separate law for the entire country that deals with violence against Dalit women, including the abolition of the devadasi system.
- Recognise hunger and starvation as grave human rights violations and ensure adequate access and availability of foodgrains to Dalit women and girls in keeping with nutritional standards. Hold administrative officials responsible for distress migration, hunger and starvation deaths.
- Supoort Dalit women to access economic resources and administrative and judiciary support to protect themselves from doestic violence.
- Protect and encourage Dalit women survivors, family members, witnesses and human rights defenders from threats/pressures to compromise and withdraw cases.

Land and Livelihood

- Expand the provisions under Art.21 to ensure ownership, control and access to asset, credit, common property resources and other adequate means of livelihood for Dalit women to prevent her dependency on dominant caste communities, often the cause of violence.
- Hold officials accountable for strictly enforing Minimum Wages Act, Equal Remuneration Act, Bonded Labour (Abolition) Act. Employment of Manuel Scavengers and Dry Latrines (Prohibition) Act. Interstate Migrant Workers Act to protect economic exploitation and violence on Dalit women.
- Take special measures to ensure that Dalit women access employment at higher levels in private and plublic spheres to prevent economic dependency.

Political Participation

- Enquire on priority basis when harassment is reported by the any elected Dalit women representative and ensure adequate protection to them for effectively exercising their Constitutional authority and duty.
- Promote the perspectives and views of Dalit women in addressing human rights violation and development concerns by providing them reservation in Assemblies and Parliaments.

Security, Protection and Progress of Dalit girl children

- Ensure that Dalit girls have equity access to adequate nutrition, health care and education services without discrimination.
- Study the causes for the high rate of dropping of Dalit girl children from education and take adequate measures to ensure she accesses quality and employment oriented education.
- Take stringent action on all concerned in all cases of physical and sexual harassment, trafficking and exploitation of Dalit girl children.

Public Education

- Orient and train police, administration and judiciary on caste-class-gender interface and vulnerability experienced by Dalit women by interfacing with Dalit women survivors and activists as resource persons.
- Launch a time-bound campaign against untouchability, discrimination and violence against Dalit women.
- Conduct legal awareness trainings for Dalit women and ensure institutional support to access justice and relief and rehabilitation.
- Include positive images of Dalit culture and Dalit women's contributions to school curriculum in training children.

Access to justice

- Undertake confidence building measures among Dalit Women by frequent visits to Dalit habitations, explain provisions available against untouchability, discrimination and violence.
- Implement the Supreme Court direction that the police registers all complaints, FIR copy is given to the complainant and senior district officials review all cases that are closed by the police on a monthly basis.
- Extend immediate and enhanced relief and long-term adequate package of holistic rehabilitation are provided to the survivor and her family members to break Dalit women's dependency on dominant communities.
- Ensure judiciary takes pro-active measures to ensure that different provisions in the SC/ST (POA) Act, especially section 4 of the Act are effectively used to support Dalit women access justice.
- Ensure judiciary takes pro-active measures to ensure that all violence perpetrated on Dalit women based on culture and tradition or superstition meet with most stringent punishments.
- Ensure just and speedy trial of cases of violence on Dalit women.

To the International Community

- Ensure that the International Women Rights organisations, movements as well as other organisations and movements extend solidarity to Dalit women's cause and concerns.
- Recognize caste and decent-work based discrimination as the prime source of human rights violation on Dalit women and Human Rights Treaty Monitoring bodies pay particular attention to ensuring disaggregated data on violence on Dalit women and girl children while examining the periodic country reports.

- Enhance self-reliance among Dalit women and International development organisations incorporate caste analysis into their country planning, review and training strategies focusing in particular on Dalit women and girl children.

CONCLUSION

Despite the growing and heinous crimes and violence against Dalit Women, the daily grind of humiliation and abuse, the unending hours of labour and hunger, the long wait for justice; Dalit women hold the splash of colours of the new dawn, the flame of hope in the depths of her heart, power of resilience in her persona and is the foundation of liberation for Indian society at large. In this battle for the reclamation of the dignity and personality of Dalit Women let us all stand together with Dalit Women.

REFERENCES

Banu, Zenab, *Tribal Women Empowerment and Gender Issues,* New Delhi: Kanishka Publishers, 2001.

—, *Disempowerment of Tribal Women: Perspectives on 73rd Constitutional Amendment,* New Delhi: Kanishka Publishers, 2004.

Buch, Nirmala, "Women and Panchayats: Opportunities, Challenges and Support" in L.C. Jain (ed.), *Decentralisation and Local Governance,* New Delhi: Orient Longman, 2005.

—, "Women's Experiences in New Panchayats: The Emerging Leadership of Rural Women" Occasional Paper 35, *Centre for Women's Development Studies* (CWDS), Delhi, 2000.

Dahlerup, Drude, "Using Quotas to Increase Women's Political Representation" *Women in Parliament,* International IDEA, 2002.

Mill, J.S., *Considerations on Representative Government,* Chicago: Reguers, 1962.

Rai, Manoj, et al, (eds.), *The State of Panchayats: A Participatory Perspective,* New Delhi: Sanskriti, 2001.

Vyasulu, Poornima and Vinod Vyasulu, "Women in Panchayati Raj: Grassroots Democracy in India, Experience From Malgudi" Background Paper No.4, UNDP, 24-26 March 1999.

Young, Iris Marion, *Inclusion and Democracy,* Oxford: Oxford University Press, 2000.

Zachariah, Mathew, "Positive Discrimination in Education for India's Scheduled Castes: A Review of Problems." *Comparative Education Review* 16(1), 1972.

9

Violation of Human Rights of Dalit Women

Introduction

All human beings have the right to live in a dignified way. Human rights are not conferred or given. They already exist in society. The concept of human rights aims at protection of rights like right to life, liberty and property. These rights are attributed to human beings irrespective of class, caste, gender, colour and religion. The Universal Declaration of Human Rights was unanimously adopted by the UN General Assembly on December 10th, 1948. The preamble of Indian constitution adequately empowers the central and state government to eliminate human rights violation in the country.

Inspite of these international and national declarations and resolutions, human rights are violated in different countries all over the world. In Indian society, due to the social barriers such as castetism, untouchability, patriarchy, disparity, superstition, religious exploitation and class variations, specific groups are becoming weaker and marginalised. These groups are facing the problems of identity crisis, deprivation, discrimination and atrocities. These marginalised groups are also identified and recognised as dalits, SCs (scheduled castes) STs (scheduled tribes), OBCs (other backward castes) NT (nomadic tribes) DT (denotified tribes) religious and linguistic minorities.

Violence on human beings in any form results in violation of human rights. Human rights of dalits and women in general are normally violated by high castes and powerful communities to practice and exhibit patriarchy and castetism. But human rights of dalit women are violated extremely and in peculiar form. Dalit women are in worst position than dalits in general, in terms of sex ratio, wages, employment, occupation, assets, education, health, social mobility and political participation. Hence, it is important to discuss the status of dalit women and various problems they face even after 60 years of independence.

This article makes an attempt to discuss basic facts, issues and concerns related to dalit women to suggest some alternatives to combat violation of their rights for social justice and equality. Explanation of relevant terms such as 'dalit', 'dalitism', and 'dalit women', is given below to broaden understanding about the issue. Further, the vulnerable situation of dalit women is also discussed in detail.

Dalit

Dalit ('oppressed' or 'broken') is not a new word. Apparently it was used in the 1930's as a Hindi and Marathi translation of 'depressed classes'. The British used this term for what are now called the scheduled caste. Dr. Ambedkar chose the term 'broken men', as English translation of 'Dalit', to refer to the original ancestors of the untouchables. Dalit Panthers, the youth activists from dalit community revived the term and in their 1973 manifesto expanded its reference to include the scheduled tribes, neo Buddhists, the working people, the landless and poor peasants, women and also those who are being exploited politically, economically in the name of religion.

Dalitism

Dalitism essentially implies conditions of subjugation; economic, political, social and cultural. Dalitism also embodies different degrees of marginalisation. It includes not only marginalised status in the economic sphere but also in cultural, political, religious and social domains. That means Dalitism symbolises marginalisation. It is a well known fact that marginalisation denies basic human rights and social justice (Punalekar, cited in Jogdand 1995)

Dalit Women

Dalit women are one of the most marginalised segments in the society. The condition of dalit women is more vulnerable than non-dalit women. Dalit women are suffering from multi-disadvantages:

(a) of being dalit i.e socio-economically and culturally marginalised section,

(b) being women and sharing the gender based inequalities and subordination.

To explore these and other crucial issues concerning dalit women there is need to discuss some basic facts concerning the vulnerable situation of dalit women.

Vulnerable Status of Dalit Women

It is easy for the historically dominating caste and gender to violate human rights of dalit women who are at the lowest rung of the hierarchical ladder. The type of violence inflicted on dalits is in the form of severest violation of human rights. Dalit and tribal women are raped as part of an effort by upper caste leaders, landlords and police to suppress movements to demand payment of minimum wages, to settle share cropping disputes or to reclaim lost lands. (Human Watch Report, 1998).

The recent incident of Khairlangi massacare is not something new. A build family had refused to let upper caste villagers build a road through their fields. Hence, on September, 29th, 2006, Bhaiyalal Bhotmange's family, wife Surekha, daughter Priyanka and two sons were killed by the villagers of Khairlangi in Bhandra district of Maharashtra. They were first attacked with huge iron chains and than abused by the other caste women of the village. Surekha and Priyanka were paraded naked and raped, and later, their bodies were mutilated and thrown into a pond.

This shows that dalit women are easy targets for any perpetrator Upper caste considers them to be sexually available. Hence they are largely unprotected by the state machinery. Further, there is prevalence of violence, making dalit women eat human excreta, parading them naked, gang-rape, murder, dacoity, robbery and burning of their huts or communities. These are the types of crime, which violate their human rights. According to SC/ST Commission report between 1981 and 1986 about 4000 dalit women became victim of rape. In 1993-94, this figure rose to 798 and 992 respectively. This means annually about 700 dalit women fall prey to sexual assault by high caste people.

The main complaints of the poorer dalit women are that they have no good houses. In urban areas most of them stay in unhygienic slums and in rural areas their houses are away from main stream society. Under conditions of grinding poverty and severe exploitation at work place, dalit women also suffer caste specific ban on water access from upper castes and may be beaten up in their own houses as well. A poem by a dalit poetess Teressama, a teacher from Guntur puts the situation in the following words:

> We go to work for we are poor
> But the same silken beds mock us,
> While we are ravished in broad daylight.
> Ill-starred our horoscopes are
> Even our tottering husbands
> Lying on the cots in the corner
> Hiss and shout for revenge
> If we cannot stand their touch.

At the outset, prevailing caste and secondary status of women in the society is largely responsible for violation of human rights of dalit women. To understand the root cause of the situation it is essential to examine basic factors responsible for their vulnerability.

Socio-cultural and Religious Factors

First and foremost dalit women are victims of social, religious and cultural practices like Devdasis and Jogins. In the name of these practices, village girls are married to God by their helpless parents. These girls are then sexually exploited by the upper caste landlords and rich men and directed in to trafficking and prostitution. In his autobiography, Kale (1994) has described a ritual called 'chira'. The literal meaning of the word 'chira', is to cut or break. In this ritual when a girl from the lower caste community reaches the age of puberty, an elderly prestigious man from the higher caste breaks the hymen of the girl child by sexual act. This ritual is performed in a way to make the girl accept this fact as a routine practice.

The 28th report of SC/ST Commission reported that in February 1986 there were about ten thousand Jogins belonging to SC in Nizamabad district of Andhra Pradesh. The survey submitted by the district collector to Schedule Caste Finance Corporation revealed prevalence of 15,850 cases. Eighty per cent of these Jogins belonged to SC (Pal and Bhargav, 1999). This data is just an example of one district of the country. Practices such as Chira, Jogins, Devdasi which are prevalent even today are harmful and threaten the dignity of dalit women and violate their human rights (P. Sainath, not dated).

Educational Status

Low level of education is a problem in itself and in turn gives rise to many other problems. (Thorat and Umakant, 2004). In 1991, literacy among the dalit women was indeed quite low. In rural areas only 19.46 percentage women were literate. A report published by Ministry of Welfare, Government of India in 1998 showed that there is much difference in the literacy rate of dalits and non-dalits in general, and gender specific. Literacy rate of non-dalits is 64.13 % and literacy rate of women is 39.29 %, where as dalit women's literacy rate is only 23.76 % (Paswan and Jaidev, 2002). There is a large disparity in the literacy rate due to widespread prejudice based on castetism and patriarchy against dalits and women in general and dalit women in particular.

Economic Deprivation and Unemployment

A careful look at the economic situation of dalit women reveals that their work force structure is such that they rarely own any land. A large majority of them are agricultural labourers. The rate of unemployment among them is also quite high. About 90% of women working in unorganised sector are mainly from lower castes (Jogdand 1999). In 1991, about 71% of dalit women workers in rural area were agricultural labourers. Only 19% of them owned land (Pal and Bhargav 1999).

It has been widely observed that Dalit women neither own any land nor are they aware of their rights on land. When enquiries were made with Strimukti sanghatana and Prerana, Mumbai based organisations working on the issue of rag picking and prostitution respectively, to ascertain the proportion of dalit women in these occupations, it was learnt that NGOs usually do not keep record of caste (Tirmare, 2004). However, Human Rights Watch Report (1998) mentioned that a large number of dalit women are engaged in unclean, inferior occupation such as sweeping, scavenging and working in dumping grounds, rag picking and also in prostitution. These women have to face steep discrimination in the matters of social relation and employment due to their engagement in these occupations.

Health and Nutrition Status

Dalit women's daily diet is the leftover of family meals, inadequate in quantity and quality. Health services are either not available in case of illness or unaffordable even if available. In addition to that, due to early marriage and too many pregnancies their health is always at risk. If birth control is practiced at all, 91% cases of tubetomy are performed on the women who have to carry the burden of family planning. In an overall situation where dalits are prone to ailments in general, women suffer from more serious and more varied kind of sickness. More than 80% of women in reproductive age group (15 to 45) are anemic. Poor health status of dalit women pushes her then into more vulnerable situation.

Political Status

Women constitute half of total population, but are unable to get equal share in active politics. Their socio-economic status directly depends on their participation in politics. Political parties in India speak much about equality of women but have totally ignored the dalit women.

Traditionally, leadership in the village was confined to 'rural elites', who were aged and belonging to higher castes. In the year 1993, 73rd amendment in the constitution granted reservation to dalits, tribals and women in local government. This amendment made it compulsory that one third of the seats reserved for dalits be filled by dalit women. In some states, there has been little or no acceptance of reservation for the lower castes and dalit women by the upper castes. This has resulted in atrocities against panchayat members including women. Dalits who stood for election were beaten, and dalit women were raped and ill-treated. The members of the higher castes, who are not prepared to relinquish power to the lower castes, grabbed their land. An easier method to retain power is to put-up proxy candidates but keep the control in the hands of the dominant castes, always men.

The incapacity of women, particularly dalit women, to assert their rights is at the root of the problem. The reservation for dalits, particularly for women, is accepted in form but seldom in substance. Any change in the status quo is resisted. Dalit women's sitting on chairs is seen as threat to social hierarchy. So, the upper castes in the village vetoed chairs in the panchayat office.

Dalit women also faced many problems in performing their duties due to illiteracy, lack of information and dependency on the male members of their families. An important obstacle is the no-confidence motion against dalit women as pradhan by the dominant sections. Rural elites are unable to accept the power, which has been given into the hands of the poorer and disadvantaged women (Manipal, 1998). Despite recognition and legal sanction for political rights, rigid caste system and patriarchy directly and indirectly has been suppressing dalit women and violating their political rights.

This proves that human rights of dalit women are violated right from her family to the society at large by one and all. All these factors are largely responsible for the precarious position of dalit women as far as their social, cultural, religious, economic, health and political status in the society is concerned. These factors force them to mutely allow violation of their civic and human rights. Thus they become victims of universal violence.

Efforts to Protect Human Rights of Dalit Women

With the realisation that violence is one of the potent threats to the peaceful existence of human beings, whole hearted and all round efforts are made at international, national and local level. The preamble to the Universal Declaration of Human Rights (UDHR) serves as a foundation and philosophy of Human rights. There are a host of international conventions including those for prevention and punishment of genocide and elimination of all forms of racial and gender based discrimination.

The World Conference Against Racism (WCAR) related to racial discrimination, xenophobia and intolerance held in Durban, South Africa in 2001, brought the issue of caste and untouchability based discrimination on the agenda of UN Conference in Durban. Among the several organisations, the National Campaign on Dalit Human Rights (NCDHR)—a collective of dalit NGOs, other NGOs, academicians', activists and large number of supporters spearheaded the national campaign in India for inclusion of the issue of caste and untouchability based discrimination in the Durban Conference.

The preamble of Indian constitution adequately empowers the central and state government to eliminate human right violation in the country. Article 17 of the constitution provides for removal of untouchability. Based on this article Protection of Civil Rights Act' (PCR), was passed in 1955. However, there was no conviction/under this Act hence, Thirty-four years after the introduction of PCR Act, the Scheduled Caste and Schedule Tribes (Prevention of Atrocities) Act 1989 was enacted to bring various forms of atrocities to an end. In this Act the complainant is given more weightage. There are stringent provisions against the police for negligence (Pandit)

Emerging Identity of Dalit Women and Formation of Dalit Women's Organisations

The focus on education of low caste women is one of the important factors responsible for the emerging identity of Dalit women. Reformist intervention by Savitribai and Mahatma Phule of opening school for untouchable girls way back in 1848 was a turning point for changing status of dalit women. Dr. Ambedkar's thought and action made important differences in the lives of dalit women. His movement and especially his organisations encouraged many dalit women to become educated to be active in public life and to gain leadership, self respect in the contemporary period encouraged women to participate in organisation for dalit women at regional, state and national level.

After independence in 1960's and 70's, the dalit movement and women's movement emerged to demand their rights against caste and gender respectively. However, specific problems of dalit women were not acknowledged by these movements. Hence in 1990's there were several special, independent and autonomous assertions of dalit women's identity; a case in point is the formation of National Federation for Dalit Women (NFDW) and All India Dalit Women's Forum

(AIDWF) at the state level. The Maharashtra Dalit Mahila Sanghatana (MDMS) was formed in 1995. A year earlier, the women's wing of Bhartiya Republican Party (BRP) and the Bahujan Mahila Sangha (BMS) was set up by the Bahujan Mahila Parishad. In December 1996, at Chandrapur, a Vikas Vanchit Dalit Mahila Parishad (WDMP) was organised and a proposal to commemorate 25th December (the day on which Ambedkar had set Manu Smriti on fire) as Bhartiya Smriti Divas was advanced. The Christi Mahila Sanghatana, an organisation of Dalit Christian Women was established in 1997. These organisations have come together on several issues such as celebration of Bhartiya Stree Mukti Divas and on the issue of reservation for OBC women in Parliament bodies. Indian Association of Women Studies (IAWS) network with dalit feminist across different regions had brought special issues on problems and identity of dalit women.

Several efforts have been made since independence to secure human rights of women in general and dalit women in particular. Despite this, human rights of dalit women are seen to be violated in different forms. Such infringement of human rights echoes the need of evolving suitable mechanism to empower dalit women to assert for equal rights and justice in order to live a dignified life.

Mechanism to Strengthen the Capacity of Dalit Women

To be human is to respond to human sufferings and pain with compassion and effective concern. It is not enough to feel with the dalit women in their pain. There is more need for effective action, otherwise it would be just sentimentalism' says Sequeira in his article 'Human Response to Dalit Women (Jogdand 1999) The needs and the problems of dalit women differ with city, village, area and caste. It is essential to keep in mind that dalit women are not mere individuals but belong to a sociological and dialectical system. Therefore to recognise the system and to prohibit violation, first and foremost proper perspectives about the issues has to be developed among all by considering following suggestions:

Awareness for Assertion

Extensive reading of available literature can be done by young generation to understand the profile and problems of dalit women. Factual incidents and success stories of dalit women namely, 'We made History Too' by Meenakshi Moon and Urmila Pawar can be included in the educational texts.

Access and Exposure Visits

Special exposure visits to dalit localities can be organised for school and college students to assess basic amenities accessible to dalit women namely, water, electricity, health and hygiene. Similarly dalit women's visit to urban structured colonies can be arranged to impress upon the importance of standard of living of non-dalits. Such purposeful visits will broaden their horizons resulting in improved living of marginalised section.

Academic Activities

Academic institutions need to be encouraged to undertake studies to assess the problems of violence and atrocities against dalit women as also the reasons therefore and to work out ways to overcome them. Thought provoking sessions on harmful social religions practices namely, Chira, Devdasi, Jogin need to be held for basic understanding and effective interventional strategies.

Campaigns and Sessions

Campaigns for equal and rational distribution of natural resources among weaker sections can be organised to secure their rightful means of livelihood. Proper rehabilitation and shelter can be provided to those communities, which are out of the social periphery (NT/DT) to protect them from the risk of sexual abuse.

Inclusion of Dalit Women in Various Systems

More dalit women in their population proportion (16.5% SC, 7.5% ST) should be given chance to enter in the system like police, judiciary, education, health and politics.

Sessions can be organised for dalit activist and women activists to sensitize them about the magnitude of torture and oppression faced by the dalit women. Legal education dealing with protection of human rights of dalits and Prevention of Atrocities Act (1989) can be organised to prevent the problems of castism.

CONCLUSION

At the threshold of 21st century, it is absolutely necessary that common people need to be sensitized about the prevailing atrocities against Dalit women. There is a growing need to capture violation of human rights of dalit women, so that talent and potential of Dalit Womens can be used for development of nation.

According to Vippal (Jogdand, cited in 1995) a nation does not prosper only on fertile soil, dense forests and everflowing rivers. It is the healthy people who make a nation. A society is made up of both men and women from all states. If women from whichever state is weak and exploited, it is not a healthy society. And when a society is healthy, then the nation will march ahead. To fulfill these dreams women in general and particularly from weaker section need to be empowered for development of the nation.

REFERENCES

Ahuja, R., *Violence Against Women,* Rawat Publication, New Delhi, 1998.

Bandhu, P., *Dalit Women's cry for Liberation: My Rights Are Rising like the Sun, will you deny this sunrise"?* Edited in Rao, 2003.

Chakravati, V., *Reconceptualising Gender, Phule, Brahmanism and Brahminial Patriarchy,* edited in Rao. *Caste and Gender,* Kali for women, New Delhi, 2003.

Chitnis, V., *Human Rights of the vulnerable groups,* Futuristic Digital, Pune, 2005.

Dietrich, G., *Dalit Movement and Women's Movement,* Edited in Rao (2003) *Caste and Gender,* Kali for women, New Delhi, 2003.

Jogdand, P., *Dalit Women, Issues and Perspectives,* Gyan Publication, New Delhi, 1995.

Kale, R., *Kolhatyachrepor,* Granthali, Publication, Mumbai, 1994.

Kumar, N., *Dalit Policies, Politics and Parliament, Shipra* Publication, New Delhi, 2004.

Kumar, N. and Raj, M., *Dalit Leadership in Panchayats,* Institute of Dalit Studies, Rawat, New Delhi, 2006.

Michael, S., *Dalits in Modern India, Vision and Values,* Vistar Publication, New Delhi, 1999.

Omvedt, G., *Dalit Women and Communalism,* edited in Jogdand, *Dalit Women, Issues and Perspectives,* Gyan Publication, New Delhi, 1995.

Pal, R. and Bhargav, G., *Human Rights of Dalits: Societal violation,* Gyan, Publication, New Delhi, 1999.

Pandit, V., Handbook on Prevention of Atrocities (SC/ST) Vidnayak Sansod Prakashan, Ujgaon, Maharashtra, 1995.

Punalekar, S., *On Dalitism and Gender,* edited in Jogadand (1995) *Dalit Women's Issues and Perspectives,* Gyan Prakashan, New Delhi, 1995.

Pillai, T., *Ambedkar's Daughters: A Study of Mahar Women in Ahmednagar District of Maharashtra* edited in Michaels (1999) *Dalits in Modern India, Vision and Values,* Vistar Publication, New Delhi, 1999.

Rao, A., *Gender and Caste,* Kali for women, New Delhi, 2003.

Thorat, S. and Umakant, *Caste, Role and Discrimination, Discourses in International Context,* Rawat Publication, New Delhi, 2004.

Zelliot, E., *Dr. Ambedkar and the Empowerment of Women,* edited in Rao (2003) *Caste and Gender,* Kali for women, New Delhi, 2003.

Webstar, J., *Who is Dalitl* edited in Michael (1999) *Dalit's in Modern India, Vision and Values,* Vistar Publication, New Delhi, 1999.

10

Devolution of Powers and Local Self-Government

Introduction

The idea of local self-government had existed in India even in ancient times. Even if we accept its beginning as an organisational concept with the Ripon's resolution it is more than a century and two decades old. In its tumultuous career it has seen many ups and downs. In spite of a formal inauguration by the Prime Minister Jawaharlal Nehru in 1959, after the Balvant Rai Mehta committee recommendation in 1957, these institutions could not take proper roots in the country. Some of the scholars even declared that Panchayati Raj Institutions (PRI) were like failed God. The Janata Government appointed the Mehta committee to rejuvenate the PRIs. But, the 73rd and 74th amendment, which were passed in 1992 and came into force in April 1994, have virtually revolutionised the idea of local self-government - both rural and urban—by bestowing constitutional status on them. These amendments were passed in the light of the experience of the Local-Self Governing Institutions in India. They have made a sincere attempt to overcome the limitations faced by these institutions.

The beginning of the idea of decentralisation in India as an organisational concept can be traced to Ripon's Resolution in 1882 which aimed at involving the 'intelligent class of public-spirited men in the management of rural areas under the British rule. In the years to come district boards and taluka boards were set up with nominated members to look after health, roads and education. But this effort did not succeed in making villages as basic unit of local self-government. A resolution of 1918 restated that the objective of self-government is to train people in the management of their own local affairs. The District Board Act of 1922 led to the reconstitution of the Boards. They were entrusted with the responsibilities of road maintenance, tree planting, hospitals, schools and drainage etc.

Panchayati Raj System

Panchayat Act of 1920 was conceived as local courts and was completely judicial in character. As there was hardly any devolution of finances and responsibilities, its role as the local unit of administration, development and rural upliftment remained non-functional.

Among the Indian leaders, Mahatma Gandhi made very strong plea for village republics. Articles 40 under the Directive Principles of State Policy included in the part IV of the Constitution, advised the government to take steps to organise village panchayats and endow them with such powers and authority which would enable them to function as units of self-government. State governments were supposed to appropriate legislation for this purpose.

The Indian planners and policy makers launched a multipurpose Community Development Programme (CDPs) with the objective of improving the conditions of the rural masses. This programme aimed at training and sending development personnel Block Development Officers (BDO), Extension Officers and Village Level Workers (VLWs) into villages. This group of officers were supposed to act as agents of change. They were expected to galvanise rural masses by encouragement, demonstration and offer of material assistance.

The failed to achieve the desired objectives. The Planning Commission requested a committee under the chairmanship of Balvant Rai Mehta to develop the ideas for a system of democratic decentralisation which would anchor the rural developmental efforts. The Balvant Rai Mehta Committee Report came up with a number of recommendations that were incorporated in the panchayat legislation of the various states in the following years. This committee recommended democratic decentralisation with a provision of a three- tier structure [village-block- district]. It also recommended for transfer of resources and responsibilities and channelisation of funds for various developmental programmes through the three- tier system. This report generated opportunity for launching block planning in states like Andhra Pradesh and Tamil Nadu and district planning in others like Maharashtra and Gujarat.

In the 1960s, Panchayati Raj Institutions were portrayed as a God that failed. One of the main reasons of failure was the sabotage by state politicians who were not enthusiastic about devolving powers to the district level or below. They were apprehensive that Panchayati Raj Instututions with real powers may pose a threat to their power and influence. Towards the end of the 1960s when Indira Gandhi was donning a progressive garb and wished to implement land reforms, it was argued that Panchayati Raj Institutions could not be involved as they were dominated by the upper caste and landed elements.

The 1960s also witnessed the advent of the Green Revolution that necessitated centralised planning and came in conflict with the ideals of decentralisation on which PRIs were based. Since rural areas in many parts of the country were still under the hands of feudal landed interest, government sponsored inputs for ushering the Green Revolution could have been monopolised by them. Both central and state government had started bypassing and thus undermining the authority and significance of the PRIs during this period. Central government created its own administrative machinery for implementing many of Indira Government programmes such as Small Farmers' Development Agency, Drought Prone Area Programme, Integrated Rural Development Programme and National Rural Employment Programme, aiming at economic justice. The lack of resources, absence of coordination, dependence on district development staff, lack of delegation of effective authority, domination by the higher castes and better off sections of society had rendered the PRIs ineffective and purposeless as institutions of decentralisation and development. By the middle of 1970s, governments both at the center and in the states had become indifferent to the PRIs. They had become defunct; elections to these institutions were not being held and at most of the places the sitting councils were either dissolved or suspended.

Reconstitution of Panchayat System

The process of rejuvenation started with the reconstitution of the Panchayats in West Bengal and by the appointment of the Asok Mehta committee by the Janata Party government in the late 1970s. The mid-seventies also marked a discernible shift of opinion in favour of conceding larger political space to local communities in the governing process. Local self-governing institutions were supposed to play an important role in reordering societal power equations.

As the Janata Party Government had pledged its commitment to the Gandhian philosophy, the overall atmosphere seemed to be conducive for the resurgence of the Panchayati Raj Institutions. Another plausible reason seems to be the fact that by the late 1970s the Green Revolution had become a decade old and it had given birth to rich peasant class that had benefited from the Green Revolution. The rich and middle peasants were fully aware of the importance of the direct access to decentralised government machinery more particularly its delivery system. Capturing village councils was very much in tune with the newly acquired econom power of this class and their motivation to count politically. The central place of the Panchayati Raj Institutions was restored.

The Asok Mehta Committee Report mentioned rooting of developmental programme through official bureaucracy, inelastic finance, dominance of local institutions by economically and socially privileged sections of society as reasons for the failure of the Panchayati Raj Institutions. Asok Mehta Committee report refused to accept the view that Panchayati Raj was a failed God. In fact, he credited these institutions for starting the process of democratic seed drilling in the Indian soil and making the citizens more consciousness of their rights than before. Among other positive fallouts was the bridging of gap between bureaucratic elite and the people. It also gave birth to a young dynamic leadership with a modernistic vision and social change oriented outlook. Mehta also averred that it helped rural people to develop a development psyche.

The Asok Mehta Committee was innovative in many ways. The participation of political parties in Panchayati Raj election was pleaded to make them more accountable and link them with the political process at the higher level. Mehta hoped that elections would translate into political powers in the hands of poor because of their numerical strength and organisation. It also made a powerful plea for women's participation in the Panchayati Raj Institutions. This report had also proposed reservation of seats for both women and weaker sections of society. The decline of the Janata government created a hostile climate for the implementation of the Mehta report. In spite of this, the non-Congress state governments of Karnataka, Andhra and West Bengal took concrete measures to reactivate the PRIs.

In Karnataka, the PRIs that came into existence incorporated most of the recommendations made by the Mehta report. While non-Congress state governments were busy implementing the recommendations of the Asok Mehta committee, the new Congress government at the center appointed other commissions. C.H. Hanumantharao's working group of 1983 and GVK Rao Committee report of 1985 emphasised the need of integration of the panchayati raj system with development programmes and administration. The concept paper on Panchayati Raj prepared by the L. M. Singhvi Committee Report of 1986 suggested that Panchayati Raj institutions should be closely involved in the planning and implementation of the rural development programmes. Both Singhvi and Asok Mehta Committees recommended democratic decentralisation on constitutional basis.

The Sarkaria Commission constituted to go into dynamics of center state relations, made a mention of the dysfunctional PR institutions and suggested legal provisions for the regular elections and sessions of Zilla Parishads and Municipal Corporations for their resurgence. The P.K. Thungon Committee set up in 1988 to suggest the type of political and administrative structure in district for district planning, advocated constitutional status for panchayati raj institutions. The Thungon Committee also favoured constitutional provisions to ensure timely and regular elections to the PRIs. According to this committee, Zilla Parishad should be the only development agency in a district.

Decentralisation

Devolution is a form of decentralisation, which seeks to create independent level of authority of government with functions and responsibilities. It is an arrangement for central or state governments to relinquish some of its functions to the new units of government that are outside its control. This can be achieved by providing for it in the Constitution itself or by ordinary law of the land. One of the major reasons for the failure of the local self-government institutions in India has been half-hearted devolution of powers to them. The 73rd and 74th amendments also contained provisions for the devolution of powers and responsibilities to rural (Panchayati Raj Institutions) and urban (Nagarpalikas) local self-government institutions. These amendments respectively provided that the panchayats at village, block and district levels would have 29 subjects of rural importance as listed in the 11th schedule and municipalities would have 18 subjects of urban importance as listed in the 12th schedule.

These amendments bestowed upon the local self-government bodies - both rural and urban - the responsibility to prepare and implement a number of development plans based on the needs of local people. They operationalise the concepts of spatial planning and micro level planning to facilitate decentralised socio economic development in India. With the help of these powers the local self government institutions are supposed to promote agricultural, industrial, infrastructural and ecological development, poverty alleviation and development of women, children, scheduled and backward castes. These development functions are in addition to the obligatory functions such as ensuring the supply of drinking water, street lighting, maintenance of schools and hospitals etc.

There seems to be plethora of debates involving the concept, utility and effectiveness of the local self- government institutions. In early village councils an arrangement of government by consent and an active sense of community prevailed over caste divisions. Since beginning, these features of the PRIs have been used to legitimise them. According to Lieten and Srivastava, the village panchayats were established as units of local self- government and focal points of development in country at large more often than not captured by autocratic and invariably corrupt leaders from among the male elite. As argued by some other scholars, the institutions were used by the rural powerful for their benefits. Paul Brass was of the view that PRIs were made to fail because of the reluctance of state politicians to devolve much powers to the district level or below because they feared that if such local institutions acquired real powers they would become alternative source of influence and patronage. Rajani Kothari argued that village councils were nothing but catchy slogans and false that promises had enabled the rulers to contain the forces of revolt and resistance and prevent public discontent from getting organised. Asok Mehta, who headed the second Committee on Panchayati Raj refused to be pessimistic about the PRIs. He thought that the process of democratic seed drilling in the Indian soil made people conscious of their rights and also cultivated in them a developmental psyche. He was of the opinion that these institutions had failed because development programmes were channelised through official state bureaucracy, finance had been inelastic and these institutions were dominated by privileged sections of society. Noorjahan Baba argues that centralised planning and administration were considered necessary to guide and control the economy and to integrate and unify new nations emerging from long periods of colonial rules. This might have been possible because as Lieten and Srivastava think, the Indian state was reputed to have an enlightened vision and a developmental mission. According to Baba in the 1960s there was great disillusionment with centralised planning because it failed to achieve equitable distribution of the benefits of economic growth among regions and groups within developing countries. Henry Maddic is of the view that there exists a triangular relationship between democracy, decentralisation and development.

The experience of the PRIs in different states of the country has not been the same. The formal beginning was made when Jawaharlal Nehru inaugurated PRIs at Nagaur in Rajasthan in October 1959. The Rajasthan model of PRIs revolved around the three tier, village panchayat, panchayat samiti and zilla parishad. The panchayat samiti at the block level was the kingpin of the Rajasthan model. In contrast to the executive role of the panchayat samiti, the zilla parishads were advisory bodies. Maharashtra and Gujarat followed a model in which zilla parishads were nodal point of action as main units of planning, development and administration. In Maharashtra, the zilla parishad executed not only the schemes under

Community Development Programme but also a large portion of progammes of various government departments.

In Karnataka, after the introduction of panchayat reform act of 1985, all functions and functionaries of development departments were transferred to panchayati raj institutions. The District Rural Development Agencies were merged with the Panchayati Raj Institutions. To give substance to the idea of decentralisation, the state budget of Karnataka was split into two providing a separate budget for PRIs. The plans and budgets prepared by Mandal Panchayats could not be altered by Zilla Parishad or state government in Karnataka. Similarly district plans of the zilla parishad could not be touched by the state government. In Andhra Pradesh, the Zilla Parishads endowed with limited functions have shown encouraging results in the filed of education. Even in Tamil Nadu PRIs have done a commendable job in the fields of education, water supply, roads and nutrition.

The PRIs had been functioning in West Bengal, Karnataka, Kerala, Maharashtra, Gujarat and Andhra Pradesh with varying degree of success. But the experience in the field of local self-governing institutions is qualitatively different after the 73rd and 74th amendments became acts because they made parliamentary democracy in our country participatory in the real sense. These amendments gave substance and meaning to the local self- governing institutions. These amendments removed the bottlenecks from the paths of empowerment of the weaker sections of society like the dalits, tribals and the women. Consequent upon the enactent of the act almost all the states and union territories have enacted their legisltation. Election to the PRIs have been held all over the country. The elections to PRIs in different parts of the country have brought out some encouraging facts. Karnataka sends maximum number of women to the PRIs followed by Kerala and Manipur. Uttar Pradesh ranks the lowest in this regard. Empowerment of women has not been a very smooth affair. There are instances of women members being accompanied by their husbands or a male member of the family. Maharashtra and Madhya Pradesh have earned the distinction of electing all women panchayats. The provision of reservation of seats for Scheduled Castes and Scheduled Tribes has ensured greater representation to people from these sections.

In many of the states local level functionaries of government departments have been placed under the control of panchayats. The governments of Gujarat, Karnataka and Kerala have passed orders to this effect. In Madhya Pradesh recruitment of school teachers have started at the block level and the powers of evaluating their performance and confirmation have been transferred to the PRIs at the block level. Rajasthan and Haryana witnessed strikes by the staffs of veterinary and education departments against the move of the state governments to transfer their services under the control and supervision of panchayats. The Apex district level development agency District Rural Development Agency [DRDA] is in the stage of its merger with the PRIs in Orissa, MP and Maharashtra. In Karnataka the merger was achieved way back in 1987. The government of Rajasthan has not been in favour of the merger. Instead it aims at securing effective coordination between DRDA and Zilla Parishad.

Constitutional Amendments

Towards the end of his tenure as Prime Minister, Rajiv Gandhi evinced keen interest in the panchayati raj institutions. The Congress had lost elections in some of the states. The whole idea of conferring power on people through PRIs was more a slogan to influence the people before the election. He held five workshops on responsive administration in which he interacted with district magistrate and collectors of all the districts in the country. These workshops unambiguously favoured constitutional provision and mandatory regular elections to the PRIs. The Rajiv Gandhi government introduced the 64th Constitutional amendment Bill in 1989. The main problem with this amendment was that it sought to establish direct links with PRIs bypassing states. As local government was a state subject, it was seen as a threat to federalism because this bill proposed to take panchayati raj from state list and include it in the concurrent list. Similarly the idea of holding elections to the PRIs under the supervision of the Central Election Commission and also the idea of providing finance to these institutions by the Central Finance Commission aroused misgivings about the intentions of the Rajiv Gandhi government.

The 73rd and 74th amendments in many ways, appeared to be a modified version of the proposals of Asok Mehta Report. These amendments bestowed constitutional status on Panchayati Raj and Nagarpalika institutions. They added part IX and part IXA to the constitution while part IX containing articles 243 to 243O relates to the panchayats while part IXA containing articles 243P to 243ZG relates to the municipalities. They provided for 33% reservation for women in both panchayat and nagarpalika institutions as well as for the position of chairpersons of these bodies. Provisions were also made for reservation of seats in these bodies for SCs and STs according to their proportion in population in that panchayat. One third of the total seats reserved for SCs and STs shall be reserved for women belonging to SCs and STs. Article 243K provides for State Election Commission. The Governor of the concerned state has powers to appoint the State Election Commissioner and assign the responsibility of preparing the electoral rolls and conducting the elections to the panchayats. Sufficient care has been taken to ensure the impartiality of the Election Commission. Once appointed, the Election Commissioner cannot be removed from the office except in like manners and on like grounds as a High Court Judge. The terms and conditions of his office cannot be changed to his advantage after his appointment. Regular elections to the local bodies after the completion of five years term and within six months of their dissolution is the responsibility of the State Election Commission. Article 243-I of Constitution provides for state level Finance Commission to review the finances. The constitution also requires the Central Finance Commission to recommend measures to augment Consolidated Fund of a State to supplement the resources of the panchayats.

The 73rd Amendment

The 73rd Amendment Act provides for a three-tier Panchayati Raj system at the village, intermediate (block or taluka) and district levels. Small states with population below twenty lakh have been given the option of not constituting panchayat at the intermediate level. This Act acknowledged the role of Gram Sabha (the assembly of people) in the empowerment of the rural people and provided for the strengthening of the Gram Sabhas for the successful functioning of the PRIs. The Act intended to make it a powerful body, the ultimate source of democratic power and an epitome of people's power at the gram panchayat level. The Gram Sabha consists of all the residents of a village, and those above 18 years of age are on the electoral rolls of a village. Almost all the State Acts mention the functions of the Gram Sabha. These functions of Gram Sabha include discussion on the annual statement of accounts, administration, reports selection of beneficiaries of anti poverty programmes. The State Acts of Haryana, Punjab and Tamil Nadu give power of approval of budget to the Gram Sabha. A Gram Pradhan is elected by the Gram Sabha. It also elects other members of the Gram Panchayat. The number of members varies from state to state, and some of them have been reserved for SCs and STs according to their population and one third of the total seats have been reserved for the women. The obligatory functions of the Gram Panchayat include provision of safe drinking water, maintenance of public wells, ponds, dispensaries, primary and secondary schools, etc. Now the Gram Panchayats have been assigned developmental functions like minor irrigation schemes, rural electrification, cottage and small industries and poverty alleviation programmes also. The Block level PRI institution is known by different names in different parts of the country. In Gujarat they are called Taluka Panchayat, in UP Kshetra Samiti and in MP they are known as Janapada Panchayat. They include (1) the Sarpanchas of the Panchayats (2) the MPs, MLAs and MLCs from that area (3) the elected members of the Zilla Parishad (4) the Chairman of the town area committee of that area.

The powers of the Panchayat Samiti include provision of improved variety of seeds and fertilizers, maintenance of schools, hospitals, roads, implementing anti- poverty programmes and supervising the functioning of the Gram Panchayats. The Zilla Parishad is the apex body of the PRIs. It coordinates the activities of the Panchayat Samitis. It includes the Pradhans of the Panchayat Samitis of the district, MPs and MLAs from the district, one representative each from the cooperative societies of the district, and also chairmen of the municipalities of the district. The Zilla Parishad approves the budgets of the Panchayat Samitis. It maintains educational institutions, irrigation schemes, and undertakes programmes for the weaker sections.

The 74th Amendment

The 74th Amendments Act provides for the constitution of three types of local self- governing institutions in the urban areas. It provides for Municipal Corporations for major cities like Delhi, Mumbai, Chennai, Kolkata, Allahabad, Lucknow, Patna etc. Middle rung cities have Municipal Councils and smaller towns have Nagar Panchayats. Every Municipal Corporation has a General Council. It has members elected by the adult citizens of the city. These members are called Councillors. Apart from the elected members, the Council also has eldermen elected by the elected Councillors. The MPs and MLAs are also the members. The Mayor is elected by the members from among themselves. Some of the states provide for direct election of the Mayor. He is known as the first citizen of the city. The Municipal Commissioner is the chief executive officer of the Corporation. The Mayor may ask the Municipal commissioner to prepare and present report on any matter.

The compulsory functions of a Municipal Corporation includes maintenance of hospitals, supplying safe drinking water, electricity, running schools and keeping an account of births and deaths.

The developmental functions of the Municipal Corporations include launching of poverty alleviation programmes for the weaker sections. A Municipality is composed of Councillors elected by the local population. Seats have been reserved for SCs and STs according to their proportion in the population of the town and one third of the seats have been reserved for women. The Presiding officer of a Municipal Board is called the Chairman who is elected by the voters of the town. In some states the Chairman of the Municipal Board has powers to appoint teachers of primary schools and even lower level staffs. An executive officer looks after the day-to-day administration of the Municipality. Among the compulsory functions are supplying electricity, drinking water, health facilities, schools and maintaining roads and keeping records of weaker sections of the society. The small towns have Nagar Panchayats. Its members are elected by adult citizens of the town. As in the case of other local self governing institutions, seats are reserved for SC/ST and women. Their functions include provision of drinking water, maintenance of primary schools and registration of births and deaths.

Limitations of the Amendments

Inspite of the revolutionary changes brought about by the 73rd Amendment it suffers from some serious limitations. Ambiguity about the functional jurisdiction of panchayats is one of its serious limitations. In the absence of properly defined jurisdiction, it is dependent upon the discretion of state legislatures for being assigned the functions. This act does not mention the powers and functions of the Gram Sabha. This amendment mentions that the Gram Sabha will perform the functions which may be assigned to it by the State legislature. The provision relating to Gram Sabha in the laws enacted by most of the states reduce the Gram Sabha to a powerless body which will routinely rubber stamp the decisions taken up by the Gram Panchayat.

The Chief Ministers' Conference held in August 1997 at New Delhi ruled that it would be necessary to vest in Gram Sabha the powers to sanction and disburse benefits in open meetings, to decide location of drinking water hand pumps etc without having to refer the matter to officials or other authorities. This conference also held that it is necessary to vest the ownership of natural resources in Gram Panchayats and also the decision - making powers concerning the management and income from such resources in the Gram Sabha. Another important limitation of the PRIs, after the amendment is that they still function in the grip of the state bureaucracy. The village Pradhan has to contact several times in a month the block office for technical and financial sanctions. Yet another omission of the act is that, there is no mention of the employees of the panchayat and their administrative autonomy. Panchayats in the past failed to deliver because they had inadequate control over people working to implement the programmes. Even when responsibilities in the field of health and primary education have been transferred, PRIs have no control over the staff and budget of these departments.

REFERENCES

Gough, Katherine, *Rural Society in Southeast India,* Cambridge, 1981.

Mencher, Joan P., "Group and Self-Identification. The View from the Bottom." *ICSSR Research Abstracts Quaterly,* New Delhi, 1973, Vol. III, 2-3.

Nagaraj, D.R., *The Flaming Feet. A Study of the Dalit Movement in India,* Bangalore: South Forum Press/Institute for Cultural Research and Action, 1993.

Omvedt, Gail, *Dalit Visions. The anti-caste movement and the construction of an Indian identity,* New Delhi: Orient Longman, London: Sangam, 1995.

11

Dalits, Panchayati Raj and Power Equations

After the new generation of Panchayats have started functioning several issues have come to the fore, which have a bearing on human rights. The important factor, which has contributed to the Dalit situation vis-à-vis the Panchayat system, is the nature of Indian society, which, of course, determines the nature of the state. The Indian society is known for its inequality, social hierarchy and the rich and poor divide. The social hierarchy is the result of the caste system, which is unique to India. Therefore caste and class are the two factors, which deserve attention in this context.

At another level, it is essential to look into the question: who are the victims of the social system and nature of the state? They are women, the Dalits, Adivasis and the poor. How can the process of decentralisation through strengthening the democratically elected local bodies tackle these issues along with defining rural development in compressed way? Whether the decentralisation process and the decentralised institutions increase human rights violations or enhance the possibility for respecting and observing human rights?

Empowerment of a New Kind

In Chhattisgarh, there has been a sharp increase in violent manifestations of casteism ever since the local government system began functioning. When the Panchayat Raj institutions have been seen by the upper castes as the tool for the lower castes to assert their right as individuals living in a democratic polity the latter have become targets of caste based discrimination and violence. This rising unrest at the local level has become a common phenomenon.

Aghru Suryavanshi, a Dalit is not in his village Goud for the past one year. His major crime is that he had defeated his rival Ballu Singh Thakur on a general seat during the last Panchayat election, which drew wrath of the upper caste. Goud is a Panchayat in Janjgir district of Chhattisgarh. Dalits in this village have long-standing story of caste assault and aggression to tell.

In the Panchayat elections of January 2000, Mithailal Lahare was elected as the Sarpanch under the reservation quota. The dominant upper caste people, who disliked his stay in the office, dismissed him after a no-confidence motion. This is yet another classical example of harassment and humiliation of Dalits in achieving their political rights under social compulsion. He stayed in the office for about 2 years after which the power automatically came back into the hands of the non-Dalits who could better manipulate the village politics.

Even after duly getting elected, the Dalits are not getting the power and status they deserve. "No confidence motion is the best way invented by the upper caste to takeover from the Dalits", says Awadh Nawrang Sarpanch of Nangaridih Panchayat in Janjgir. Devkuwar Sarith Sarpanch of Bada Darha Panchayat expressed her ambiguity saying, "untouchabilty practises are touching unpredictable magnitudes and there is an unvarying threat from the upper caste segment to bring in no-confidence and overthrow me. Women face it the worst. How will I work freely under this circumstance?"

In the last one year, there were 34 cases of no-confidence motions in Dalit Panchayats. Reservation being the modus by which Dalits could get into power sharing is seen as a means of disgrace by the upper caste segment thereby instigating a lobby to dismantle all reservations. What has happened in the last few decades is a gradual, sensible and rationale growth in the level of awareness among the Dalits. Questions relating to caste issue have been challenged that intimidates the very existence of the caste politics within the Panchayat Raj itself. In recent time these question were more related to the aspects like delivery systems, mid-day meal, etc. Scores of such cases frequently occupy space in the media.

Mounting Caste Violence

Violent attacks on Dalit bastis have been reported at many places in the state. In the background of these cases, in some way or other, is the power equation in the Panchayat. In 2004 there was an attack on Dalits in Gumka of Durg district by the upper caste segment. According to a report by Dalit Study Circle, the setting conditions of this began with the last Panchayat elections when the Dalits supported a candidate against the whims of the caste Hindus.

Similar incident happened in Goud in 2005, here there were several rounds of violence against the Dalits, beginning with the social boycott to refusal of worship rights of village goddess and finally converging into several rounds of violence. However, the tension was set much before with the coming of a Dalit to power as Sarpanch.

In September 2005, a third incident of similar style was reported from Bhokludih village of Mahasamund district. Here the tension detonated with the mid-day meal scheme run by the non-Dalit Sarpanch. According to Tamaskar Tandon member of Dalit Mukti Morcha (DMM), "these assaults are expressions to survive the challenge to the caste hierarchy".

With strong presence of caste disparity, utilizing the government machinery like the police has happened in a number of cases. The Pipariya Police on the instruction of the Sarpanch of Khairwar Panchayat in Kawardha district on 5th October 2004 detained one Bannu Satnami. Next day morning his body was found lying in front of the police station. During the year 2004-05 there were as many as 13 custodial deaths in

Chhattisgarh, of which 11 were Dalits, a self-explanatory figure showing how police is deployed as a tool of caste atrocities.

Defining Discrimination

In the village, there is clear discrimination on the lines of caste. DMM activist Guddu Lahare says, "in the Panchayat there are two major means of discrimination. One is that the Dalits are kept away from the Panchayat proceedings, developmental work, schemes, etc. and another is that wherever Dalits are in power by virtue of reservation they are targeted and their posts are declared null and void after a certain period of time".

This is seen in good number in many Panchayats. For example the development work in the Panchayat in the Dalit bastis are not properly done. Nor the Dalits are involved in the planning and implementation process. Hence these settlements are still lying under bad condition.

Secondly, the Dalits who are in positions like Sarpanch or Panch they are toppled within a short period by bringing in a no-confidence motion. This has barred many Dalits off exercising their rights in the Panchayat institutions. Those who had survived are only based on the principles set by of the caste masters or by applying corrupt politics.

In Hasda village of Raipur the Panchayat has served the Dalits cultivating the land since 1965 with a notice of evacuation. Paul Ratre served with a similar notice says, "it is another form of discrimination synthesised with the Panchayat Raj, where the power at the grassroot is being manipulated by the caste Hindus to take away even the remaining resources and subjugate the Dalits." Dalits are socially boycotted; anyone who dares will have to pay the penalty of 10000/- rupees.

Landlessness and land alienation is a major issue of Dalit reality. In one village near Baramkela of Raigarh district nearly 200 families are landless and also their homestead land is also going out of their hands since they had been notified by the

Panchayat to leave the land. The land is said to be government land. However they had been living on this land for the past many generations.

Mid-day meal and discrimination against Dalit children in the schools are very high. DMM and other Dalit organisations have undertaken the fact-finding investigations in several villages. Similar investigation needs to be undertaken in different places too. Here again there is a social boycott imposed on Dalits.

In earlier days, the boycott was mostly imposed by the caste Panchayats, but in recent time the Panchayat itself is undertaking it, under the guise of land encroachment. Scores of such cases from each district had come into the limelight through local media. Hirri village of Bilaspur, Salkhan in Raipur are the latest victims.

CONCLUSION

While analysing these cases, such incidences happened only when Dalits began to assert their political rights through Panchayat institution. It is evident that the upper castes controlled the affairs of the village cannot tolerate the changes being brought about by the decentralised democratic institutions. In the backdrop of such incidences an array of question raises with reference to Panchayat Raj vis-à-vis Dalits. The initial prediction of decentralisation envisioned through Panchayat Raj hasn't become a reality. It also tells us how Panchayat Raj is utilised as a tool of disempowerment of Dalits and consolidation of caste system.

In conclusion one may say that, the new Panchayat Raj as it will weaken the bureaucratic stranglehold is welcome and attempts should be made to strengthen it against the feudalist casteism, bureaucracy and state government. But how far it has helped the Dalits to come into the centre stage is absolutely questionable.

REFERENCES

Bhadouria, B.P.S., *Panchayati Raj and Rural Development*, Commonwealth Publishers, New Delhi, 1981.

Kanango, Suhla Deh, "Panchayati Raj and Emerging Women Leadership", *An Overview, Social Action*, Jan.-March, 1996.

Kaushik, Susheela, *Women and Panchayati Raj*, Haranand Publications, New Delhi, 1993.

Jain, Devaki, *The Vocabulary of Women's Politics*, Fredrich Ebert Stiftung, Delhi, 2000.

Moghe, Kiran, "Who Killed the Women's Reservation Bill?" One Indian One People, *Women in Politics*, March, 2004.

Thakkar, Usha and Rohini Gawankar "Women in Panchayat: March towards Empowerment", One India, One People-Special Number on *Women in Politics*, March, 2004.

12

Powerful Women in Panchayati Raj System

Through the introduction of the 73rd Constitutional Amendment Act, the degree of control has been given to women at grassroots over physical, human, intellectual and financial resources and also an opportunity has been provided to them to become a source of individual and social power. Further, the presence of "critical mass" of women in governance is the grand impetus for change in the condition and position of women in the patriarchal Indian society. The space provided for women in politics is expected to create an impact upon the political agenda, political culture and public policy. The power bestowed upon women contemplates to make significant changes in the process of governance.

However, the dynamic and relational nature of power transmission from the government to the people, from men to women, from privileged to underprivileged is not an innocuous task. It is a multi-layered and prolonged process, where changes have to be made at different levels. The threshold level of women through 33.3 per cent reservation of seats ensuring adequate political representation is the beginning of this process and it is about to make a purport. Now, women in power, reaching a certain size, known as "critical mass", will bring qualitative change in the nature of performance in governance and thereby, transform the institutional culture, norms and values. But, before putting their ideas into "critical action", they need to grapple with several ordeals. This study tries to explain the problems and performance of women in the process of exercising their power and how the "critical mass" of women transforms to "critical action" for the upliftment of the whole human society.

Backdrop of the Statement

The social divisions such as gender and caste through the institution of family, religion, education, media, the law, etc. have created a great impact on the condition and position of women and their status remains low when compared with men. And, hence, different degrees of power are sustained" and perpetuated through this division. The power and control exercised over them for a prolonged period of time has placed women at the lowest stratum of society. This was established by patriarchy which stresses the prevalence of unequal power equation between men and women. Patriarchy has been prevalent though several theories disprove that there is a natural justification for patriarchy based on biological differences between men and women. This discrimination ultimately gets reflected in the Human Development Index where one-half of the human beings have failed to make progress in the ladder of development. When looking into the corrective measures, suggestions came in the form of empowerment process of women, by which women gain greater control over material and intellectual resources and challenge the ideology of patriarchy and the gender-based discrimination in all the institutions and structures of society. In this concept of empowerment, organising women and acknowledging them as a political force is the primary requirement.

In the Indian context, this has been implemented through the 73rd and 74th Constitutional Amendment Act. Now women are made to represent not only the problems of women but also the society at large. Generally women's perspectives are significantly different from men's as they are much associated with "welfare and protective" activities. If these activities are twined with the concept of power -the result might be potentially remarkable. The space created for women in governance is expected to bring such a conspicuous change.

The need for women's presence in politics should not be judged merely in terms of "equity"; i.e., giving reservation. Rather the process should enable women to participate effectively for more socially responsive governance. But, this is not going to be an easy task since this process strikes at the root of existing power relations. The existing power structure in the form of patriarchy, ideology and other institutions are ought to show stiff resistance to change and the present phase becomes critical where the empowerment process is with this backdrop, the present study analyses the position of women in grassroots governance, the problems they encounter and their performance in village Panchayat with particular reference to Tamil Nadu.

Women in Power

Women are pushed forward into the local political arena through the method of reservation of seats and this is how they form "critical mass" which ought to result in governance more responsive to women. Even though the process of women empowerment is ongoing, this space for women in politics has become an important area of analysis, because the socialisation process has created differences between men and women both positively and negatively and has placed men at the top of the hierarchy, who would not allow women to exercise their political power. This problem is multi- faceted and a single solution cannot be offered since complex factors and situations form the core of the problem.

It starts from the socialisation process of women where women's perceptions are moulded with the ideology which she imbibes from the socialisation process and also the external factors which try to bridle women by domination and restriction. The conundrum faced by women in this transmission process can be broadly classified under three heads *viz.*, ideological level, pragmatic level and domain level.

Ideological Level

For a long period, women have been subordinated to uphold male power and this is deeply embedded in the consciousness of women. Ideology is a complex structure of beliefs, values, attitudes, and ways of perceiving and analysing social reality -virtually, ways of thinking and perceiving. Even though the objectives and policies of the state may be superficially egalitarian, the ideology has an upper hand in performing its task of sustaining unequal power structure. But, the dominance of ideology is not static- making rule for a longer time and can be challenged by stiff resistance (which should be continuous in nature). This can be challenged by the collective force where powerful and marginalised sections of society raise its voice and make itself the source of social power. Therefore, the "critical mass" of women has to perform "critical action" to shake the basic source of dominance against them.

Pragmatic Level

When women in power deal with their proceedings, repression of patriarchy takes its own course in the form of domination, oppression, character assassination, agitation and all other activities which rapidly subjugates women. Men in the fear of losing their traditional power and control over women and other resources react sharply against women in power. They may not be ready to free themselves from their role as oppressor and exploiter, and through various ways and means try to re-establish their power and strike women hard, mostly trying to shackle them with psychological blow (where women are vulnerable mainly due to their socialisation process). Therefore, the process of women's empowerment should co-opt men and make them realize that this process will relieve men from gender stereotyping. Changing gender-relations will bring a fruitful result in the power-relations also.

The burdens of male and female can get exchanged and thus lead to the insurance of using the power resources sanely and safely.

Domain Level

At the domain level, the state is not women-friendly. This has been witnessed in many areas like, in framing legal framework, policies and programmes etc. These are mostly gender-neutral instead of gender- transformative and ameliorative. In the era of globalisation, the state is dominated by market factors and everything is equated in terms of production and profit. In this milieu, women are worse affected. In many cases it is observed that when women show resistance, the legal framework fail to rescue them. The dominance shown by these factors ultimately affects the performance of women and the state fails to create conducive environment to empower them. This can be solved only by adopting a strategy -by creating enabling conditions to change women's position. The collective voice from women will serve as a catalyst.

In all these three dimensions, the power balance is tilted towards men, hence the notion of power has to be re-defined. On the whole, the process should enable women to challenge and change these three dimensions. Even though this is a multi-layered and a prolonged process, the presence of women in grassroots governance for more than half-a-decade proves their capacity so far. Their able leadership provided in terms of pro-poor, pro-nature, pro- community, pro-women, pro-dalit activities is a great stimulant to the empowerment process of women.

Without considering the voices of women in governance, the concept of human development will be full of flaws. Therefore, the state has to create enabling conditions to change women's position; men should co-opt themselves in this process; and finally women have to bring a change at their ideological level to quicken the process further. Based on this assumption, a few cases have been selected from Tamil Nadu to explain the problems faced by the women as Gram Panchayat Presidents. These cases reflect their promising performance amidst the colossal problems.

CASE STUDIES

Problem Faced by Dalit Woman Panchayat President

Pappa, a dalit President of Athankaraipatti Gram Panchayat in Madurai district, is a strong lady who fought with many adverse situations with ease. As a woman and as a dalit, she faced many problems. She said that the Dalit leaders have been facing a volley of problems at different levels. To glorify the existing order, people give statistics to prove that many dalits are in power in the Panchayat system. She felt that all the Acts passed in favour of dalits are not used where they are needed. On most of the occasions they are misused.

At the grassroots, dalits are suffering a lot at the hands of the dominant caste groups. The sufferings of dalits can be felt or understood only by a dalit. Other communities have only one type of suffering, that is, economic poverty, whereas dalits face human indignity also. To remove such indignity, dalits need the support of many organisations and associations for which an alliance has to be formed.

Another problem she encountered in her Panchayat Administration was related to the financial provision. She narrates an incident when the government sanctioned *Rs.2,60,000* for drought relief works. The councilors and contractors asked the Panchayat President to hand over the money to them for executing works, to which she refused. As a result they influenced people at a higher level and stopped the funds. She fought through the Federation of dalit and women Panchayat Presidents to get the money released. Even officials do not follow procedures and rules. Instead they join hands with the dominant elements. Audit is an evil weapon used by the officials to make the Panchayat leaders obey them.

She said that she has to manage the dominant caste groups, officials and opponent groups. She is of the opinion that people of all castes are good as individuals, but they are misled by caste leaders and political leaders and become dishonest for personal reasons.

Similarly, Kaliammal of Therkkupatti Gram Panchayat of Karur district, said that women dalit Panchayat Presidents are struggling in society. When she won the election, another Schedule Caste (SC) leader convened a meeting of 500 members and brought allegations against her and submitted them to the District Collector. It was written in the petition that the Panchayat leader has got Rs.5000/- as bribe to allot Indira Awas Yojana houses to the poor. Kaliammal petitioned the District Collector to conduct an inquiry. Accordingly, an inquiry was conducted and it was found that the allegations were false. Having failed in this attempt, the opposition group brought another trouble when the Panchayat President took steps to provide water supply by laying a pipe across their street. In this conflict, the President's husband was assaulted and he was in hospital for one month. Since she belonged to SC, the dominant caste groups created the game by selecting an SC group to work against her. It is said that the poverty of the SC people can be exploited by anyone.

Collective Strength

Bhavani Ilango, the President of Merpanaikadu Gram Panchayat, Pudukkottai district was totally opposed by a section of the men folk. She was kidnapped by the opposition group from where she escaped. She decided to move closely with other women. She formed 23 self- help groups (SHGs). These SHGs helped the Panchayat in desilting a tank, which provided drinking water to the entire area. Valuing the work done by the women worth Rs. 60,000/-, the officials helped the Panchayat by laying a pipeline for the supply of drinking water. She is confident that the Panchayats, especially women-headed Panchayats, can achieve many more things if they get the support of other women. She felt that men have not changed their perception and attitude towards women even after seeing the transformation effected by the women leaders in Panchayats. They are to be conscientised on the concept of gender and its implications.

Women and Social Development

Chinnammal, the President of Urathupatti Gram Panchayat, has prepared a plan for the development of her Panchayat. As per her perception, the Panchayat is nothing but a wishlist as it is the desire of the people. Carrying out the plan is a difficult task as the President has to get the money. Panchayats do not have adequate finance to carry out Panchayat works. Mobilizing the people for plan preparation is easy. They do participate in all common action, but governance is not in their hands as it is in the hands of the officials. She further said that the Panchayat leaders have to struggle a lot to fulfill the needs of the people. After the preparation of the plan, she first paid attention to the implementation of the nutritious noon meal scheme in the schools. She provided a nail cutter to the *anganwadi.* She made the ration shop function as a public shop. She made efforts to provide safe drinking water to the schools.

She reiterated that if people are mobilised and organised at the grassroots, the government will abide by the wishes of the people. She says that the Panchayat leaders have to be accommodating and should have patience in tackling the issues. Panchayat leaders especially women have to work under severe pulls and pressures. Unless they are capacitated, it is very difficult to manage the Panchayat. The initiative taken by Chinnammal is an instrument to mobilize people and pressurize the government.

Lady with Determination

Jesu Mary, the President of Michaelpattinam Panchayat of Ramanathapuram district is a lady with a strong determination. There was no water source in the village. According to her, providing drinking water supply was the first priority in her village. She fought with the Tamil Nadu Water and Drainage (TWAD) Board and got her village included in the TWAD Board drinking water supply scheme. When she attended a training programme, she was sensitised by the Secretary of Rural Development on the importance of rainwater harvesting. She realised the importance of this new idea, but its implementation in the village was not so easy. With the help of SHGs, she installed the structures in all the 340 houses, but it took several months for the people to realize the importance of these structures. People started believing only when they saw the water level rising in their wells. In the whole state it was the first Panchayat to do rain water harvesting in all the houses in the Panchayat. This activity has credited her with the award by the World Bank and she was sent to Washington to receive the award.

Jesu Mary got five other Gram Panchayat women leaders interested in this work and then five other Panchayats also carried out this work because of her influence. Seeing this success, the Government of Tamil Nadu made it mandatory to install rain water- harvesting mechanism in all the buildings of Tamil Nadu. According to Jesu Mary for all her success, her opponents are responsible. Whenever she wants to introduce anything she discusses with them. She feels that critics are needed for a healthy democracy. Critics' arguments will help the Panchayats to perfect the administration. *Courtesy: Report of the Workshop on New Panchayati Raj: Trials and Triumphs, Gandhigram: Rajiv Gandhi Chair for Panchayati Raj Studies,* 2003.

Passion for Governance

Marudambal, the President of Panchampatti Gram Panchayat in Dindigul district, is a progressive leader with a high level of passion for governance. She said that women Panchayat leaders can do wonders but their achievements are unnoticed and are always under watch. There are people to belittle their achievements and to indulge in character assassination. Police cases are registered against them. One advantage that the women leaders have in Panchayats is that they have more enemies than men and these enemies are the watchdogs of the Panchayats. Being assertive in nature and affirmative in action, she takes each and every step consciously and once she decides her strategy of action, she never goes back. She often looks into gender issues in her Panchayat and through negotiation solves most of the problems. If it is beyond her control, she takes the issue to the police station. She does not have faith in the legal system as she feels that the proceedings and judgment psychologically affect women and they not women- friendly. This is her second term in office and in the next Assembly Election, she wants to contest for the post of MLA. She wants to grab more political power so that she can extend her sphere of activity. She feels that even though MLAs and MPs have no power/control over the Panchayats headed by women, they think that the women leaders have to obey their orders (even if they are against the rules and provisions of the Act). This scenario needs to be changed and this can happen by continuous training (for women) and strong alliance-building with like-minded organisations.

Women as Agents of Change

Rani Sathappan, the President of K. Rayavaram Gram Panchayat in Pudukkottai District, is in her second term. Sections/groups in a village community had a clash due to difference of opinion, particularly in a case related to temple celebrations. Two different groups claimed that the 'Muthal Mariyathai' i.e., the first honours, had to be given to its leaders. This resulted in the discontinuance of temple celebration for a decade. The Panchayat Council decided to bring the two opposing parties to a peaceful solution. Rani took special interest and played a vital role in bringing about a settlement between those groups and, at last the temple 'Kumbabisekam' was performed successfully along with the festival celebrations.

During the initial period, her focus was on the provision of minimum basic amenities to the villagers. In course of time she came to understand the problems of farmers. On several occasions, during the Gram Sabha meetings, the village elders and the members of traditional committee urged her to take up activities related to protection and promotion of common property resources, especially irrigation tanks and *ooraines* in the village. There were three *ooranies* and four *kanmais* in her Panchayat. Two *kanmais* belong to the PWD and two are under the Union Panchayat, when there was an encroachment on the inlet channel by an individual belonging to a nearby village. The Panchayat decided to deal with the issue carefully, otherwise there would be a clash between the two villages. They petitioned the District Collector and the Chief Minister. Rani attended the monthly grievance day and brought the matter to the attention of the District Collector, who arranged for an inspection by the revenue officials. The revenue officials twisted the matter, and threatened that they would become enquiry officers and book the Panchayat President, if she did not obey the officials. But the President complained against the revenue officials. Due to this difference of opinion and egoism, it was delayed.

It is more than three years of struggle with the bureaucrats, but the encroachment is not yet removed. "Efforts will bring about change" is the slogan printed on her official letter pad.

Another significant achievement is that she made her village plastic-free. Nearly ten animals died after swallowing polythene materials dumped in dustbins. Taking this tragedy to the Gram Sabha, she discussed this issue with the people. Having convinced the people she evolved the norm that no one should use plastic articles in the Panchayat area and that individuals who violated it would be penalised.

Pioneer in Communal Harmony

Jamrud Beevi, President of Devipattinam Village Panchayat of Aamanathapuram district, from a Muslim community has moved towards the public space. Devipattinam is a Hindu pilgrim center but is dominated by Muslim families and both lead a peaceful life in this village. Jamrud's concern was to keep her village protected in the days of communal and caste rivalry. There are nine deities inside the sea and the place is known as 'Navabashanam'. People have to cross the water by boat or on foot, walking in the water. To reduce the inconvenience of the pilgrims, she thought of constructing a small bridge for about 90 feet, for which she approached the District Collector. She obtained a grant of Rs. 13 lakhs from the district administration and constructed a bridge around the deities and provided a sodium vapour light to the Agraharam and a bathroom complex. She also made efforts to keep the entire area neat and clean by removing encroachments.

Proxy War against Dalit Women Panchayat President

The stubborn refusal by an elected representative (a caste Hindu who "purchased" the Vice-President post for Rs. 27,000/-) to cooperate with the dalit woman President of Pottlupatti in Usilampatti taluk in Madurai district, has rendered the village Panchayat inactive. The Vice-President refuses to sign cheques; most of the work remains unfinished, creating widespread disappointment among the villagers against the President, S. Mani. Even the Council has passed a unanimous resolution cancelling cheque signing powers from the Vice-President who is said to have been waging a "proxy-war" against the illiterate Dalit President ever since she refused to obey his instructions and has refused to remain puppet. "He wants to recover the money he paid for the post", she says. The village committee auctioned it and he emerged successful. "But, when the village failed to save me from a dalit, I demanded the money back", he says. The committee returned the money.

Concern for Ecology

In Vanduvancherry district, Rani Muniyakannu is waging a battle against the silicon sand miners in her Panchayat. The village falls in a coastal area, so it gets filled with saline water on digging pits and that affects the ground water and the plantations. Rani passed resolutions against mining, boycotted the Parliamentary election in 1998, coordinated silicon sand mining and picketed the lorries. She was arrested and then released when the villagers blocked the roads. Rani also presented her village's case in a people's Forum at Tamil Nadu, held in February 2002 in Chennai.

Eswari, the President of Appipalayam Gram Panchayat of Karur district, also faces a similar problem. Environmental degradation has become acute and as a result people have lost their source of drinking water. In Karur area, people have sold their lands to industries which manufacture dyes. The waste coming out of these industries is dumped in land and the waste pollutes the soil and water resources. As a Panchayat President, she started her agitation against these industries and filled cases in the court, but government officials showed apathy and supported the powerful industrialists. They cited false complaints against her under Section 205 of Tamil Nadu Panchayat Act, 1994, which curtails the power of village Panchayat President, but she emerged successfully. The people have extended support to her to fight against such atrocities and even now with the help of the people she is striving hard to save the environment from encroachment.

Observations

From the above cases, several inferences can be drawn out and these cases show the present condition and position of women in power. Women being naive to power are performing amazingly in spite of the problem posed to them by society. What they need is a helpful platform for their action. They consider the difficulties as an opportunity to show their ability but the hard fact is the mental trauma they undergo. This is pathetic and substantive measures should be taken in this regard by the civil society and the state. The major inferences drawn from these cases are briefly analysed as follows:

Commitment to the Society

Through these cases, women's commitment to the society is obvious. Their concern for even simple things brings a remarkable change in society. Jesu Mary case is the finest example where she first convinces her opponents to make her task easier. On the other side, the consideration shown by a Muslim woman, Jamrud Beevi, for communal harmony shows that women think differently. Similarly, the involvement of Eswari to save her environment from pollution shows her high commitment level.

Focus on Social Development

Focus of these women Presidents to cater to the felt need of the people is appreciable. Their plan for social development ranging from care for children and their development towards upliftment of poor (socially and economically) will surely result in the development of the nation.

Ability to take Initiative

The initiative taken by these women to mobilize the people for a common cause proves that women can influence the society with positive ideas and perform their action collectively. The initiative taken by Rani Sathappan in all her activities ended in victory since she was backed by the larger group.

Resourcefulness

Women's ideas are significantly different from men and are much more resourceful. Their ideas are mostly centered on the optimal utilisation of resources. Their idea on generating more income for the Panchayat by planting fruitful trees in the Panchayat area and auctioning them enhances their financial resources. Intellectually also, they get succeeded by performing collective action without any hesitation and ego, whereas men sometimes get caught by these poor characteristics.

Resoluteness

The firmness of these women shows that they are able leaders. Steps taken by Bhavani Ilango in spite of stiff resistance through male dominance; Pappa's affirmative action against the politicians and bureaucrats; and Rani's action against the usage of plastics are a few examples of their resoluteness. Women act as an agent of change and once decided they will achieve their desired result in spite of all the hurdles. They are changing their position from

(i) Subordination to resistance

(ii) Curbs to challenge

(iii) Suppression to co-optation

Of course, this phase is going to be the toughest phase for the whole society and women in particular, but there is a hope that change in power relations will bring favourable situation for development.

CONCLUSION

The state intervention in the form of reservation of seats for women through 73rd and 74th Amendment Act can, indeed, become a real source of power. But, this political space is highly contested and men, the "previous stakeholders, may not easily accept the shift in power equations. This is the beginning of a long process and collective action is necessary to quicken the process further. Moreover, the process should challenge and change the meaning of 'power' in itself. The power exercised by women should be meant for social, political, economic and cultural development.

So, first women have to articulate their oppression collectively since the critical mass has been evolved and it will be easier for them to raise their voice collectively. Secondly, in this process women should enter into collaborative action with other multi-lateral organisations, which work for the same cause. Finally, the critical action taken consciously by integrating the activity and strategy will show better results, which may help women to utilise the space for political participation effectively.

REFERENCES

Calman, Leslie J., *Toward Empowerment, Women and Movement Politics in India,* Boulder, San Francisco, Oxford West view Press, 1992.

Giri, V. Mohini, *Emancipation and Empowerment of Women,* Gyan Publishing House, New Delhi, 1998.

Kanango, Suhla Deh, "Panchayati Raj and Emerging Women Leadership", *An Overview, Social Action,* Jan.-March, 1996.

Kaushik, Susheela, *Women and Panchayati Raj,* Haranand Publications, New Delhi, 1993.

Santosh, *Cultural Pattern and Economic Participation of Women,* Radha Publications, New Delhi, 1995.

Patel, Vibhuti, *Women's Challenges of the New Millennium,* Gyan Publications, Delhi, 2002.

Thakkar, Usha and Rohini Gawankar "Women in Panchayat: March towards Empowerment", One India, One People-Special Number on *Women in Politics,* March, 2004.

Bibliography

Alsop, Ruth, *et al,* "Inclusion and Local Elected Governments: The Panchayati Raj System in India" Social Development Paper 37, *World Bank, South Asia Region, Social Development Unit,* Washington D.C., 2001.

Banerjee, A., P. Gertler, and M. Ghatak, "Empowerment and Efficiency: Tenancy Reform in West Bengal", *Journal of Political Economy,* 110(2), April 2002, pp. 239-80.

Banu, Zenab, *Disempowerment of Tribal Women: Perspectives on 73rd Constitutional Amendment,* New Delhi: Kanishka Publishers, 2004.

—, *Tribal Women Empowerment and Gender Issues,* New Delhi: Kanishka Publishers, 2001.

Bardhan, P., "Decentralisation of governance and development," *Journal of Economic Perspectives,* Fall, 2002.

Baviskar, B.S., "Impact of Women's Participation in Local Governance in Rural India" in L.C. Jain (ed.), *Decentralisation and Local Governance,* New Delhi: Orient Longman, 2005.

Besley, T. and R. Burgess, "Land reform, poverty reduction and growth: evidence from India," *Quarterly Journal of Economics,* 105 (2), May, 2000, 389-430.

Bhadouria, B.P.S., *Panchayati Raj and Rural Development,* Commonwealth Publishers, New Delhi, 1981.

Buch, Nirmala, "Women and Panchayats: Opportunities, Challenges and Support" in L.C. Jain (ed.), *Decentralisation and Local Governance,* New Delhi: Orient Longman, 2005.

—, "Women's Experiences in New Panchayats: The Emerging Leadership of Rural Women" Occasional Paper 35, *Centre for Women's Development Studies* (CWDS), Delhi, 2000.

Bystydzienski, Jill M., (ed), *Women Transforming Politics: Worldwide Strategies for Empowerment,* Bloomington: Indiana University Press, 1992.

Calman, Leslie J., *Toward Empowerment, Women and Movement Politics in India,* Boulder, San Francisco, Oxford West view Press, 1992.

Castles, Stephen, "Studying Social Transformation," *International Political Science Review* Vol. 22, No.1, 2001, pp. 13-32.

Centre for Women's Development Studies, "From Oppression to Assertion: A Study of Panchayats and Women in M.P., Rajasthan, and U.P.", *CWDS,* New Delhi, 1999.

Chauhan, Abha, "Women's Participation in Panchayats in Scheduled Areas With Special Reference to Madhya Pradesh", *A Decade of Women's Empowerment Through Local Government in India,* Institute of Social Sciences/South Asia Partnership Canada/International Development Research Centre, October 20-21, 2003.

Chowdhary, Prem, *The Veild Women: The Shifting Gender Equations in Rural Haryana-1980-1990,* Oxford University Press, New Delhi, 1994.

Crook, R. and J. Manor Deaton, A. and J. Dreze, "Poverty and inequality in India: a re-examination," *Economic and Political Weekly,* September 7, 2002, 3729–3748.

Dahlerup, Drude, "Using Quotas to Increase Women's Political Representation" *Women in Parliament,* International IDEA, 2002.

Fox, Richard and Jennifer Lawless, J., "Entering the Arena? Gender and the Decision to Run for Office," *American Journal of Political Science,* Vol. 48, No.2, 2004, pp. 264-280.

George, Abey and Jyothi Krishnan, "From the Other End: Tribals and Democratic Decentralisation in Kerala", *IDPAD,* 2006.

George, Alexander and Andrew Bennett, *Case Studies and Theory Development in Social Sciences,* Boston: MIT Press, 2005.

Ghatak, M. and M. Ghatak, "Recent reforms in the panchayat system in West Bengal: toward greater participatory governance?," *Economic and Political Weekly,* January 5, 2002.

Ghosh, Archana, "Women's Reservation in Urban Local Bodies: A Perspective from Chennai Municipal Corporation Election, 2001", *Urban Management*, 10th Issue, 2002, pp. 42-64.

Giri, V. Mohini, *Emancipation and Empowerment of Women*, Gyan Publishing House, New Delhi, 1998.

Government of India, "Report of the Committee of the Status of Women in India". Ministry of Education and Social Welfare, New Delhi, 1975.

Government of India, *Administrative arrangements for rural development—a perspective: proceedings of the national workshop held at NIRD*, Hyderabad: National Institute for Rural Development, 1985.

Government of India, *National Human Development Report*, New Delhi: Planning Commission, March, 2002.

Government of India, *Report of the Eleventh Finance Commission*, New Delhi: Ministry of Finance, 2000.

Government of India, *Report of the task force on Panchayati Raj institutions*, New Delhi: Planning Commission, December, 2001.

Government of India, *Report of the working group on decentralized planning and Panchayati Raj institutions*, New Delhi: Ministry of Rural Development, November, 2001.

Helmke, Gretchen and Steven Levitsky, "Informal Institutions and Comparative Politics: A Research Agenda," *Perspectives on Politics*, Vol. 2, No. 4, 2004, pp. 725-740.

Hust Evelin, "Political Representation and Empowerment: Women in the Institutions of Local Government in Orissa after the 73rd Amendment to the Indian Constitution", *Heidelberg Papers in South Asian and Comparative Politics*, Working Paper No.6, August 2002.

Institute of Social Studies Trust, "Beyond Practical Gender Needs —Women in North-Eastern and Hill States", *Study for the UNDP-Panning Commission National Research Programme on Growth and Human Development*, ISST, New Delhi, July 2005.

Institute of Social Studies Trust, "Women in Leadership Positions: A Scoping Paper", ISST, New Delhi, July 2005.

International Fund for Agricultural Development, "India - Participation of Tribal Women in Village Organisations", *IF AD,* 19 January, 2007.

Jahan, Raunaq, "Women in South Asian Politics", *Mainstream, Delhi,* August 15, 1987, pp. 35-44.

Jain, Devaki, *The Vocabulary of Women's Politics,* Fredrich Ebert Stiftung, Delhi, 2000.

—, *Women's Quest for Power.* Vikash Publishing House Pvt. Limited, Sahibabad, 1980.

John, Mary, "Reservations and Women's Movement", *Economic and Political Weekly, Review of Women's Studies,* Bombay, Vol. XXXV, Numbers, 43-44, pp.ws 22-ws 60.

Kanango, Suhla Deh, "Panchayati Raj and Emerging Women Leadership", *An Overview, Social Action,* Jan.-March, 1996.

Karnard, Raghu, "A Thar Spring: A Women Sarpanch Rewrites the Script of an 'Injured' Rajasthan Village", *Outlook,* October 15, 2007.

Kaushik, Susheela, *Women and Panchayati Raj,* Haranand Publications, New Delhi, 1993.

Kenworthy, Lane and Melissa Malami, "Gender Inequality in Political Representation: A Worldwide Comparative Analysis", *Social Forces,* Vol. 78, No.1, September 1999, pp.235-268.

Kohli, A. Kohli, *The state and poverty in India,* Cambridge: Cambridge University Press, 1987.

Leiten, G.K., "Panchayats in Western Uttar Pradesh: 'Nameless Member", *Economic and Political Weekly,* XXXI, No. 39, 1996, pp. 2700-2705.

Mahbub ul Haq, 1996*Reflections on Human Development,* Oxford University Press, New Delhi, 1996.

Manor, J., *The political economy of democratic decentralisation,* Washington, D.C.: World Bank, 1999.

Mansbridge, Jane, "Should Blacks Represent Blacks and Women Represent Women? A Contingent "Yes"," *The Journal of Politics,* Vol. 61, No.3, 1999, pp.628-657.

Marine, S. Shaul. "Victims of Sudden Affluence", *India Today,* December, 15, 1997.

Mathew, G., "Panchayat elections: dismal record," *Economic and Political Weekly,* January 20, 2001.

Mathew, George, "Panchayati Raj Institutions and Human Rights in India", *International Council in Human Rights Policy,* 2002.

Maxine Molyneux, *Panchayati Raj from Legislation to Movement,* Concept Publishing Company, New Delhi, 1994.

Mehta, A., "Report on Panchayati Raj Institutions", GOI, Ministry of Rural Development, New Delhi, 1978 .

Mill, J.S., *Considerations on Representative Government,* Chicago: Reguers, 1962.

Moghe, Kiran, "Who Killed the Women's Reservation Bill?" One Indian One People, *Women in Politics,* March, 2004.

Mookherjee, D., "Combating the crisis in government accountability: a review of recent international experience," *Boston University Institute for Economic Development Discussion Paper* No. 117, December, 2001.

Moser, Caroline, O.N., "Practical and Strategic Gender Needs and the Role of the State" in Caroline Moser (ed.), *Gender, Planning and Development: Theory, Practice and Training.* London: Routledge, 1993.

Murthy, Ranjani (ed.), *Building Women's Capacities: Interventions in Gender Transformations,* New Delhi: Sage, 2001.

Nandal, Santosh, "Gender Justice: Some Issues", *Women's Link,* Vol. 9, No. 1, January-March, 2003.

Palanithurai, G., "New Panchayati Raj System in Tamil Nadu", *South Asian Journal of Socio-Political Studies,* January-June 2001.

Panchayati Raj Update, Institute of Social Sciences, Vol. VIII, April 2001.

Pande, Rohini, "Can Mandated Political Representation Increase Policy Influence for Disadvantaged Minorities." *The American Economic Review* 93(4), 2003, pp. 1132-1151.

Patel, Vibhuti, *Women's Challenges of the New Millennium,* Gyan Publications, Delhi, 2002.

—, "Adivasi Women on the Warpath", Miranda Davies (Ed) *Third World- Second Sex,* Zed Press, 1987.

—, "Emergence and Proliferation of Autonomous Women's Groups in India: 1974-1984" in Rehana Ghadiali (Ed) *Women and Society in India,* Sage Publications, 1988.

—, "Emergence and Proliferation of Autonomous Women's Groups (1974-1984) in Neera Desai (ed.), *A Decade of Women's Movement in India,* Himalaya Publishing House, 1988.

—, "Ideological Debates Among Autonomous Women's Groups in India" in Susheela Kaushik (ed) *Women's Participation in Politics,* Indian Association for Women's Studies, Vikas Publishing House, 1993.

—, "Women's Movement in India and Anti-rape Campaign", in J.P. Singh(Ed) *The Indian Women-Myth and Reality,* Gyan Publishing House, 1994.

—, "Women's Action Groups and the State Machinery", in Maithreyi Krishnaraj (ed) Women and Violence, *Research Centre for Women's Studies,* SNDT Women's University, Bombay, 1991.

Phillip, Anne, "Democracy and Representation: Or, Why should it Matter Who Our Representatives Are?" in Anne Phillips (ed.), *Feminism and Politics,* New York: Oxford University Press, 1998.

—, *The Politics of Presence,* Oxford: Clarendon Press, 1995, Reprinted 2003.

Pitkin, Hanna F., "Rethinking Representation", *American Political Science Review,* Vol.97, No.4, 2003.

—, *The Concept of Representation,* Berkley: University of California Press, 1967.

PRIA, *The State of Panchayats: A Participatory Perspective,* New Delhi: Samskriti, 2001.

Rai, Manoj, et al, (eds.), *The State of Panchayats: A Participatory Perspective,* New Delhi: Sanskriti, 2001.

Rai, Shirin M., "Reserved Seats in South Asia: A Regional Perspective", *Women in Parliaments Beyond Numbers* 2005.

Rajaraman, I., "Fiscal features of local government in India," in *Governance, decentralisation and reform in China, India and Russia,* ed. Jean-Jacques Dethier, Boston: Kluwer Academic Publishers, 2000.

Rajaraman, I. and M.J. Bhende, "A land-based agricultural presumptive tax designed for levy by panchayats," *Economic and Political Weekly,* April 4, 1998.

Ravi, Venkata *et al,* "Women participation in Decentralised Local Self Governance" *South Asia Politics,* Vol. 3, Issue 4, August 2004, pp. 26-30.

Santosh Nandal, "Equality and Development: Gender Issues in India", *Women's Link,* Vol. 8, No. 1, January-March, 2002.

Santosh, *Cultural Pattern and Economic Participation of Women,* Radha Publications, New Delhi, 1995.

Seabright, P., "Accountability and decentralisation in government: an incomplete contracts model," *European Economic Review,* 40, 1996, 61-89.

Sivaraman, Mythily, 'Blow to Goodness', *The Hindu,* May 18, 1997.

Thakkar, Usha and Rohini Gawankar "Women in Panchayat: March towards Empowerment", One India, One People-Special Number on *Women in Politics,* March, 2004.

Thakur, Rekha "Should It Be Caste or Gender?" *One India One People,* March, 2004.

Tiebout, C., "A pure theory of local expenditures," *Journal of Political Economy,* 64, 1956, 416-424.

Uma Prachar (A Resource Letter on Panchayati Raj), Vol. 13, No. 1, 2006.

Vijayanand, S.M., "Issues related to administrative decentralisation and administering decentralisation: lessons from the Kerala experience," Workshop on Decentralisation, Institute for Social and Economic Change, Bangalore, May 31-June 1, 2001.

Vyasulu, Poornima and Vinod Vyasulu, "Women in Panchayati Raj: Grassroots Democracy in India, Experience From Malgudi" Background Paper No.4, UNDP, 24-26 March 1999.

Williams, Melissa, "The Uneasy Alliance of Group Representation and Deliberative Democracy" in Will Kymlicka and Wayne

Norman, eds., *Citizenship in Diverse Societies,* New York: Oxford University Press, 2000.

Wolpert, Stanley, *A New History of India,* Oxford: Oxford University Press, 2000.

Young, Iris Marion, *Inclusion and Democracy,* Oxford: Oxford University Press, 2000.

Zachariah, Mathew, "Positive Discrimination in Education for India's Scheduled Castes: A Review of Problems." *Comparative Education Review* 16(1), 1972, pp. 16-29.

Index

J

K

L

M

R

S